PLOTS & PANS

PLOTS & PANS

Recipes and Antidotes from The Mystery Writers of America

Illustrated by Gahan Wilson • Introduction by Isaac Asimov
Edited by Nancy & Jean Francis Webb

WYNWOOD™ Press
New York, New York

Excerpt from *Dead Run* by Richard Lockridge. Copyright © 1976 by Richard Lockridge. Reprinted by permission of Harper & Row, Publishers, Inc.

Adaptation of the appendix from *My Foe Outstretch'd Beneath the Tree* by V. C. Clinton-Baddeley. Copyright © 1968 by V. C. Clinton-Baddeley. Reprinted by permission of Victor Gollancz, Ltd., London, and William Morrow and Co., Inc.

Excerpt from *Season of Snows and Sins* by Patricia Moyes. Copyright © 1971 by Patricia Moyes. Henry Holt and Company, Inc. and Patricia Moyes.

Illustrations © 1989 by Gahan Wilson

Library of Congress Cataloging-in-Publication Data

Plots and pans.

Includes index.
1. Cookery. 2. Literary cookbooks. I. Webb, Nancy.
II. Webb, Jean Francis. III. Mystery
Writers of America.
TX714.P62 1989   641.5   89-5761
ISBN 0-922066-01-9

Copyright © 1989 by Mystery Writers of America
Introduction copyright © 1989 by Isaac Asimov

Published by WYNWOOD™ PRESS
New York, New York

Printed in the United States of America

Contents

5

Introduction

I suppose those of you who have never met a mystery writer have a firm impression as to what they're like.

Keen-eyed, you'd say. World-weary from gazing at the seamier side of life. Drawn and lined from long hours spent in studying the criminal mind. Stoop-shouldered from hunching over micro-portable typewriters balanced on knees while sitting in the judge's chambers. Walking the mean streets in the small hours to forget, yet finding no surcease.

How sad it is!

Or rather how sad it would be if there were an atom of truth in it.

I have met any number of mystery writers in my professional capacity as one of them, and they are pussycats, one and all.

You have never in your life seen such a cheery, gentle bunch. Take them away from their typewriters and the gore which, a moment before, had been dripping from their fingers and forming a sticky puddle all around their desks, vanishes as by magic. Their fangs retreat into their jaws. Their scowls melt. Their malignant eye-glares become sunny twinkles and they metamorphose into the kinds of people to whom you would cheerfully entrust an infant toddler, knowing full well that each would meet a three-year-old on an equal level of purity and innocence.

And what do mystery writers do when away from the typewriter and when there are no three-year-olds for them to cuddle? Why, with a happy cry, and a merry clap of hands, they rush into the kitchen to cook and to prepare savories of all sorts. Off with chillery and on with cheffery. Off with mayhem and on with mayonnaise. Off with blackmail and on with black beans.

Finally, looking up from their ragouts and sauces and chutneys and bouillabaises and nut-brown ales, they all cried out with gleeful laughter, "Why not a Mystery Writers of America cookbook?"

Why not indeed?

Let us all share in the gentle treasures produced for the taste buds by the rarest spirits of all—those kindly Jekyllish men and women who supply us with crime and terror at such times as they Hydishly sit down at the typewriter.

But wait—an introduction is required.

But by whom?

Why, by the one mystery writer whose absence of decency and whose lack of mildness of disposition are notorious in the profession—by the one mystery writer who can't cook and who isn't certain which room in his apartment is the kitchen.

By me, to put it briefly.

The last time I tried to boil water, I scorched it. I have yet to figure out which side of a frying pan is down. I'm the one who was unable to use an electric stove once because I couldn't light the pilot light.

So would they ask me for a recipe? Not on your life!

"Recipes are to be obtained from pussycats," there came the stern cry. "You may write the Introduction, for you are fit for naught otherwise."

So here it is.

—Isaac Asimov

The Mystery Writers of America is a rugged outfit that swashbuckled its way from the depths of Butcher's Row . . . and finally (I hope) came to rest in the tree-lined Elysium of West Twenty-seventh Street.

How many previous meeting places? I can remember a few. We ate at Cheerio's and Guffanti's. We sat in a dozen or more restaurants, a few good ones and a few bad ones, but, most of them—well, we kept the costs down, even though a detachment of gourmets usually excused themselves and skipped off somewhere else for dinner.

There are places and moments to remember, for instance, the memory of what we called the Blue Grotto. It had blue walls surrounding a toilet and an old-fashioned bathtub. It was the favorite promenade of Twenty-fourth Street roaches. They were dedicated mystery fans who attended all meetings and scurried precariously across the long table at which we sat. We swatted them on sight, and some survived and some did not. *Sic transit gloria scriptororum.*

—Lawrence Treat

Foreword

Mystery Writers of America

Once upon a time—the way we always began when I was much younger and still of a romantic turn of mind—people who wrote mystery fiction were considered to be second-class citizens in the world of writers. They were labeled as such by those whose economic success entitled them to a first-class rating; and, unhappily, also by themselves.

In those early days, pulp magazines flourished. Mystery writers had a market where they could earn a cent a word or two cents a word, or, if they were miraculously successful, three cents a word. Forty years ago many pulp writers turned out anywhere from twenty to fifty thousand words a month. They lived quite well in a noninflated time with moderate income taxes. But they were second class. Writers for the "slick" magazines made a great deal more money, acquired a great deal more prestige and fame. The mystery writers of the time signed inferior contracts, almost literally gave away secondary rights. They took what was offered and it was second class, from start to finish.

And so it was that once upon a time, in 1944, a group of these second-class citizens got together to form the Mystery Writers of America. A slogan was born: "Crime Does Not Pay—Enough." The names of those founders are in the records. They should be in line for eventual sainthood.

This new organization was to operate outside and independent of The Authors League. Some writers refused to join on that account. Some of those original members saw M.W.A. as a fighting union. But in the 1940's many interpreted "union" as a dirty word. In all the arts it is difficult to get the artist to strike for his rights. He is too hungry. He cannot bear to see "No Sale" rung up on the buyer's cash register.

The more militant members of this new organization proceeded to fight to improve their lot. Many others joined for the guild and craft aspect of it. The fiction writer's job is a lonely one, unlike the cooperative ventures for writers in stage, screen, radio, and television. Those fiction writers knocked on the doors of some shabby headquarters, the best M.W.A. could then afford, and came to know one another for the first time. They discovered that very few of their peers had two heads. They came to respect their fellow craftsmen. In the process, they developed a new respect for their own abilities.

The social aspects of M.W.A. have grown over the years. An annual dinner has enlarged into an Edgar Awards ceremony, as important in its field as filmdom's Academy Awards or the theater's Tony Awards. Excellence is honored and announced to the world.

It would be satisfying to report that the aims of the founders of M.W.A. in the 1940's have been fully achieved. Unfortunately, people get so much free entertainment from television that there is little reason to buy overpriced reading matter not on the best-seller lists. The well-made book, like the well-made play, struggles to survive.

The mystery writers of this generation face the same kinds of problems that the founders of M.W.A. faced. But they are better equipped, more knowledgeable and more courageous than their forebears—thanks to M.W.A. Personally, I view them today as first class in a second-class society. Perhaps, now, their problem is how to become successfully second class. The music goes round and round.

The members of M.W.A., writers of taste and special skills, have demonstrated over several decades that they have courage. That's what it takes to put out a cookbook in a world flooded with "how to" volumes.

I recommend it to you without hesitation, and I wish you good reading and good eating.

—Hugh Pentecost

EDITOR'S NOTE: It has been suggested (surely in jest?) that today's M.W.A. motto might be somewhat revised to read "Crime Would Not Pay if the Government Ran It." No action on this matter has been officially considered by M.W.A.

Edgars and Ravens

The high point of each Mystery Writers of America year is the mid-spring Edgar Awards Dinner in New York City. At this event, Edgars and Ravens are presented for the best work done in various mystery-allied categories. An Edgar is the mystery writer's equivalent of a Hollywood Oscar, a Broadway Tony, or a Television Emmy. A Raven is bestowed for some special service or contribution in the field, generally one of a nonwriting character.

Both are ceramic figures. The Edgar is a likeness of Edgar Allan Poe, detective fiction's patron saint. The Raven is a facsimile of the brooding bird in Poe's most famous poem.

—Jean Francis Webb

Hors d'oeuvres

The Lady with the martini said, "Really? And do you write under your own name?"

"Not necessarily. Sometimes I write under the name of Agatha Christie and sometimes Josephine Tey and occasionally Hillary Waugh."

"My goodness! And how in the world do you think up those marvelous plots?"

"They come to me giftwrapped. The only trick is to open them without damaging the contents."

"And do you write other things than mysteries?"

"Yes, ma'am. I did a series once. It was called *The Rover Boys on Fanny Hill.*"

"And are all writers like you?"

"Exactly. Put us in a box and you can't tell us apart. Why, Phyllis Whitney and Rex Stout . . ."

"Now I know you're teasing me."

"Well, Rex does have a beard. And Phyllis is prettier. Would you like another drink? I'll be happy to get . . ."

"Do all writers drink?"

"Some, the fortunate ones, also eat. There are publishers who don't think we ought to, but that's a matter of opinion."

—Richard Martin Stern

Hors d'oeuvres

Green Olives

  1 16-ounce can green olives   *1 clove garlic, mashed*
1½ teaspoons dried basil leaves   *Juice of 2 lemons*

Drain the olives. Bruise them with your thumb so that they will accept the seasonings, and store in a covered jar in the refrigerator at least 24 hours before serving. Shake occasionally.

"I stole this, or at least the idea for it, from the wife of my British publisher on whose spiced olives we gorged ourselves one evening with drinks before dinner. I warn you, served as canapes these do tend to disappear rapidly; and you will find all available ashtrays filled with olive pits."

—Richard Martin Stern

EDITOR'S NOTE: Pitted black olives may also be used. They take seasonings well and obviate the need for so many ashtrays.

Writer's Cramp Hors d'oeuvres

½ cup butter   *1 8-ounce can chopped green chilis*
10 large eggs   *1 pint small curd cottage cheese*
½ cup flour   *1 pound Monterey Jack cheese,*
1 teaspoon baking powder   *shredded*
Dash salt

Preheat oven to 400° F. Melt butter in a 13″ x 9″ x 2″ pan. Beat eggs lightly. Stir all ingredients except melted butter into eggs. Blend thoroughly. Pour into buttered pan. Bake for 15 minutes. Reduce heat to 350° F. and continue to bake for 35 to 40 minutes. Cut into 1½″ squares. Serve hot. Yield: approximately 60 squares.

"In the unlikely event that some is left over, it may be frozen and reheated without damage. A few years ago, I felt obliged to provide a snack for a group of mystery writing friends. I decided to try my mother's famous chili-cheese appetizer called *Queso con Huevos*. Though I'm not much of a cook, everyone

17

in the group requested a copy of the recipe. From that time on, I've called the snack *Writer's Cramp Hors d'Oeuvres* for the recipe's crippling effect on my fingers."

—Richard Laymon

Water Chestnut Canapes

Canned water chestnuts   *Brown sugar*
Bacon strips, halved   *White sugar*
Toothpicks   *Cinnamon*

Amounts depend on quantity needed.

Preheat oven to 325° F. Drain water chestnuts and wrap each in bacon. Roll in equal parts brown and white sugar, to which has been added a good shake of cinnamon. Fasten bacon strips with toothpicks. Place in pie pan and bake at 400° F. until bacon is nearly crisp, or about 20 minutes. Yield: 4-6 chestnuts per guest.

—Gary Madderom

Purchase liquamen from your neighborhood sauce dealer. Until its famous disaster, Pompeii, for instance, produced some of the best liquamen. This combination of boiled-down salted fish entrails, mashed and formed into a sauce, is an ideal disguise for the following—which otherwise would lack pungency and seasoning.

Cut up a number of mushrooms, stalks and all, into an earthenware pan with seasonings of liquamen, lovage (try Chinese parsley or its Italian cousin), honey and oil. Cook and serve.

This dish was offered to the Emperor Claudius at his home on the Palatine in Rome on the night of October Augustan Celebrations in 54 A.D. He did not die until the next morning. But it is presented in my novel *Death in High Places* that the recipe itself was harmless. I contend that the emperor died of poison administered on the point of a feather wedged between his teeth in an effort to make the sick man yield up the food that had caused his indigestion.

According to Apicius, the well-known cookery expert, the recipe was a positive godsend in some families. One has only to consider the Empress Agrippina (Claudius's widow). By one of those coincidences so dear to historians, her second husband—Claudius was third—also died after eating mushrooms.

Even as today, one then had to be careful where one picked mushrooms. And also with whom one ate them.

—Virginia Coffman

Mushroom Treat

½ pound small mushrooms
1 tablespoon oil

½ teaspoon curry powder
Lemon juice

Remove mushroom stems and save for another dish. With a wet thumb, wash each cap. Heat oil in a heavy pan. Mix in curry and a few drops of lemon juice. Add mushrooms and cook slowly until all the natural juices have evaporated. Then, if you have a coal or wood stove, place on rear of stove. If you have a gas or electric one, set at lowest heat. The purpose is to allow very low heat to reach the mushrooms. They are being dried as well as cooked. Stir occasionally. This whole process may take from 8 to 20 hours, and may be interrupted if necessary. Delicious as an *hors d'oeuvre*, the mushrooms are ready for eating when they are hard like hazelnuts.

—Rose Treat

Mushrooms Penzler

12 medium-to-large mushrooms
¼ cup minced onion
¼ cup melted butter
2 tablespoons minced cooked ham
2 tablespoons minced cooked chicken

⅛ teaspoon seasoned salt
⅛ teaspoon garlic powder, optional
¼ cup freshly grated Gruyère cheese
 (or mixture of Gruyère and
 Parmesan)

Preheat oven to 350° F. Wash mushrooms. Remove stems, leaving crowns intact. Dry thoroughly and set aside. Mince stems. Heat 2 tablespoons of the melted butter in saucepan. Add minced onion and sauté over low flame until soft. Place mushroom stems in cheesecloth and squeeze briefly to remove moisture. Add to saucepan and stir. Add ham, chicken and seasoning to saucepan; mix thoroughly and simmer for 1 minute. Place mushroom crowns, gill-side down, in shallow baking pan. Brush with remaining butter, then invert and brush top edges only. Add half the grated cheese (2 tablespoons) to saucepan and mix thoroughly. Fill mushroom crowns with stuffing. Bake for 15 minutes. Remove from oven and sprinkle remaining cheese on caps. Replace in oven for 5 minutes. Serve hot. Yield: 6 servings as first course.

—Otto Penzler

Bludgeoned Garlic Dip

1 19-ounce can chick peas
4-6 cloves garlic, mashed
½ cup yogurt
Juice of 1 lemon
⅓ cup sesame seed paste*

Salt and pepper, to taste
Herbs of your choice
Raw carrot sticks
Raw celery sticks

Puree chick peas in blender, a few at a time; or force through fine sieve. Mix with remaining ingredients except vegetable sticks. Chill. Serve with carrot and celery sticks. Yield: approximately 2½ cups dip.

* Seasame seed paste, also called Tahini, is available at Middle Eastern, Oriental groceries, and health food stores.

"This is a dip with a sort of Near Eastern flavor, sometimes known as hummus. After you have eaten this up you should go off by yourself because the garlic will hover around you transcendentally for days."

—Jane Langton

Millionaire's Antipasto

2 cups olive oil
1¾ 12-ounce bottles catsup
1½ 5-ounce bottles Worcestershire Sauce
½ cup cider vinegar
2 medium carrots, scraped and cut into chunks
1 pound green beans, cut up
1 head cauliflower, cut in florets
6 stalks celery, cut up
¼ bottle Tabasco

2 6-ounce cans tuna, drained and broken up
2 3-ounce cans small sardines, halved
6 medium dill pickles, sliced thin
6 sweet gherkin pickles, sliced thin
2 bottles capers
1 10-ounce can small stuffed green olives
2 5-ounce cans button mushrooms
1 jar hearts of artichoke, cut in quarters

Combine oil, catsup, Worcestershire Sauce, and vinegar in large kettle. Add the vegetables, cover and boil over low heat until vegetables are crisply tender (about ½ hour). Stir often to prevent burning. Add all remaining ingredients and marinate from 24 to 48 hours. Chill and serve as first course, or as salad at a summer lunch. (Pour remainder into container and freeze.) Yield: 12-24 servings.

—Robert Fish

Soups

What ever happened to poison? It has been completely superseded by that trite instrument, the Saturday Night Special. The last case of poisoning I recall was done by Margaret Holben Fisher who confessed that on May 26, 1960, she put one-quarter teaspoon of a rodent killer in her husband's asparagus soup.

Cases like Mrs. Fisher's point up the lack of readily available "untraceable" poison. I am working on that problem now; I think I have the answer. Perhaps soon you will see in the bookstore on the shelf for self-help books a small volume entitled *A Garden Book for Poisoners*.

—Thomas M. McDade

One-Minute Gazpacho

1 *large cucumber, peeled and chopped*
2 *16-ounce cans tomato sauce with onions (or 1 large can if obtainable)*

1 *pint sour cream*
Salt, pepper, and celery salt, to taste
Croutons

Put all ingredients except croutons into a blender. Blend until smooth. Chill thoroughly and serve with croutons. Yield: 4 servings.

—Robert Fish

Cold Apple Soup Anne McCaffrey

4 cups peeled, chopped, and cored
   tart apple
Grated rind of a lemon and all its
   juices
1/2 cup sugar

1 tablespoon cinnamon
Dash salt
2 tablespoons melted currant jelly
3 cups red wine

In a large saucepan, combine apples, grated lemon rind, sugar, cinnamon, and salt. Mash the apples slightly to extract some juice. Simmer over low heat until soft, about 15 to 20 minutes, stirring occasionally to prevent sticking. Puree the apples, add lemon juice, currant jelly and wine (the jelly will probably melt by itself in the hot apple puree). Mix well, cover, and chill several hours or overnight. Yield: 4 servings.

—Elsie Lee

The Ambassador's Cook's Borscht

4 medium beets, peeled and chopped
1 small onion, chopped
1 stalk celery, chopped
1/2 teaspoon salt

1 cup beef stock or bouillon
1/2 cup yogurt
1/4 cup sour cream
1 teaspoon lemon juice

Simmer first five ingredients until vegetables are tender, about 20 minutes. Cool slightly. Place in blender with remaining ingredients and puree. Chill before serving. Yield: 4 servings.

"Having once been hired as a private secretary for a man who had been dead two months, and another time as a chimpanzee babysitter, I am now a full-time writer. I discovered this recipe while living in West Africa, where I also discovered American mystery fiction (in French) and made the decision to be a mystery writer (in English)."

—Jane Beckman

Chilled Cream of Avocado

1 cup chicken stock or canned broth
1½ cups cream
1 cup water
2 green onions, finely chopped (including 2 inches of green tops)

1 medium avocado
Cucumber slices
Black pepper

Combine stock and 1 cup of cream in saucepan over low heat. Stir until blended. Stir in onion. Simmer 10 minutes. Chill. Peel and remove pit from avocado and puree in blender. Add to chilled soup. Blend in remaining ½ cup of cream. Serve garnished with thin slices of cucumber sprinkled with pepper. Yield: 4-6 servings.

"This was served by Becky to the family on the hidden key in *Eight Candles Glowing*."

—Patricia Muse

Green Summer Soup

1 11-ounce can condensed cream of green pea soup, undiluted
⅔ cup water

½ cup sour cream
1 teaspoon bottled horseradish
¼ teaspoon Worcestershire Sauce

Combine soup and water. Blend well. Add remaining ingredients. Beat until smooth. Chill. Yield: 3-4 servings.

"In *The Clue of the Faceless Criminal*, my heroine, Cherry Ames, discovers a deadly undercover situation next door to—and affecting—a children's camp where she is camp nurse for the summer. In the course of making friends and enemies that summer in the mountains of Pennsylvania, Cherry acquires from a young farm woman the recipe for Green Summer Soup."

—Helen Wells

Scotch Broth with Peas

2 pounds mutton neck or breast
    bones
1 tablespoon bacon grease
1 minced onion
1 cup dried peas, soaked overnight
2 teaspoons salt
3 quarts water

1 large beef or lamb soup bone, op-
    tional
1 cup fresh peas
1 cup diced carrots
1 cup diced potatoes
1 cup chopped cabbage
2 tablespoons minced parsley

Sear mutton bones in bacon grease. When half seared, add onion and brown. Do not burn. Drain dried peas. Add salt, water, and dried peas. Cover and simmer 2 to 3 hours, stirring occasionally. After 2 hours, add remaining ingredients. Stir and simmer 1 hour longer. Remove meat from bones if desired. Return meat to soup. Serve hot. Yield: 6-8 servings.

—Lillian de la Torre

EDITOR'S NOTE: Lamb may be substituted, but it gives a less distinctive flavor.

Soup Bone Soup

1 large beef bone with meat, 1-2
    pounds
1 small bunch parsley, chopped
1 large onion, sliced
1 bay leaf
2 carrots, scraped and sliced

Salt and pepper, to taste
3 stalks celery, chopped
3 quarts water
1 1-pound 4-ounce can whole toma-
    toes

Place all ingredients except tomatoes in a soup kettle. Bring to a boil and cover. Simmer for approximately 2 to 3 hours. Remove from stove and refrigerate. Let stand overnight. In the morning, remove hardened fat. Add tomatoes. Simmer again for at least another hour. Yield: 8 servings.

—Stephen Wright

Mother's Famous Bean Soup

1-pound package beans (white kidney, baby lima, navy or lentils)

1 quart water, or enough to cover beans

Salt, to taste

1 onion, chopped fine

1 large or 2 medium-size carrots, chopped fine

2 stalks celery, leafy tops included, chopped fine

1 cup V-8 juice

1 clove garlic, chopped, or garlic powder, to taste

Basil, fresh or dry, to taste

Black pepper, to taste

2 bay leaves

Any leafy vegetable: lettuce, bok choy, chard, spinach (not green pepper, broccoli or cauliflower which don't take kindly to long simmering), optional

Cover beans in pot with water. If you have time, soak overnight, but if not, turn on the heat and bring to a boil. Salt water to taste. Lower heat to a slow simmer. Check the pot fairly often. When the beans look wrinkled add remaining ingredients. Turn the heat down very low. There exists an odd-looking steel platform often called a "flame-tamer," which can be put under the pot to keep everything under control for long, long simmering. An electric slow cooker also controls the heat well, but the soup seems to taste better when cooked slowly on a gas stove. Stir the pot every hour, and be sure that when hunger (yours or theirs) finally intervenes, there'll be a hearty meal ready. All that's needed to go with it is a salad and some crunchy French bread. Yield: 6-8 servings.

"Use soy sauce instead of salt, if you like. It gives a nice color and the taste blends well.

"Ham hocks, or smoked neck bones, or other bits of meat or sausage can be added, but I mostly make a vegetarian version these days.

"I've been making Mother's Famous since before I was a mother. It didn't

28

have a name then. It was just good, plain, peasant food. I think white kidney beans are the best.''

—Joyce Harrington

Potage à la Reine

¼ pound bacon, cubed	3 quarts canned chicken stock
1 whole chicken, about 3 pounds	Salt, to taste
1 medium onion	¼ teaspoon white pepper
2 whole cloves	1 cup soft white breadcrumbs
1 carrot, cut in chunks	2 tablespoons finely chopped blanched
Pinch of thyme	almonds
8 parsley sprigs	3 tablespoons cooked green peas
2 bay leaves	12 spears canned asparagus
1 stalk celery with leaves, cut into	2 tablespoons sweet butter
1-inch pieces	Chicken Forcemeat (below)

Put cubed bacon and whole chicken in large soup kettle. Stick whole onion with cloves and add to the kettle. Then add carrot, thyme, parsley sprigs, bay leaves, celery, and 1 quart of the chicken broth. Add salt and white pepper. Bring to a boil, uncovered, skimming occasionally. When broth is clear, heat remaining stock and add to kettle. Cover and simmer slowly, turning the chicken frequently so the meat left uncovered by the stock does not dry out. Continue simmering until chicken falls from bones, about 3 hours. Remove the chicken from kettle. When it is cool enough to handle, remove skin and bones and discard them, reserving the meat. Save the dark meat for future use. Dice the white meat finely and mix with breadcrumbs. Force through a meat grinder, using finest blade. (A blender may be used.) Strain the broth and return to a simmer. Stir the chicken–bread mixture into the simmering broth. Add the almonds. Heat to boiling and add the peas, asparagus and butter. Just before serving, add the chicken forcemeat balls. Ladle into heated soup plates from a heated tureen. Yield: 6 servings.

Chicken Forcemeat:

Cooked meat from 2 small chicken breasts	*1 cup dry breadcrumbs, sieved*
Salt and pepper	*1 blade mace*
Pinch nutmeg	*3 tablespoons butter*
Pinch powdered cloves	*2 egg whites, stiffly beaten*
1 cup half-and-half	*2 egg yolks, beaten*
	Deep fat for frying

Cut chicken into chunks. Chop it along with salt and pepper, nutmeg, and cloves in a food processor; or feed chicken through meat grinder and add spices. In a large saucepan scald half-and-half and add breadcrumbs and mace. Remove from heat and stir in butter and ground chicken. Fold in egg whites. Shape chicken mixture into walnut-size balls. Dip in egg yolks and fry in 350° F. deep fat until golden. Drain on paper towels. Yield: approximately 2 dozen balls.

—Jean Francis Webb

Mulligatawny Soup

½ cup chopped onion	*4 cups canned chicken broth*
¼ cup diced carrots	*1½ cups canned tomatoes*
1 clove garlic, mashed	*Salt and pepper*
1 large apple, sliced but not peeled	*1 cup diced cooked chicken*
4 tablespoons butter	*½ cup cooked rice*
4 tablespoons flour	*½ pint unsweetened heavy cream,*
2 teaspoons curry powder, or to taste	*salted and whipped*

Sauté vegetables and apple slices in butter until limp but not too brown. Stir in flour and curry powder. Add broth and tomatoes. Simmer slowly for 1 hour, adding more stock if necessary. Strain through fine sieve. Discard pulp, and add chicken and rice to soup. Top with dabs of whipped cream. Yield: 4 servings.

—Jean Francis Webb

Oyster Stew Yates

1 quart shucked oysters, reserving
  liquid
½ cup water
1 tablespoon butter
Salt

Freshly ground pepper
1 bay leaf
Dash celery salt
1 quart ice-cold milk

Cook oysters slowly in saucepan in their own liquid and ½ cup water until they begin to curl at the edges. Then add tablespoon of butter, sprinkle with salt and freshly ground black pepper. Add bay leaf and dash of celery salt. The minute the butter is melted, dash in whole quart of ice-cold milk. (This immediately stops the cooking of the oysters, leaving them tender.) Allow the milk to heat slowly to the proper temperature for serving at once. And *do* serve at once. Yield: 6-8 servings.

"Did you know that what makes Lynnhaven oysters so fine is that they feed on water celery? That is why celery salt brings out the full oyster flavor. Be sure to use a *level* tablespoon of butter. And remember that overseasoning ruins the whole thing."

—Margaret Taylor Yates

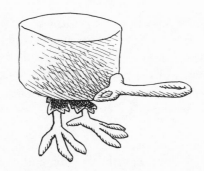

Dr. Sam: Johnson, Epicure

"Oats," Dr. Sam: Johnson quipped in his dictionary, contemptuous of Scottish cuisine, "a grain, which in England is generally given to horses, but in Scotland supports the people."

"Ay," replied a hardy Scot, "and England is famous for her horses . . ."

But this interchange took place before the dictionary-maker visited Scotland.

On Wednesday, August 18, 1773, Dr. Sam: Johnson set out from Edinburgh to visit the Western Islands of Scotland. With him in the chaise rode James Boswell, Scotch advocate, already self-destined to be his biographer. For two months the pair journeyed from island to island, from chieftain to chieftain, from table to table, and in his little book James Boswell noted down everything that Dr. Johnson said and everything that he ate.

"Dr. Samuel Johnson's figure and manner," Boswell began his account, "are, I believe, more generally known than those of almost any man, yet it may not be superfluous here to attempt a sketch of him. His person was large, robust, I may say approaching to the gigantic, and grown unwieldy from corpulency. His countenance was naturally of the cast of an ancient statue, but somewhat disfigured by the scars of that evil which it was formerly imagined the royal touch could cure. He wore a full suit of plain brown clothes with twisted-hair buttons of the same colour, a large bushy greyish wig, a plain shirt, black worsted stockings, and silver buckles. Upon this tour, when journeying, he wore boots and a very wide brown cloth greatcoat with pockets which might almost have held the two volumes of his folio dictionary, and he carried in his hand a large English oak stick."

It was this singular traveler who turned in at the New Inn, Aberdeen, accompanied by spry, sharp-nosed young Boswell. At the New Inn, Dr. Johnson got his first taste of Scotch cooking. At dinner he ate several platefuls of Scotch broth with peas in them, and was very fond of the dish.

"You never eat it before, sir," Boswell pointed out the novelty to him.

"No, sir, but I don't care how soon I eat it again," replied Johnson, scooping up the succulent mouthfuls. He and Boswell topped off their platefuls of broth with skate, roasted lamb, chickens and tarts.

Besides the Scotch broth with peas, Aberdeen offered to the ponderous doctor the freedom of the city. It was curious, Boswell thought, to see him walking about the streets with the document stuck in his cocked hat, as the custom was.

"This is the first time," exclaimed Dr. Johnson, angrily glaring at the fare offered at the Red Lion Inn, "that I have seen a dinner in Scotland which I cannot eat!"

I am sorry to say that the uneatables before him included a dish of Scotch collops. Dr. Johnson was to meet many a supremely eatable dish of collops later on. A collop is a slice of meat, as it might be a steak or a chop. "Collops and eggs" is the Scotch version of ham and eggs. Most people have sampled collops under their aliases, *Scaloppine* or *Escalope.*

The next stop was Inverness. There at the inn, Johnson and Boswell, with two Scottish friends, supped on roasted kid. It was an occasion the Scotsmen never forgot. Full of good food, Johnson was in high spirits. He assured the Caledonians that the scientific expedition of Sir Joseph Banks had discovered in New South Wales an extraordinary animal called a "kangaroo." The better to characterize this beast, he rose from his chair and volunteered an imitation of the animal. The visitors stared as the tall, heavy, grave-looking Englishman stood erect, put out his hands like feelers, and, gathering up the tails of his huge brown coat so as to resemble the pouch of the animal, made two or three vigorous bounds across the room!

At Inverness the chaise was abandoned, and the travelers bestrode two sturdy little Highland ponies. The bulky doctor was quite a sight in this situation.

They rode along the bank of Loch Ness. A good way up the loch, Boswell spied a little Highland hut with an old woman standing at the door.

"Let's go in," said he.

Accordingly in they trooped, Boswell, Johnson, and a Highland guide to interpret the old woman's Gaelic speech.

Johnson was curious to know what the old woman ate. His nose soon told him. There was a pen full of goats at one end of the room, and a pot of goat stew steaming over a peat fire. Some of the smoke went out at a hole in the roof.

Dr. Johnson was also curious to inspect the old woman's sleeping arrangements. The guide put the request in Gaelic. The old woman's answer was shrill and indignant. Her virtue, the guide explained, was alarmed. Johnson and Boswell were merry over the misunderstanding as they rode on.

"She'll say," predicted Johnson, " 'There came a wicked young fellow, a wild young dog, who I believed would have ravished me had

Plots and Pans

there not been with him a grave old gentleman who repressed him. But when he gets out of the sight of his tutor, I'll warrant you he'll spare no woman he meets, young or old.'"

"No," Boswell came back. "She'll say, 'There was a terrible ruffian who would have forced me, had it not been for a gentle, mild-looking youth, who, I take it, was an angel'. . . ."

At Glenelg the ponies were left behind, and the travelers took boat for Skye. It was here, at the hospitable tables of the chiefs and tacksmen, that Dr. Johnson really learned to appreciate Scotch cooking. Mr. Mackinnon, a jolly big man, welcomed them at his farm of Coirechatachan. He set before them a large dish of minced beef collops; a large dish of fricassee of fowl; a dish which Boswell understood to be fried chicken or something like it; a dish of ham or tongue; some excellent haddock; some herring; a large bowl of rich milk, frothed or whipped; a bread pudding full of raisins and orange or lemon peel; all served up on a good tablecloth with china, silver spoons and dinner napkins, and washed down with porter for those who liked it or with Dr. Johnson's favorite tipple, punch.

Eleven people sat down to this feudal repast. Dr. Johnson did it full justice. Boswell took notes on everything. He was wrong about the "fried chicken." It was friar's chicken, that is, chicken broth with eggs poached in it.

From Skye, bulging with such food, the travelers proceeded to the Isle of Raasay. Their escort was that very Malcolm MacLeod who was celebrated in '45 for aiding the escape of Bonnie Prince Charlie; a stout, well-made man; quick and lively of eye; bronzed; rough-bearded; dressed in brogues and tartan hose, a purple kilt, a gold-corded green coat, and a blue bonnet with a gold thread button. Boswell admired him much.

The boat trip was rough, and Johnson's spurs were somehow lost overboard. This bizarre misfortune annoyed the good doctor.

He was soothed when they arrived at the laird's house and found a sturdy tea prepared: tea and coffee, marmalade, currant jelly, and for those who had come off the sea, mutton chops and tarts, with porter, claret, and punch. First the travelers had to join in a *Scalck*—a dram of brandy filled round according to Highland custom. After they had eaten, a fiddler appeared and a little ball began.

Boswell must have been in ecstacies with this entertainment. In

34

the first place, he was so fond of currant jelly that he once wrote a poem about it:

Long ere the cups were filled, I'd eager rise
(The love of jelly flaming in my eyes),
A slice of nicest cut, and spoon, would seize.
And with my usual much-becoming ease
Would the ambrosia plentifully spread
In mode genteel upon the wheaten bread.

In the second place, the Highland *Scalck* hit just the right spot. Boswell adopted the custom with such enthusiasm that he began each day with a *Scalck* before breakfast, until Johnson had to remonstrate with him about it.

In the third place, all over the Highlands, Boswell was wont to leap and caper to the fiddle after dinner. "My exertions as a dancer," he remarked with self-satisfaction, "are all forced by a reflex desire to promote lively good humour."

Boswell carried his lively good humor on a picnic on Raasay. Johnson stayed behind, perhaps because the expedition started before six in the morning, with only a dram (that *Scalck* again!) and a bit of bread to stay the stomach. The happiest hours of a man's life, in Dr. Johnson's opinion, were those he spent lying in bed in the morning.

But five spry Scotchmen climbed to the top of Duncaan and picnicked on cold mutton and bread and cheese, with plenty of brandy and punch. Then Malcolm MacLeod sang a Highland song, which brought to the fore Boswell's desire to promote lively good humor. While Malcolm rendered an encore, the picnickers danced a reel on the mountain top.

Left behind to his meditations, Dr. Johnson may have been composing the only recipe known to have fallen from his pen. It took form in Scotland as a burlesque *Meditation on a Pudding*.

"Flour that once waved in the golden grain and drank the dews of the morning. Salt which keeps the sea from putrefaction, contributes to a pudding; and milk is drawn from the cow, that useful animal. It is made with an egg, that miracle of nature which the theoretical Burnet has compared to creation."

Obviously this is an untested recipe, and should be approached with caution.

Though Dr. Johnson took no *Scalck*, it was breakfast in Scotland which drew from him the *amende honorable*. Primed with his *Scalck*, Boswell grew lyrical about Raasay's breakfasts; goat's whey brought to the bedside, chocolate, tea, bread and butter, marmalade and jelly, and very good scones, or cakes of flour baked with butter.

In spite of misunderstandings, Johnson was loyal to the stout-hearted Scotch breakfast. True, it turned out to be a little *too* stout-hearted at Lochbuie. Lady Lochbuie proposed to serve cold sheep-head. This rusticity annoyed another of the guests, but Boswell said:

"I think it is but fair to give him an offer of it. If he does not choose it, he may let it alone."

"I think so," said the hostess.

"Do you choose any cold sheep-head, sir?" she greeted her late-rising guest.

"No, madame," replied the traveler from London, indignantly.

"It's here, sir," she pressed him, as if he had refused it to save her the trouble of producing it.

Cold sheep-head was but an ill accompaniment to the whisked chocolate which Boswell liked to his breakfast. There was no end to crosspurposes at Lochbuie.

"Are you," bawled the bull-voiced old laird at their first meeting, "of the Johnstons of Glencoe, or of Ardnamurchan?"

"Neither, sir," replied the Sassenach visitor.

The Highlander's brow creased in puzzlement. A Johnston had to be one or the other. Finally light dawned.

"Then," he exclaimed, "you must be a bastard!"

Back in London, Dr. Johnson wrote up his travels. Forgotten were the bastardy and the sheep-head. He licked his chops as he thought of those Highland breakfasts, and he wrote: "If an epicure could remove by a wish, in quest of sensual satisfaction, wherever he had supped, he would breakfast in Scotland."

—Lillian de la Torre

EDITOR'S NOTE: Lillian de la Torre is the author of more than two dozen stories featuring Dr. Johnson as their detective. Most of them first appeared in *Ellery Queen's Mystery Magazine*, and have since been collected in book form.

Chupe

2 onions, minced
1 tablespoon lard or butter
2 large ripe tomatoes, peeled and cut
   up, or 2-3 canned tomatoes
5 medium potatoes, peeled and quartered
1 teaspoon salt
Pinch of cayenne pepper

½ teaspoon marjoram
6 cups water
¼ cup rice
1 3-ounce package cream cheese
2 eggs
1½ cups milk
½ pound cooked shrimp, optional
6 eggs, poached, optional

Sauté the onions in lard or butter until golden. Add tomatoes and potatoes. Simmer until potatoes are yellow and transparent at the edges. Season with salt, cayenne pepper, and marjoram. Add the water and rice and simmer 20 minutes or until potatoes are tender. Dissolve the cream cheese in potato mixture. Turn off the heat and stir in eggs beaten with milk. Season to taste and serve at once. As a luncheon or supper soup, add the shrimp or poach an extra egg in the soup for each person before adding the combined egg-milk mixture. Yield: 6 servings.

—Lillian de la Torre

Sandwiches

Feeding Miss Seeton

Short notice, but by applying some pressure in the right quarters, he could give a dinner party tomorrow, have some music and watch the effect of Miss Seeton's appearance on his wife and secretary. Stemkos got to his feet.

"You will both dine with me—informal, a snack, at such short notice. What," he asked Miss Seeton, "is your choice?" She rose but was too surprised to speak. "There must be some dish you have missed since you left England. Name it."

She thought of the overindulgence, the overabundance of rich food that she had suffered recently. Something that she had missed? How kind of Mr. Stemkos. Well, actually there was. One would so enjoy plain. . . . "Scrambled eggs," said Miss Seeton.

The menu proved the chef had tried:

> Scrumbledeggs Miss Seeton
> Ritz de Veau Emilie
> Boeuf en croute Dorothée
> Pommes Nouvelles   Haricots Verts
> Bombe Miss Seeton en Surprise

Reading her individual menu, Miss Seeton's appetite shrank. If this was Mr. Stemkos' idea of a snack, what, she wondered, must be his idea of a full-course meal. Also his little joke of putting her name to the different courses. So embarrassing. However, she comforted herself that few of the guests, some twenty in all, were likely to detect the teasing. . . .

—Heron Carvic

40

Sandwiches

Scrumbledeggs Miss Seeton

4 eggs	Bread slices
4 tablespoons cream	Lemon juice
1 jar lumpfish roe, finely chopped	Cayenne pepper
1 spring onion, finely chopped	Chopped chives or parsley, optional

Lightly scramble eggs with cream in a double boiler. Put in refrigerator to cool and set. Mix lumpfish roe with onion. Toast bread. Spread egg mixture on toast for open-faced sandwich, heaping some roe on top and giving each sandwich a good squeeze of lemon juice and a firm shake of cayenne pepper. Garnish if desired with chives or parsley. Yield: 1 sandwich per slice of toast.

"The same procedure will produce canapés if small buttered biscuits are substituted for toast."

—Heron Carvic

EDITOR'S NOTE: Try this also using melba toast rounds.

Fletch's Fried Egg Sandwich

2 slices bread	Thick slice raw onion
1 teaspoon butter	Catsup
1 egg	

Butter 1 slice of bread, one side. Fry egg, sunny side up, and put on buttered bread. Add onion. Douse liberally with catsup. Top with second slice of bread. Yield: 1 sandwich.

"Important! Do not expect to halve or quarter this sandwich! To be eaten while taking a shower, preferably before bed."

—Gregory Mcdonald

One-eyed Bessarabian Sandwich

1 slice bread
2 tablespoons bacon or chicken fat, or
   butter

1 egg
Salt and pepper

Cut hole in center of bread with cookie cutter or shot glass. Heat fat in skillet. Place bread slice in fat. Break egg into hole. Cook over medium heat until bread is brown and egg partially set. Turn over and cook until egg reaches desired doneness. Sprinkle with salt and pepper. Serve hot. Yield: 1 open-faced sandwich.

"W. C. Fields called this a 'One-Eyed Egyptian Sandwich.' His mistake. This is the fastest breakfast on record. You take a slice of bread and a shot glass and by pressing the shot glass down hard on the slice of bread you cut out a circular chunk of bread. Place slice with hole in a frying pan, skillet, spider, depending on what your region calls what is after all the same damned article. Where were we? Oh yes! You will have already melted a bit of fat or grease or heated some oil. And then comes the fun—simply crack the egg and drop (plop!) the yolk right into it. Hyunkle, hyunkle, hyunkle. The white spreads over the slice and into the pan. Cook to taste. Turn over or not, as you like. It's toast and egg in one piece. Use circle of bread to dip or wipe with. Pour shot into shot glass. Down the hatch!"

—Avram Davidson

Sandwich Romano

2 pieces rye or whole wheat bread
1 slice provolone cheese
4 anchovies

1 tablespoon mayonnaise
1 tablespoon butter

On slice of bread, place provolone. Top with anchovies. Spread second slice of bread with mayonnaise. Put, mayonnaise side down, over anchovies. Brown on both sides in butter, about 1 minute per side. Yield: 1 sandwich.

—Catherine Barth

Sandwiches
The Flynn Sandwich

2 slices dark rye bread
1 slice corned beef
1 slice Swiss cheese

1 cup chicken liver pâté, approximately
Cucumber dill pickle

On a slice of fresh, warm, dark rye bread, double over a slice of delicatessen corned beef. Add a slice of Swiss cheese. Top with an ice-cream scoopful of chicken liver pâté. Cover with second bread slice. Eat quickly, alternating bites with a cucumber dill pickle. Yield: 1 sandwich.

—Gregory Mcdonald

EDITOR'S NOTE: This is sublime with beer.

Avocado Club Sandwiches

3 slices toast
1 avocado, mashed
Lemon juice

2 tablespoons peanut butter
3 slices bacon, fried crisp
1 lettuce leaf

Spread slice of toast with avocado. Sprinkle with lemon juice. Place a second slice of toast over the first. Spread with peanut butter. Cover with bacon and lettuce leaf. Top with remaining toast slice. Cut into 4 pieces. Yield: 1 sandwich.

—Mary Higgins Clark

EDITOR'S NOTE: If "A Stranger Is Watching" you as you sample this taste treat, he well may slay you out of jealousy.

The Fletch Sandwich

1 slice pressed ham   *Cream cheese*

Thickly spread a slice of pressed ham with cream cheese. Roll into cigar shape. With toothpicks, run the sandwich through 3 times to hold. Yield: 1 sandwich.

"Blatantly leave the penetrating instruments (toothpicks) in the corpse. Do not even think of using bread."

—Gregory Mcdonald

Increase ("Inky") Proffit and the role he played in the stirring days of the War of Independence are unknown to almost all Americans. Neglect of the man justly called "the Godfather of the American Revolution" must be rectified. If we celebrate our heroes, it is only fair (especially for mystery writers) to look as well at our criminals.

For the truth is that without Increase Proffit's attempts to turn a dishonest shilling, there might have been no American Revolution!

As Crown and Colonies approached the confrontation from which there could be no turning back, cooler heads on both sides strove for reconciliation. But they were thwarted.

What made the Boston Tea Party such a sore point with both Americans and British, for instance, was not the dumping of the tea into Boston Harbor so much as its resale by Proffit. Proffit employed a team of swimmers in the recovery of the broached tea chests, which the English saw as turning a political protest into simple hijacking.

The fact that the tea was completely spoiled by soaking in salt water enraged Proffit's American customers. They had expected to get a bargain. Thus both Tory and Patriot tempers were further inflamed. The prospect of compromise receded.

—D. R. Bensen

Sassie Fleming's Boston Tea Party Sandwiches

4 slices bread
1 cucumber, sliced

Pepper
¼ cup mayonnaise

Cut crusts off bread. Spread lower slice with cucumber slices, and pepper lightly. Spread upper bread slice with mayonnaise and place over lower slice. On a solid surface, punch sandwich hard with flat of hand. Quarter sandwich and repeat process. Yield: 8 sandwiches.

"A little practice at this violent punch will allow you to squirt the mayonnaise and shoot the cucumber seeds into the usual American air-blown bread exactly right. If slices of cucumber shoot out between slices of bread into the general environment, then you are being excessively violent. Mix up the sandwich quarters on serving plate, so the palm print will appear less obvious; or at least, not be identifiable as yours. This kitchen violence is also helpful in keeping you calm and gracious subsequently at the tea table."

—Gregory Mcdonald

Eggs and Cheese

If you know the *Suisse Romande*, you have probably eaten *Raclette* in a cafe, for it is one of the specialties of the region; and I know that a good many foreigners find it a little disappointing. Briefly, the idea is to take a Bagnes cheese (no other will do), which roughly resembles a disk about the diameter and depth of a scooter tire, cut it in half, and apply the cut surface to the hot embers of a fire. As the cheese begins to melt and bubble under the heat, it is scraped off onto your plate and eaten with small potatoes boiled in their skins, pickled onions, and gherkins. Each helping of melted cheese is quite small, and the idea is to see how many scrapings you can manage to eat. Seven or eight is about average, ten or twelve is good, and the record is alleged to be around forty.

As I say, in spite of the particularly delicious and delicate taste of the Bagnes, some people find *Raclette* rather banal. This is because they have eaten it only in stuffy restaurants, prepared on electric grills. The proper way to eat *Raclette* is as follows:

Take a large rucksack. Into it put half a Bagnes cheese; a kilo of raw potatoes; a jar of mixed onions and gherkins; a saucepan; a plate, glass, knife and fork per person; a large knife for scraping the cheese; and a couple of liters of local white wine (don't forget the corkscrew). An old ski glove is also useful to prevent burned fingers.

Next climb your mountain with the rucksack on your back. As you go, look out for certain geographical features—a stream, a flat clearing with plenty of large gray stones to make a hearth, and pine trees for kindling and fuel. When you find your ideal site—remember it should have a fantastic mountain view and be surrounded by flowering meadows—you pitch your camp.

Having constructed your hearth, you light your fire, fill the saucepan from the stream, and boil the potatoes. Open the first bottle of wine. By the time the potatoes are done, the embers of the fire will be red and glowing, and you can make your *Raclette*. Each member of the party toasts his own cheese, holding the Bagnes against the red-hot wood ash with his ski-gloved hand. The second bottle of wine has, of course, been cooling in the ice-cold running water of the stream and is now ready to accompany your meal. The pines are green, the sky is deep blue to match the gentians, the distant peaks are capped with white. The smell of wood smoke and toasted cheese drifts deliciously upward through the crystal air. The stream burbles busily and the wine glows golden in the sunshine. Now you know what *Raclette* is all about.

—Patricia Moyes
(From *Season of Snows and Sins*)

Ed Gorgon's Pre-Game Omelette

Filling:

½ *bunch watercress*   1 *large banana*
 1 *tablespoon butter or margarine*

Chop watercress and set aside. In a small skillet, melt butter or margarine. Slice banana in ⅛-inch slices into hot butter. Sauté over medium heat for 1 minute. Remove banana slices, mix with watercress, and set aside.

Omelette:

4 *eggs*   *Salt and pepper*
1 *tablespoon cold water*   1 *tablespoon butter or margarine*

In a bowl beat together first 3 ingredients with a whisk or rotary beater. Heat butter or margarine in small skillet until bubbles disappear. Pour in the

49

egg mixture and cook over a high heat until done. On half of omelette, spread mixture of banana and chopped cress. Fold remaining half over the mixture and serve at once. Yield: 2 servings.

"Ed Gorgon, the umpire-detective who solves sports-related mysteries, says:

'Baseball players only spend half their season on the road. But we poor umpires—aside from being booed, insulted and generally unappreciated—spend our whole season on the road. (Make that eleven-twelfths of the season for those who live in one of the cities in the League, which I don't.)

'Needless to say, we get mighty tired of hotel food and restaurant food, even if we frequent the best places in town. (And we usually leave those to the players with their six-figure salaries.) Whenever I have a chance, I prefer to cook for myself. I've snuck out my traveling omelette pan in hotels from coast to coast to make myself this light pregame meal. It serves two, so I often invite another ump in to share it—preferably a skinny ump. Or in a pinch I eat it all myself. Then I'm ready to go to work. Play ball!' "

—Jon L. Breen

Calvin Trillin's Scrambled Eggs That Stick to the Pan Every Time

This is my only dish. I turn it out every school morning for my two daughters. They hate it.

Egg. Milk. If you can find it (back behind the lettuce, hidden by the shadow of the Chinese take-out leftovers), butter.

Burn the butter while looking for sandwich bread for lunch or discussing riboflavin contents of various cereals. Apologize to your daughters for your daughters. Put a little milk (if you can find it) with the eggs, and scramble away until you're afraid the butter might burn again. Shove the eggs around in the pan until you remember that the toast is about to burn. Turn back to the eggs which, by this time, have stuck to the pan.

Serve with burnt toast and a wan smile.

—Calvin Trillin

Lorraine Omelette

1 tablespoon unsalted butter
3 eggs, at room temperature
1 tablespoon cold water
1/2 teaspoon salt
1/8 teaspoon white pepper

2 tablespoons coarsely grated Gruyère cheese
1 tablespoon minced parsley
2 slices bacon, cooked crisp and crumbled

Warm butter in an 8-inch omelette pan over low heat while you mix eggs. Beat eggs, water, salt and pepper vigorously with a fork or whisk for 30 seconds, or until blended and frothy. When butter is bubbly, but not brown, tip to coat sides of pan and pour in eggs. Turn heat to medium-high. With a fork, draw edges of eggs in toward center of pan as they cook. At the same time, tilt and gently shake the pan so runny portions flow underneath cooked egg. Continue until omelette is just set and top is creamy and moist. Take pan from heat at once. Loosen omelette edges with fork, shaking gently. (If omelette should stick, slide a dab of butter underneath and tilt pan so butter runs over bottom). Top omelette with Gruyère cheese, parsley and bacon. Fold omelette in half as you slide it out onto a warm plate.

—Lesley Egan

EDITOR'S NOTE: Instead of the cheese, you might try a dollop of red caviar topped with sour cream and omit the bacon; even beluga may be substituted.

Soufflé Surprise, Sans Mort

1½ envelopes unflavored gelatin
1½ cups water
 1 cup milk
 ¾ cup sugar
 ¼ teaspoon salt
 2 tablespoons instant coffee

3 eggs, separated
1 teaspoon vanilla extract
Whipped cream, unsweetened
Sweet chocolate, grated
Candied ginger, finely chopped

Mix gelatin with water, milk, sugar, salt, and instant coffee. Place in top of a double boiler and heat until mixture is scalded and gelatin dissolved. Add 3 slightly beaten egg yolks and cook until mixture coats a spoon, stirring constantly. Remove from heat, mix in vanilla and chill until syrupy. Fold in the 3 egg whites, stiffly beaten. Pour into individual sherbet glasses or a serving bowl, and chill until firm. Top with whipped cream and sprinkle with chocolate and ginger. Yield: 6 servings.

"*Soufflé Surprise*, the famous short story by Vincent McConnor, is like a perfect suspense recipe with all the ingredients of tension, surprise and intrigue properly mixed and measured. Author McConnor has exceptional skills in evoking the sights, sounds, and smells of the old Les Halles markets, the River Seine, sidewalk cafes, the picturesque restaurants—plus the chilling, deadly rivalries between chefs—in memorable, lovely Paris. The above recipe, delicious really, omits its original ninth and lethal ingredient. I have added a new one of my own, the topping, which will not kill you. Except, of course, in calories."

—Maureen Daly

The British Merchant's Cook's Quiche

½ cup thin strips cooked ham
 1 onion, chopped
 2 tablespoons butter
 3 eggs

Salt and pepper
½ cup milk
¾ cup grated Swiss cheese
 1 9-inch unbaked pie shell

Preheat oven to 375° F. Sauté ham and onions in butter until onions are soft. Remove from heat and cool slightly. In bowl, beat eggs and add salt,

52

pepper, milk, and ham-onion mixture. Stir in cheese. Pour into pie shell. Set pie pan on cookie sheet and place in oven. Bake 30 minutes or until center is firm and top slightly browned. Yield: 4 servings.

—Jane Beckman

EDITOR'S NOTE: You might try a layer of crab meat, either fresh or canned, instead of the ham.

Quiche Lorraine

1 cup grated Swiss cheese	Butter
1 9-inch piecrust	5 eggs, beaten
1 medium onion, chopped	1 8-ounce container plain yogurt
1 cup fresh or canned mushrooms, sliced	

Preheat oven to 375° F. Sprinkle cheese over bottom of piecrust. Sauté onion and mushrooms in small amount of butter. (If canned mushrooms are used, drain prior to cooking.) Sprinkle over cheese. Combine eggs and yogurt, and pour over other ingredients. Bake for 35-40 minutes or until custard is firm. Yield: 4 servings.

—Cylvia Margulies

EDITOR'S NOTE: If any custard mixture is left over, it may be baked in custard cups and served cold with sliced fruit as dessert at a later meal.

Marine Corps Omelette

4 large eggs
½ cup milk, approximately
Oil, as needed
½ cup grated sharp cheddar cheese,
½ cup minced Spanish onion
1-2 cloves garlic, finely chopped

¼ cup finely chopped pepperoni
¼ cup finely chopped ham
¼ cup minced chives
Salt and pepper, to taste
¼ cup finely chopped green pepper

Beat eggs in a martini pitcher. Add milk until mixture is consistency of medium cream. Heat flat skillet (preferably rectangular). Grease with oily paper towel. Pour egg mixture on skillet and immediately sprinkle with all remaining ingredients except green pepper. Cook until bubbles in center remain open, as in cooking pancakes. Sprinkle with green pepper and, using a spatula, roll up like a jelly roll. Remove to platter and serve hot. Yield: 2 servings.

—Rex Burns

Fletch's Garbage Eggs

6 whole eggs
½ cup skim milk
1 tablespoon butter
10 chopped pimiento-stuffed olives

1 fresh tomato, chopped
1 green pepper, chopped (or chopped parsley or chives)
1 slice of cheese, chopped

Crack eggs into mixing bowl, removing any bits of shell. Beat lightly. Mix in other ingredients. Cook in buttered frying pan, stirring constantly. Serve immediately.

"Confusion should be caused in the bowl by vigorous stirring with a fork. Only when elements are as mixed up as defense evidence when presented to a jury should contents be scrambled into a frying pan. Eyes are best closed or averted during commission of this particular crime, if one expects one's taste to witness results without prejudice."

—Gregory Mcdonald

Mystery books and gourmet recipes are like the little girl (or is it a little boy now?) who has a little curl right in the middle of the forehead. When they are good, they are very, very good; when they are bad, they are horrid.

—Dorothy B. Hughes

Stuffed Eggs

6 hard-cooked eggs
Salt to taste
1 teaspoon vinegar (or to taste)

Prepared mustard, to taste
Mayonnaise
Chili powder

Peel cooked eggs under running cold water while they are still hot. Cut in half lengthwise. Remove yolks, reserving whites. Mash yolks with salt and vinegar. Add mustard and mayonnaise until desired consistency is reached. Stuff mixture into reserved whites and sprinkle with chili powder. Store in plastic wrap in refrigerator. Yield: 4-6 servings.

"As chili powder uncooked has little or no taste or bite, it's mostly for decoration—only a faint flavor. Just take a sampling as you're mashing up the yolks, and you'll know what you want in taste."

—Dorothy B. Hughes

EDITOR'S NOTE: Try curry powder for a change instead of the chili.

Scotch Eggs

½ dozen small eggs hardboiled (pullet
   eggs are good)
Salad oil for deep-frying
Sage
Freshly ground black pepper

Flour
1 pound hot sausage meat, the hotter
   the better
1 uncooked egg to beat up
Fine breadcrumbs

Hardboil the eggs the previous day. The secret of success is very dry eggs and very moist sausage meat.

When ready to roll, start heating oil. Shell eggs. Mix plenty of sage and black pepper with a little flour into the meat. Divide the mixture into six parts. Spread the first part evenly across your right hand and lay one egg in the middle. This is the hardest part. Now ease the meat evenly around the egg. Then dip the meat-covered egg in flour, beaten egg and fine breadcrumbs. Continue with second egg. When all six are prepared, place them in the hot oil and deepfry for 7 minutes per side (you may have to turn them over). Fish them out with a spoon, and drain. Yield: 3-6 servings.

"Some say one can eat such eggs hot. But I wait and then cut them into four bite-size pieces, to serve with drinks. A few cherry tomatoes and a sprinkle of fresh parsley make this an attractive platterful.

"If your first egg falls apart, try again. The secret is in sealing the sausage meat around the egg. Remember to keep the eggs dry and the meat and your hands moist!

"This is a specialty of British pubs. The mysterious element is how the eggs get into the sausage meat."

—Helen Lillie

"A Spanish tortilla like this one was served to Janie and David on the Madrid-Bilbao train in *Steps to Nowhere*. Scene, the dining car:

> The jounce and hustle of the train were evident here, making a pleasant slosh in the mineral water bottle and a challenge of the wine, a matter of due attention to the eccentric rhythms of the car. Plate after plate was dealt to them—crusty bread, antipasto, Spanish tortillas, steak—while the countryside rushed past, a changed view now of vineyards and sheep and here and there a plow drawn by oxen. Something about the scrabbly, difficult land and flicks of rain slanting across the windows served to heighten the sense of privilege and plenty inside.
>
> 'It's going to be all right,' David said warmly. 'There's usually a simple explanation of these things, you know. And then we'll get back to what we were doing, like having fun, remember? That's the point of this exercise. Every day a holiday, every meal a banquet. . . .' "

—Constance Leonard

Tortilla a la Española

2 small potatoes	Salt
2 tablespoons cooking oil	4 eggs

Peel potatoes, slice thin, dry on paper towels, then fry in hot oil in round pan until lightly browned and tender. Pour off oil. Salt potatoes. Beat and salt eggs and pour over potatoes in the pan. When omelette is firm and brown on one side, turn and brown on other. Yield: 2 servings.

"The Spanish tortilla is really a hearty potato omelette, very common in Spain and subject to all kinds of variations—onions come first to mind. On the train it was served as one course in a big meal; most Americans would find it an adequate main dish for lunch or supper—or a farm-type breakfast."

—Constance Leonard

Huevos Rancheros

(Ranch-Style Eggs)

1 tablespoon butter
1 16-ounce can refried beans
1 cup shredded cheddar cheese
2-3 onions, finely chopped
1 tablespoon olive oil
1 8-ounce can hot Mexican chili sauce
1 8-ounce can tomato sauce or tomato puree

¾ teaspoon crushed oregano
Salt, to taste
6 tortillas
Cooking oil
12 eggs, poached or fried
2 ripe avocados
1 bottle green chili sauce (salsa jalapeña)

Cut butter into refried beans and spread in a shallow buttered casserole. Sprinkle thickly with the cheese and bake, uncovered, in a 325° F. oven for 18 minutes. Sauté onions in olive oil, gradually adding Mexican chili sauce, tomato sauce, and oregano. Salt to taste. Keep warm until ready to use. Fry the tortillas in a small amount of cooking oil until crisp, turning often. Drain on paper towels. Dip tortillas in the warm sauce and place on individual dishes. Spoon remaining sauce over tortillas and top with 2 eggs. Garnish with avocado cut in thick slices. Pass heated beans and green chili sauce. Yield: 6 servings.

"The green chili sauce should be added by the individual diners, according to their tolerance for very hot food. If tortillas are not available in your local market, they can be made very simply. They are nothing but an unleavened bread made of dehydrated masa flour (corn flour), or regular flour. To 2 cups

58

of masa add 1½ cups of warm water and mix until the dough holds together. Shape the dough into a smooth ball and divide it into equal-size pieces. If you have a tortilla press, you'll know what to do next. If you don't have one, flatten a small ball of dough slightly and place it between two damp cloths. Roll with a rolling pin until the cake is about 6 inches in diameter. Trim to a round shape and put between two squares of waxed paper.

"To cook, peel off the top of the waxed paper and flip tortilla into a preheated, ungreased hot griddle or heavy frying pan over a medium heat. As the tortilla warms, you will be able to peel off the remaining paper. Turn tortilla frequently and cook until it is dry and is slightly flecked with brown specks, approximately 2 minutes. Homemade tortillas are much better if they are put in the icebox for 24 hours before cooking.

"If masa flour is not available, use 2 cups of unsifted flour, a teaspoon of salt, ⅓ cup lard and ½ cup of warm water. If green chili sauce is not available, you can fake it with Tabasco, or any available commercial hot sauce, blended with either catsup or puree of tomato. There is no real substitute for refried beans. If they are not available, I would suggest that you forget the whole dish.

"Huevos Rancheros makes an excellent breakfast dish, a good lunch, a fine supper, and may also be served as a dinner, especially if accompanied by a hefty salad. Irrespective of what meal you select, the proper accompanying beverages are virtually mandatory. As a prelude, several ounces of 100-proof imported tequila on the rocks with a twist of lemon. Ladies and authors of Gothic novels may substitute a Margarita without being considered in disgrace. During the meal, the only proper drink is imported Mexican beer. The meal may be topped off with a piping hot cup of chocolate coffee (no cream, no sugar) laced with brandy; or an ethnic purist may return to the tequila."

—Lionel White

Hermione Slocum's Cheese Wafers

1 pound sharp cheddar cheese
1/2 pound butter, softened
1 teaspoon dry mustard

1 teaspoon Worcestershire Sauce
1 teaspoon salt
2 cups sifted flour

Grate the cheese. Allow it to soften and knead it into the butter with hands. Add seasonings. Add flour gradually and knead into a firm dough. Form the dough into rolls (like ice box cookies), wrap in waxed paper, and chill until hard. Slice as thin as possible, and place on greased cookie sheets. (This dough will not rise, nor spread very much in baking.) Bake in 350° F. oven for 20 to 30 minutes, depending on thickness of slices. Wafers should be lightly browned. Let cool before serving. Yield: about 36 wafers.

"These wafers are delicious with cocktails, with soup, or salad. The dough is best made a day or more in advance."

—Warner Law

Cheese Puff

7 slices white bread
2 cups (1/2 pound) grated American
  cheese, divided
1/2 teaspoon salt
1/4 teaspoon pepper

Paprika, optional
3 eggs
2 cups milk
Mustard, to taste

Preheat oven to 350° F. Cut crusts from bread. Fit half the bread into bottom of well-greased rectangular baking dish. Cover with half the cheese. Sprinkle with salt and pepper, and paprika if using. Cover with remaining bread and cheese. Sprinkle with salt and pepper. Beat eggs, milk, and mustard together. Pour over bread. Place baking dish in larger pan of hot water and bake until custard is set, about 40 minutes. Serve very hot. Yield: 4 servings.

—Helen Wells

EDITOR'S NOTE: This is a perfect accompaniment to any leftover cold meat—turkey, ham, roast beef.

Fish and Seafood

The Old Shell Game

As a former (reformed?) mystery writer who now sells sea shells, I am frequently asked why I do not take time out to write a story in which a mollusk serves either as the weapon, the motive, or the milieu for murder.

The shell as weapon has been done—notably by Phyllis A. Whitney in *Columbella* and by Baynard Kendrick's whodunnit with the lethal harpoon of a Textile Cone. *Conus textile*, whose beautiful shell rarely measures over four inches, can kill a fully grown man who fails to understand who is collecting whom. It does not do this with malice aforethought but is driven by instinct to immobilize anything it encounters that moves, in order to satisfy its carnivorous appetite.

On the other hand, a mollusk with a perfectly terrible reputation is actually much maligned. The so-called Killer Clam, *Tridacna gigas*, is a gentle vegetarian. Yet who in early childhood or on the late, late show has not seen him devouring the likes of Johnny Weismuller, with or without relish?

A shell might quite logically serve as the motive for homicide. Some of them cost in the thousands. However, the perpetrator would have to be some kind of nut. One of two kinds of nuts: A) the recluse who likes to gloat over his treasures alone in a locked room and never dares show them to anybody; or B) a feckless thief who is so dumb that he would probably steal a Rembrandt and then discover that he could not sell it to anyone but A. The shell world is so small that the theft of a rare specimen would instantly flash around it, making the property too hot to handle.

The best story possibilities lie in shells and shelling as a milieu, a way of life which frequently is a way of death. It involves diving at great depths, usually with a buddy. But what if the buddy harbors a secret grudge? What neater way to dispatch a rival than to scuttle his scuba?

The professional abalone divers who work out of Santa Barbara, California, have even simpler means at their disposal. They do not use scuba (self-contained-underwater-breathing-apparatus). It is more economical, and in some instances obligatory, to have air pumped down from a boat by a topside partner, called a tender because he tends to everything except the actual diving and gathering of abalone, or *ab* as it is called.

You don't have to be crazy to be an ab diver, but it helps. Their days begin at dawn or shortly before, in waterfront diners where guys sit around and try to think up reasons for not going out that day. The rewards are great, three- or four hundred dollars *per* lucky *diem*. The hazards are enough to give anyone pause, and are both external and internal.

It is part of the camaraderie of divers that each must have a nickname, usually insulting. I shall call my composite here Hapless Hal (short for *Haliotis*, the generic name of the Abalone family). He has been diving for four of his twenty-six years, which puts him twelve months ahead of his boyhood chum who now serves as his tender. A year ago Hal rescued his friend, who had dived a little too deep and suffered the intoxication called "rapture of the deep," making it impossible for him to save himself.

Hal pays fifteen dollars a year for a license to collect. There is no limit on how many he may take, but strict limitations as to where from and how small. The where extends roughly from the middle of the California coast southward to the Mexican border, in water at least twenty feet deep. Usually the pickings are better deeper than that, all the way down to two-hundred feet.

Minimum size requirements have been precisely set for each species. The principal tool of Hal's trade is an "ab iron," a bar of heavy metal with which he jimmies the abalone off the rock to which it so tenaciously clings. The bar is marked with notches or projections between which each specimen is measured at time of capture. (If it is a hair's breadth undersized, back it goes on the rock.) Later, aboard the boat, Hal or his tender must measure it again. If a mistake was made due to haste or poor visibility, he must return the critter to exactly whence it came. Not just in the general direction: *exactly*. He is under constant surveillance by the patrols of Fish and Game. Taking underlimit abs in offlimits waters can cost him a five-hundred-dollar fine, six months in jail, confiscation of equipment, or all three.

The patrol boats are not the only adversaries in hot pursuit of Hal's livelihood. The jolly sea otter practically takes the bread out of his mouth. Unlicensed, these outlaws take every abalone on which they can lay their paws, at any depth they choose. Then they float on their backs, smash the shell with a stone, and daintily eat their favorite cuts, throwing the rest away. To a man, professional ab divers loathe otters.

So much for the external dangers. The gravest internal dangers are, quite literally, internal. Hal's lungs, liver, and lights take a terrible beating from the sea. Among his associates there are bound to be several who have suffered the "bends" from too swift an ascent after a deep dive. Three or four such seizures can prove fatal; but even one can leave its victim as barmy as a punch drunk fighter. Seeing too many of these can make a diver lose his nerve. Once that happens, it's time to change jobs.

Most abalone meat is frozen and shipped to Japan. However, some of it remains in the United States and may be purchased. This is easier to do if you live on the west coast, but wherever you are it is worth the effort. Poets and epicures have vainly tried to describe its flavor and usually end up by saying it tastes like nothing else, certainly like no other seafood.

—Veronica Parker Johns

Abalone Casserole

2 pounds abalone steak	1 tomato, peeled, seeded, and chopped
2 eggs, beaten	1 teaspoon prepared mustard
1 cup cracker crumbs	Juice of 1 lemon
1/2 cup peanut oil	1 tablespoon minced parsley
1 cup hot water	1 clove garlic, crushed
1 small onion, minced	Salt and pepper, to taste

Slice abalone steaks and pound with wooden mallet until tender. Dip slices in egg, then cracker crumbs. Heat oil in large skillet and quickly fry slices until golden brown. Remove to casserole. Pour hot water into skillet and add remaining ingredients. Simmer for 5 minutes, stirring constantly. Pour over abalone. Bake, covered, in a 300° F. oven for 1 hour. Yield: 6 servings.

"If you can obtain the shell as well as the meat, treasure it. It's gorgeous!"

—Veronica Parker Johns

Fish and Seafood

Abalone Steak

3 pounds abalone steak
2 tablespoons melted butter
2 tablespoons mayonnaise

Salt, to taste
Pepper or paprika
Juice of 1 lemon

Cut steak into ½-inch slices against the grain. Pound thoroughly with wooden mallet until tenderized. (Abalone *must* be pounded to make it edible.) Combine remaining ingredients* and marinate abalone for 15 minutes. Arrange strips on greased broiler pan. Place in preheated broiler, 2 inches below heating unit. Broil 5 minutes, or until golden brown. Turn strips, brush with remaining marinade, and broil 10 minutes longer. Yield: 6 servings.

* Double or triple all marinade ingredients if broiling a large steak.

—Veronica Parker Johns

Prawns Paradise

1 3-ounce package cream cheese
1 11¼-ounce can of clear jellied beef
   consommé

1½ pounds small shrimp, or prawns,
   cooked

Mix cream cheese and consommé in blender, reserving about ½ inch of the consommé in the can. Divide shrimp among 4 soup cups. Pour evenly divided contents of the blender over shrimp. Pour what is left of consommé onto the surface of the mixture in each cup to make a nice glazing. Place in refrigerator until mixture has jellied. Yield: 4 servings.

"Some consommés work better than others. The final result should be fairly firm, textured, but not runny. Poor-grade consommés don't have enough gelatin in them. But this is delicious. I could eat it every day of the week. I doubt you have seen it before. And I doubt you have ever tasted anything so good. It is a first course."

—Roald Dahl

EDITOR'S NOTE: This recipe is as versatile as it is delicious. Try it with sliced avocado instead of shrimp and jellied chicken consommé instead of beef. Or substitute sliced pimiento and sliced black olives.

Forty years ago, when England was celebrating the end of the war by a period of unusual austerity, with rationing as tight as ever and a general feeling that rejoicing was unseemly and suffering good for the soul, the newly married Gilberts acquired the habit of taking all their holidays in France—a habit which has persisted.

Travel might be on foot or by third class rail. But the francs saved could be spent on meals—*real* meals. The *Tournedos Henri Quatre*, each topped with its little pastry basket of *foie-gras*, eaten at Angers in 1948, are still as fresh in my memory as the *Poularde au Vapeur* of that prince of cooks, Alexandre Dumaine at the *Côte d'Or* at Saulieu. So are certain fresh trout cooked in butter and goodness knows what else that we ate after driving through the Massif Central in a thunderstorm so terrifying that even the French lorry drivers had to draw up at the side of the road while water ran past us like a stream.

Much though I love it, I have only (very rarely and very cautiously) attempted to introduce the delights of French cooking into a crime story.

On reflection, I think the instinct was sound. Do cuisine and crime really mix? They may do so functionally, if the cookery is part of the crookery. But as an ornament it seems to me distracting. On only one occasion, when my hero wished to seduce his secretary, I did think it kinder to both parties to allow him to do so to the accompaniment of a first class French meal:

He ordered *Quenelles de brochet*, deciding regretfully against lobster sauce as being too rich, followed by guinea fowl *à la belle maman* with a salad of watercress.

"After that," he suggested, "we shall pause for breath, and see if we can manage something ambitious to finish up with, or perhaps just a sorbet."

I see that I suggested that on such an occasion the appropriate wines would be a *Sancerre* to go with the *Quenelles* and a *Chambertin* with the guinea fowl. This was, I think, more important than the food. A good bottle of wine undoubtedly adds something to either a meal or a story.

But a word of warning. The minutiae of wine can be a terrible trap to the unwary. It may have been only a printer's error when Evelyn Waugh referred in *Brideshead Revisited* to *Clos de Bère*, when he clearly meant *Close de Bèze*. But what can have come over the meticulous Dorothy Sayers when she allowed that unmatched wine lover, Lord Peter Wimsey, to refer to Hermitage as a claret?

If you are lucky enough to possess a first edition of *Busman's Honeymoon*, you will find that she took this gaffe so much to heart that she insisted the publishers insert an erratum slip at page 335: "For 'Hermitage' in the last line of this page read *'Léoville'*." I am even a little doubtful of this correction. Would an expert refer to *"Léoville?"* There are no fewer than three chateaux which incorporate this name: *Léoville-Barton, Léoville-Lascases* and *Léoville-Poyferré*.

It just shows how careful you must be.

—Michael Gilbert

Gratin de Fruits de Mer

½ pound halibut, cod, or haddock
1 cup milk
1 bay leaf
¼ pound mushrooms, sliced
2 tablespoons butter, divided
1 tablespoon flour

¼ cup grated Gruyère or cheddar
  cheese
¼ pound prawns or small shrimp,
  cooked and cleaned
Salt and pepper, to taste
2 cups boiled rice

Poach fish, until just tender, in milk to which bay leaf has been added. Drain, reserving milk. Sauté mushrooms in half the butter. Make a cream sauce of the remaining milk by simmering milk and adding remaining butter. Sprinkle in flour slowly to thicken sauce. Stir in grated cheese, mushrooms, prawns or shrimps, and poached fish. Season to taste and serve over boiled rice. Yield: 4 servings.

"We have enjoyed this dish in France, and have reproduced it, in a simplified form, in our own kitchen."

—Michael Gilbert

Moules Marinières

3 quarts mussels, in shell
¼ cup dry white wine
¼ cup minced shallots (or green
  onions, if you must)

1-2 parsley sprigs
2 tablespoons butter or olive oil,
  optional

Put all ingredients in a large uncovered kettle. Bring quickly to a boil and boil about a minute to reduce wine a little. Cover tightly and continue cooking over medium-high heat. Cook until shells open—about 5 to 8 minutes—shaking kettle once or twice. Ladle mussels into bowls. Pour broth over mussels, but leave a little broth in the kettle to avoid pouring out the sand. Yield: 3-4 servings.

—Aaron Elkins

Seafood Supreme

2 11-ounce cans mushroom soup
1 cup hollandaise sauce
3 tablespoons grated Parmesan cheese
1/2 cup white wine
1/2 cup heavy cream
1 cup grated cheddar cheese
Salt and pepper, to taste
Lemon juice, to taste
Curry powder, to taste
Worcestershire Sauce, to taste
Sherry, to taste
Seafood, cooked (shrimp, crab, lobster, fillet of sole, oysters, mussels, at least three)
1 bunch asparagus, cooked
Breadcrumbs
Butter

Combine first 11 ingredients in top of double boiler. Simmer over hot water, stirring constantly until smooth. Stir in seafood. Place asparagus in buttered casserole. Pour sauce over asparagus. Cover with breadcrumbs, dot with butter and brown under broiler. Yield: 6 servings.

—Nancy Webb

Lucy Freeman's Shrimp Dish

1 pound raw shrimp, shelled and cleaned
Boiling water
1/4 pound butter
1/4 cup white wine
1 cup fresh breadcrumbs
1 clove garlic, minced
Salt and pepper
Chopped parsley
Toast points, rice or boiled fish

Cook shrimp in boiling water for 3 minutes. Drain. Melt butter in saucepan and add shrimp, wine, breadcrumbs, garlic, salt and pepper. Bring to boiling point, stirring constantly. Serve sprinkled with parsley over toast or rice, or as sauce for boiled fish. Yield: 4 servings as main dish, 6-8 servings as sauce.

—Lucy Freeman

Shrimp Shannon

3 cups water
1½ teaspoons sea salt
2 11-ounce cans shrimp soup
1 pound small shrimp, cleaned,
  shelled and deveined (if frozen,
  thaw and dry)

1 pound fresh mushrooms, chopped
  (or 6 ounces canned, drained)
3 cups instant rice, uncooked
1½ cups fresh large peas (or 1 package frozen, thawed)
Parsley, to taste

Add salt to water in a large pot and set aside. In a smaller pot, spoon in the thick canned soup and heat it slowly. Allow to thicken. Add shrimp to heating soup. Add mushrooms. Stir and let heat to just below a simmer. It won't matter how long you hold it like that if you don't let it boil which would break down the flesh of the shrimp.

Boil the water. Add the instant rice and stir. Cover and let stand for 5 minutes or more. At the last minute, add the peas to the rice. Stir them through to warm the peas a trifle. Spoon out a generous helping of rice and peas and ladle over the thick, salmon-colored sauce. Garnish with parsley. Yield: 6 servings.

"This is a light sea-side dish, but filling enough for a working fisherman. I serve with it a thoroughly heated long loaf of Italian bread, and butter which I've let soften for an hour on the table."

—Shannon O'Cork

Fred Tobey's Old Tavern Shrimp

2½ cups sliced raw mushrooms
½–¾ pound raw large shrimp or
  cooked lobster meat
¼ cup butter, divided
4 teaspoons flour
2 tablespoons fresh lemon juice
2 teaspoons soy sauce
2 teaspoons honey (preferably
  clover)

Dash Tabasco
¼ teaspoon salt
⅛ teaspoon pepper
½ teaspoon ground ginger
½ cup water
2 tablespoons sherry
2 cups boiled rice, optional

Simmer mushrooms in small amount of slightly salted water until crisply tender. (Do not overcook.) Drain, reserving liquid. Cook shrimp in mushroom water 4 minutes. Drain, discard water. Peel and clean shrimp and cut into bite-size pieces. Melt half the butter. Add flour and cook until lightly browned, stirring constantly. Add remaining butter but do not allow to brown. Combine remaining ingredients except sherry and rice. Pour slowly into roux, stirring constantly, until thickened. Remove from heat, add sherry, shrimp and mushrooms. Heat and serve over rice or as a side dish. Yield: 2 servings as main dish, 4 servings as side dish.

—Fred S. Tobey

EDITOR'S NOTE: The flavor of the dish is improved by refrigerating overnight and reheating the next day. Do not allow to boil.

Shrimp Basquaise

2 teaspoons minced shallots
1 tablespoon butter
12 large raw cleaned shrimp
⅔ cup heavy cream

1 teaspoon minced chives
1 teaspoon minced parsley
2 tablespoons green Izarra
2 cups boiled rice

Sauté shallots in butter over low heat until golden. Add shrimp and sauté 5 minutes over medium low heat, turning to pinken all sides. Reduce heat to low, stir in cream, chives and parsley. Cover and bring to a boil, stirring occasionally, over low heat. Add Izarra, mix gently to distribute through the sauce, and serve with plain boiled rice. Yield: 2 servings.

"Perhaps Bunter would prepare this for Lord Peter Wimsey and his first *diner à deux* with Harriet Vane?"

—Elsie Lee

EDITOR'S NOTE: Izarra is a Basque liqueur, rarely stocked by local stores. You may substitute green Chartreuse. The flavor is similar.

Big Fat Shrimp

24 raw jumbo shrimp	2 tablespoons minced onion
4 tablespoons anchovy paste	½ teaspoon freshly ground black
4 tablespoons unsalted butter,	pepper
creamed	Flour for dusting
1 cup breadcrumbs	Batter
2 tablespoons lemon or lime juice	

Peel shrimp, leaving on tail, and devein. Butterfly for stuffing. Combine anchovy paste, butter, breadcrumbs, lemon or lime juice, onion, and pepper. Stuff shrimp with this mixture and dust lightly with flour. Refrigerate while making batter.

Batter:

1 cup all-purpose flour	1 egg, separated
1 teaspoon salt	Oil for deep frying
1 tablespoon unsalted butter, melted	Parmesan cheese, freshly grated
1 cup flat beer	

Sift flour and salt into large bowl. Make well in center. Pour butter, beer and egg yolk into well. Mix and set aside in warm place. Beat egg white until stiff. Fold into batter. Dip stuffed shrimp into batter, and fry in deep hot oil, 2 or 3 at a time. Drain on paper towels. Keep warm. When all shrimp are fried, sprinkle with Parmesan cheese. Serve immediately. Yield: 4-6 servings.

—Tobias Wells

Fish and Seafood

Bouillabaisse à la Bloch

2 large leeks, washed and diced
2 large onions, diced
½ clove garlic, minced
2 tablespoons olive oil
1 cup raw potatoes, diced
½ cup celery, diced
½ large green pepper, diced
1 1-pound 4-ounce can peeled whole
    tomatoes
Bottled clam juice or water
1 tablespoon parsley, minced

¼ teaspoon thyme
¼ teaspoon marjoram
1 bay leaf
5 10-ounce cans whole baby clams
1 pound cooked shrimp, peeled and
    drained
1 pound cooked lobster meat, shelled
1 pound cooked scallops
1 pound cooked crab legs or crab
    meat, shelled
Salt and pepper, to taste

In a large, heavy pot sauté leeks, onions, and garlic in olive oil until soft but not brown. Add potatoes, celery, green pepper, and tomatoes in their juice. Add sufficient bottled clam juice or water to make 2 quarts. Add herbs and simmer 1 hour, stirring occasionally. Add clams, shrimp, lobster, scallops, and crab meat. Simmer for ½ hour longer. Add salt and pepper. Serve in heated soup plates. Yield: 6-8 servings.

"Every time I essay the role of gastronomer, I run the risk of accenting the first syllable. But somewhere in my checkered-tablecloth career, I developed a fondness for bouillabaisse—the dish itself, not the spelling or pronunciation. And most emphatically not the turgid soup offered in most restaurants, with its profusion of shell-encased objects which cannot be properly dealt with unless one has a master's degree in engineering and a complete set of plumber's tools.

"Bearing this in mind, my wife Eleanor devised a recipe of her own. Gone is the mushy potato soup colored by tomato paste. Gone are the encrusted crustaceans playing the old shell game with the hapless diner. Here is a gourmet delight which can be enjoyed without a napkin around the neck before or an indigestion remedy down the throat afterwards."

—Robert Bloch

EDITOR'S NOTE: Serve with hot garlic bread and a dry white wine.

Deviled Scallops

1½ pounds bay scallops
½ cup butter, at room temperature
1½ teaspoons strong Dijon mustard
¾ teaspoon salt

2 dashes cayenne pepper
1 cup milk
Buttered crumbs (about ½ cup tossed
with 2-3 tablespoons melted butter)

Preheat oven to 350° F. Rinse and drain scallops and set in baking dish. Mash together butter, mustard, salt and cayenne until smooth. Spread over the scallops. Add the milk and top with the buttered crumbs, spreading evenly. Bake, uncovered, 20 minutes. Yield: 4 servings.

—Elsie Lee

EDITOR'S NOTE: You might try this with poached sole fillets; also with cooked shrimp.

Crab Cakes Oxford Style

1 pound cooked crab meat (fresh),
    shredded
½ small onion, chopped
1 tablespoon prepared mustard
Sprinkling of dry mustard (about one
    teaspoon)
1 egg, unbeaten

Salt, to taste
¼ cup butter, melted
3 slices white bread, crumbled
2 tablespoons mayonnaise
Flour
Fat for deep fat frying

Combine all ingredients except flour and fat. Mix with fork or fingers. Form into 8 cakes. Chill between waxed paper overnight or for at least 8 hours. Dip in flour. Fry in deep fat, uncovered, until brown. Or sauté slowly in butter until cooked through. Yield: 4 servings.

NOTE: Chilling in refrigerator, *not* freezer, is important. Otherwise, the cakes may fall apart in frying.

"A crab cake delicate in flavor, juicy in texture, yet light in quality. Certain guests have been known to eat four at a single sitting."

—Lucille Fletcher

Seafood Risotto with Vegetables

9 tablespoons butter, divided
1/2 cup finely chopped onion
1/2 cup finely chopped carrots
1/2 cup finely chopped celery
1 teaspoon thyme
1 bay leaf
Salt and pepper, to taste
1 1/2 pounds fresh lobster meat
1/3 cup cognac
1 pound cooked jumbo shrimp,
   peeled and deveined
1/3 cup cream sherry
Juice of 1 lemon
1 teaspoon fresh dill

1 tablespoon olive oil
1 teaspoon grated fresh ginger root
1 large onion, chopped
1 medium zucchini, chopped
1 carrot, chopped
1 green pepper, seeded and chopped
1 1/4 cups raw Carolina long grain
   white rice
5-6 cups rich chicken stock
1 cup heavy cream
1 cup grated Parmesan cheese
2 tomatoes, peeled, seeded and
   chopped

Melt 4 tablespoons butter in a large skillet. Stir in 1/2 cup onion, 1/2 cup carrots, 1/2 cup celery, thyme, and bay leaf. Sprinkle with salt and pepper. Cook over low heat for 5 to 8 minutes or until carrots are tender. Cut lobster into large pieces and add to skillet. Cook over medium-low heat until lobster is heated through. Add cognac. Flame. Cover and cook 1 minute longer. Remove lobster and combine with shrimp in large bowl. Sprinkle with sherry, lemon juice, dill, olive oil, and ginger root. Marinate in refrigerator for 1/2 hour. Remove vegetables from skillet and reserve, discarding bay leaf. Melt remaining butter in large, clean skillet. Add remaining chopped vegetables and stir briefly. Add rice and mix well. Cook over medium-low heat for 7 minutes. Stir in 5 cups of stock, one cup at a time. After each addition cook, stirring constantly, until liquid is absorbed. When rice is almost tender, add remaining ingredients, the reserved lobster and shrimp, the marinade and vegetables. Stir until rice is tender and heated through. Serve immediately. Yield: 5 servings.

—Fred Jarvis

I enjoy cooking, but I am fearful that any recipe which I might contribute would be looked upon with great suspicion on the part of the reader as to the source of the ingredients. And I am not a vegetarian.

Many years ago I went up to Westchester County to do an autopsy on an exhumed body. I had taken Mr. John Brennan with me to take the stenographic notes. It was a long autopsy. On the way back we took the train. I had a heavy bag, much heavier than when I started out, with some materials for chemical examination which involved a suspected case of poisoning. We hadn't had lunch and we stopped off at the Oyster Bar at the station. I carried the bag. Brennan was suffering from asthma at the time and I wanted to spare him the physical strain of carrying that heavy bag with instruments, jars, etc., inside. We walked into the checkroom, and I carried the bag and placed it on the floor. When we finished our lunch I claimed the bag. The young lady who picked it up for me remarked, "You'd think that there was a body inside!"

I said, "You would be surprised," and she gaped at me. But a recipe might worry some of your readers.

—Milton Halpern, M.D.
Former Chief Medical Examiner
City of New York

Oyster Casserole Oxford

1 quart oysters
1 bag crumbly stuffing mix (not the
  crouton type)

Milk
1 tablespoon butter

Preheat oven to 400° F. Pick, drain and wash oysters, reserving the liquor. Grease a baking dish and place a layer of oysters in the bottom. Spread over it a layer of stuffing mix, then another layer of oysters and another layer of stuffing. Add oyster liquor and enough milk to moisten the mixture. Dot with butter and bake for 35-40 minutes or until top layer is golden brown. Yield: 6 servings.

"It is quick to prepare and yet tastes complicated. It's particularly delicious when served with country ham, a green salad and plenty of biscuits."

—Lucille Fletcher

New Orleans Oysters au Gratin

6 slices white bread
Butter
2 eggs, slightly beaten
½ cup milk
1 teaspoon salt

1 teaspoon dry mustard
½ teaspoon paprika
½ pound sharp cheddar cheese, grated
1 pint oysters

Preheat oven to 350° F. Cut crusts from bread. Butter slices and cut into quarters. Combine eggs, milk, seasoning and cheese. Grease casserole. Alternate layers of oysters with squares of bread. Pour liquid mixture over all. Top with layer of bread squares. Bake 50 minutes. Yield: 4-6 servings.

—Hildegarde Dolson

Meats

Cooking à la Eberhart

Recently, having invited my goddaughter, her sister, their husbands, and a cousin to dinner, I found I was to cook it. It's in this book, if you care to look at it. I did everything just right—*just right*—but I forgot to turn on the oven. Consequently my guests were obliged to stem their appetites with appetizers and such, while I began to fear that I was pressing liquor on these young things.

Eventually, the roast reached the stage where it was at least a little brown. If one carved too deeply, it was simply bloody. It makes it worse when I confess that I did the same thing a few weeks before that, under even more humiliating circumstances, for one of my guests, a dear and lovely French woman, who is also practically a cordon bleu. I was ready to serve them a completely *raw* three-rib roast. I have now put a sign on my oven saying, *"Turn Me On!"* These two memories are too sharply engraved upon my soul.

However, since I have kept house for many more years than I care to mention, I do have sense enough to keep a housekeeping and guest book. Therein are special recipes, charts of where the guests sat at table whenever in my house, what they liked and didn't like, any allergies, preferences as to wine—all those multitudinous items which a good housekeeper can and does store away in her mind and doesn't have to write down anywhere.

I secreted several recipes from all eyes but mine. (They will be found in these pages.) One of them is more than a little vague, for the magnificent cook who was generous enough to give it to me was so expert a cook that she would say "a pinch of this," "stir until you think it's thickening," "until it bubbles," or "take so much butter." You've all heard these recipes with perfectly frustrating directions. However, I did—twice, I think—follow this very recipe and it is heavenly and oozing with calories.

Well—happy cooking! And remember always to turn on the oven.

—Mignon G. Eberhart

Meats

Goddaughter Leg of Lamb

4-5 *pound leg of lean lamb*
  2 *tablespoons butter or margarine*
Salt and pepper

1¼ *teaspoons dried rosemary*
  1 *cup dry white wine*

Preheat oven to 500° F. Rub lamb with butter. Season with salt, pepper, and rosemary. Place in roasting pan in oven for 20 minutes, or until lamb is browned. Reduce oven heat to 300-350° F. Continue cooking until lamb is done, figuring 25 minutes per pound including browning time. Remove to serving platter. Serve pan juices in sauce dish with the lamb. Yield: 5-6 servings.

—Mignon G. Eberhart

Rara Ovis

1 *small leg of lamb (not over 4½*
   pounds)
8 *cloves garlic, slivered*

¼ *cup flour*
2 *cups double-strength black coffee*
1 *cup claret or Burgundy wine*

Preheat oven to 350° F. Wipe the lamb with paper towels and make slits with a sharp knife all over, into which insert thin slivers of garlic. (Do not skimp. That lamb should be fragrant clear into the livingroom!) Rub flour completely over the lamb, by hand and not missing a pinspot. Bake for 20 minutes, until the flour browns slightly and a bit of pan juice has developed. Mix coffee and wine and pour ¾ cup over the lamb. Baste every 5 minutes thereafter. Add more coffee/wine whenever pan juice is getting skimpy, which is usually at 12-15 minute intervals. Do not cook roast longer than 1 hour in all. Remove from oven, cover, and let stand for 20 minutes, keeping warm on top of stove. Pour pan juices into a sauce dish to serve separately, and slice meat wafer thin. (It will be pink but not raw or indigestible.) Yield: 4-6 servings.

"You must have a timer and a kitchen pad and pencil. To start the five-minute basting, set the timer and make a mark on the pad. Use a roaster baster to anoint every inch of the lamb every time the bell rings, removing pan from the oven for this operation. Reset timer as pan is replaced and make another mark on your pad. Do not rely on mental counting, or you are certain to lose track. When you have eight marks the lamb is done, whether or not you think so."

—Elsie Lee

EDITOR'S NOTE: The actor Alfred Lunt prepared a leg of lamb this way but added a jar of melted currant jelly to the gravy.

Baked Breast of Lamb with Pickled Fruit Sauce

2 tablespoons fat
1 onion, finely minced
4-pound breast of lamb
Salt and pepper, to taste
½ teaspoon paprika
⅛ cup flour
½ teaspoon monosodium glutamate,
*   optional*

½ cup white wine
½ cup ginger ale
1 8-ounce can sliced peaches
1 8-ounce can purple plums
1 8-ounce can white grapes
2 tablespoons orange marmalade
3-4 tablespoons brown sugar
3 tablespoons (or more) vinegar

Heat fat in a small roasting pan. Add onion and sauté until soft. Place lamb on top. Sprinkle with paprika, flour, and monosodium glutamate. Add wine and ginger ale. Bake in 325° F. oven for 1¾ to 2 hours, or until the lamb is tender. Meanwhile, combine undrained fruits, marmalade, brown sugar, and vinegar. Bring to a rolling boil. Cook until syrup thickens. Pour fruit sauce over lamb. Turn heat to 400° F. and bake, uncovered, for another 10 to 15 minutes until the top is a golden glaze. Yield: 6 servings.

—Dan Ross

In my own books I always describe a meal if it is mentioned in the text. Not for me are those writers who say, "Samson and Delilah sat down to a delicious dinner." If it's delicious I want to be able to taste it!

The recipe for Lyon's Lamb I dreamed up once when I was having writer friends for dinner at my little redwood shack in Los Gatos. We ended up the evening in front of my outdoor fireplace with a bottle of brandy. The fact that one of my guests fell into the fireplace did not diminish the evening.

—Dana Lyon

Lyon's Lamb

4½-6 *pound leg of lamb*
  2 *tablespoons finely chopped garlic*
  1 *tablespoon chopped parsley*

½ *teaspoon salt*
¼ *teaspoon black pepper*
Pinch of rosemary
  1 *bottle dry white wine (750 ml)*

Wipe leg of lamb and bring to room temperature. Two hours before cooking time, mix garlic, parsley, salt, pepper and rosemary into a thin paste. Cut deep slits into lamb and force paste into them. (The number of slits and the amount of paste in each does not matter.) Put lamb in deep bowl and pour wine over it. Marinate for 2 hours, turning frequently. Remove lamb from liquid and pat dry with paper towels. Preheat oven to 350° F. Roast until medium-rare, basting occasionally with marinade. Remove from oven and carve. Serve with a sauce made by combining pan drippings with marinade. Thicken sauce with flour or cornstarch if desired. Yield: 4-6 servings, depending on size of roast.

—Dana Lyon

Menu Menu Tekel Upharsin

Before the Fact
Pâté McGerr • Oeufs à la Roos • Little Grey Celeri Remoulade

Body of the Crime
Inspector Dover Sole (or Heel) • Filet of Robert L. Pike
Roast Mother Goose • Chicken à la Queen
Sleight of Ham • Gordon Hashe • New England Boiled Diner
Sgt. Velie Cutlets • Smersh Kebab, Served on Flaming Skewer

Ron Goularsh • Book-of-the-Month Club Steak

The Specialty of the House

LAMB AMIR STAN ELLIN

One Man's Meat. . .

All the Above Served with Little Caesar Salad and Elizabeth Daly Bread

Strong Poison
May Gret Wine • Rex's Stout
First Draft Beer in Large Aaron Marc Stein

Antidotes
Homi Cider • Perrier Mason
William Irish Coffee • Josephine Tea • Fred Dannyade

Unjust Desserts
Reggie Fortune Cookies • Crime Puffs • Salt Water Toff
Cornstarchy Goodwin Pudding • Baked Alaskan

AN MWA FIRST!
TWO TOPLESS WAITRESSES!!
ANNE BOLEYN AND MARY QUEEN OF SCOTS!

Orange Thyme Lamb

8 lean lamb chops
Juice of 4 oranges
2 tablespoons grated orange rind
Large stalk chopped celery

Salt and pepper, to taste
Several sprigs fresh thyme
2 tablespoons chopped parsley
2 cups boiled rice

In heavy, covered baking dish arrange chops in single layer. Add orange juice, rind, salt and pepper, and thyme. Cover tightly and cook until chops are tender, 3 to 4 hours, in 275° F. oven. Sprinkle with parsley and serve with rice. Yield: 4 servings.

"This is my winter recipe for a Working Writer's Lunch—that's when you want to spend the morning at your typewriter, but have somebody coming for lunch."

—Joan Aiken

Dulma

(Stuffed Grape Leaves)

2 pounds lean boneless lamb stew
    meat
1¼ pounds rib lamb chops
1 onion
3 green onions
2 cloves garlic
1 bunch cilantro (Chinese parsley)
    or fresh coriander

2 tablespoons fresh dill
Pepper, to taste
½ cup cooked rice
1 quart jar grape leaves
1 tablespoon butter
3 cloves garlic, sliced
1 8-ounce can tomato sauce
1½ cups cold water

Dice lamb into ½-inch cubes. Rinse with cold water and place in mixing bowl. Chop onion, green onions, garlic and cilantro and add to lamb. Rinse rice in cold water and add to mixture along with dill and pepper. Stir ingredients well. Wash grape leaves with cold water, snip stems, and place leaves on counter, shiny side down. Place 1 tablespoon of meat mixture on center of each leaf, near stem. Roll leaf once, fold in corners, and continue rolling. Place lamb ribs on bottom of 3-quart pan. Place stuffed grape leaves in layers in pan. After layering, top with small chunks of butter and 3 sliced garlic cloves. Add 1½ cups water. Top with layer of flat grape leaves and 3 lamb ribs. Simmer for 1½ hours. When liquid starts boiling, add can of tomato sauce to juices. May be served hot or cold. Yield: 6-8 servings.

—William Rivera

Rice Damascus

½ cup each uncooked brown rice, bulgar wheat, white rice, vermicelli
Chicken broth
Fresh lemon juice
Pine nuts
2 pounds ground lamb
4 onions, chopped

Garlic, to taste
Olive oil, as needed
Allspice
Salt and pepper, to taste
White meat of chicken, cooked and shredded
Plain yogurt, chilled

Cook grains and vermicelli according to separate package directions, substituting chicken broth and lemon juice for water. The ratio of broth to lemon juice should be 2 to 1. Sauté pine nuts, lamb, onions, and garlic in olive oil until tender. Add to cooked grains. Season with allspice, salt and pepper. Add chicken. Mix well. Serve hot topped with chilled plain yogurt. Yield: 4-6 servings.

"This recipe is my mother's invention, and one of my favorites."

—William Peter Blatty

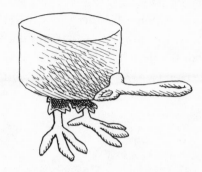

H. Allen Smith, God rest his restless soul, did not move to Sarasota because on an exploratory visit somebody swiped his camera from a restaurant chair while he was eating, and he vowed he would not live in a place where they stole a man's camera while he was at feed. He went to the Southwest instead and tried to turn himself into a chili expert. Alas, a man does not become an expert by merely claiming to be one. His chili was glutenous and unforgiveably mild.

—John D. MacDonald

Joe Cook's Chili Con Carne

2 cloves garlic, chopped
2 medium-size onions, chopped
2 green peppers, seeded and chopped
¼ cup olive oil
2 pounds ground chuck
¼ teaspoon cayenne pepper

2 tablespoons chili powder
1 teaspoon salt
3 16-ounce cans red kidney beans
1 1-pound 4-ounce can tomatoes,
    cut up
Chopped parsley

Sauté garlic, onions, and green pepper in olive oil. Add meat and seasonings. Stir steadily while cooking. Meanwhile, heat beans and tomatoes with their juice in a large kettle. When meat is medium-well done, add to beans and tomatoes. Simmer for 30 minutes. Add chopped parsley 5 minutes before serving. Serve with crackers and *crudités*. Yield: 8 servings.

"In the golden days of vaudeville, Joe Cook was a comedian of consummate charm and subtlety. Those of us with memories of the theater that predate the tube remember him fondly. Whenever he was not on the road his great house at Lake Hopatcong (he called it Sleepless Hollow) was filled with weekend guests—comedians, midgets, jugglers, journalists. His golf course boasted a golf ball tree. Guests were asked to refrain from picking the ones he'd painted green. Those were to be left to ripen. His basement bar housed his enormous collection of objects smaller than a man's hand. Friends felt challenged to find him something smaller than a man's hand that was not already in his collection. By birth a Mexican, in early childhood Joe had been adopted by a family named Cook. Chili, however, was in his genes. This is his recipe."

—Miriam-Ann Hagen

EDITOR'S NOTE: This freezes well. If freezing, do not add parsley until serving time.

Jail House Chili

¼ cup oil or shortening	1 teaspoon dried oregano
3 pounds beef, cut into 1-inch cubes	1 teaspoon dried marjoram
1 pound ground beef	½ teaspoon red pepper
1 quart water	1 tablespoon sugar
5 tablespoons chili powder	3 tablespoons paprika
3 teaspoons salt	3 tablespoons flour
1 tablespoon monosodium glutamate, optional	3 tablespoons cornmeal
	4 cups red pinto beans, optional
10 cloves garlic, chopped	2 cups chopped onion, optional
1 teaspoon cumin	

Heat the oil, add all meat and sear. Stir constantly over high heat until meat is grey (not brown). Add water, cover, and simmer 1½ to 2 hours. Add remaining ingredients except flour and cornmeal. Excess fat from the meat will rise to the top after the spices are added. Skim it off. Simmer another 30 minutes. Blend flour and cornmeal with 2 cups water. Add to other ingredients. Simmer 5 more minutes. More thickening or more water may be added to achieve the consistency you prefer. Serve with red pinto beans (cooked until tender) and chopped onion, if desired. Yield: 8-12 servings.

"Chili became popular in the American Southwest of the 1880s when some unknown (but blessed!) cook discovered that the combination of chili peppers and spices could render palatable cheap cuts of beef and tough game, such as jackrabbit. The economy factor made the dish a favorite with frontier jails; and certain jails achieved fame on the quality of the chili they served. Legend has it that Billy the Kid made his celebrated escape from Lincoln County Jail not because he feared hanging but because he couldn't stand its chili. While the story may be apocryphal, Jail House Chili is not."

—Whit Masterson

Tolbert's Chili for One Hundred

30 pounds lean stewing beef, in
    ½-inch cubes
Cooking oil
 1 pound kidney suet, rendered
90 red chili peppers, stemmed, seeded,
    scalded (reserve pepper water),
    peeled, and ground
 1 cup dried oregano, heaping
 1 cup crushed cumin seed, heaping
 1 cup salt

 1 cup powdered cayenne pepper
 1 cup Tabasco
20 garlic cloves, chopped
 3 level cups Masa Harina (ground
    Mexican cornmeal)
Unchopped chili pods, stemmed,
    skinned and seeded
 1 quart "mystery ingredient" (prob-
    ably Tequila)

Sear beef, a little at a time, in oil. As it browns, remove to huge kettle centered over driftwood fire. Add suet and ground chili peppers and enough pepper water to cover meat. When boiling, remove to edge of fire so it will simmer. After 30 minutes, remove from fire, add the next 6 ingredients, and return to center of fire. Bring to a boil and, when boiling, bring kettle to edge of fire and simmer for 45 minutes. Keep kettle covered except for frequent stirrings. Add more pepper water to keep from drying out. (If all pepper water is used, add plain water.) The chili, however, should be thick; so add liquid as sparingly as possible, just sufficient to prevent burning. Remove from fire, skim off fat, stir in corn meal and return to edge of fire for 30 minutes more. Taste frequently and add some unground chili peppers, about ½ cup at a time, if the chili lacks authority. After last addition of peppers, simmer 30 minutes more. Remove from fire and stir in "mystery ingredient." Yield: 100 servings.

"Tolbert's Chili is featured in a Travis McGee 1977 adventure. The character Meyer, who prepares it for a large gathering, calls it 'variations . . . so I can improve the chili based on the Frank X. Tolbert experiments.' This recipe appeared in Tolbert's book *A Bowl of Red*. But Meyer somewhat altered it.

"So this is not identical. It retains the taste of the original, the perfect, the incomparable chili. Maxwell Penrose Wilkinson, that gourmet and bon vivant who happens to be my agent, has certified that the Tolbert chili is historically genuine. Meyer's few minor changes hew to the original line".

—John D. MacDonald

If I have a current ambition, other than wealth beyond the dreams of avarice, it is going to be something like learning to pace a novel as well as Alfred Bester does, create atmosphere as well as Arthur W. Upfield did, and write first-person English anywhere near as well as Rex Stout did. That ought to keep me busy until the Tricentennial.

All through 1975 I couldn't sell a mystery novel and had to work the other side of the street for a while. One whodunit outline was recast as a Western called *Last Stage to Benbow*. This one had a hero with an appetite as big as mine, and halfway through the book he made the acquaintance of Texas Red, a chili "so strong and authoritative that he wound up loosening his collar in mid-bowl to get a little air. His eyes burned; the skin across his temples seemed to stretch tight; he bellowed for more beer. The dish was fresh, tough chunks of steer meat cut in cubes and cooked with hellishly hot chilis."

Writing this, I got so hungry that I hollered for my wife Jackie, whose recipe this is. (She's the daughter of a Swiss-trained chef who used to cater places like the Sulgrave Club, the more posh DC embassies, and the White House.) And we went right out and bought the fixings. Matter of fact, I'm getting hungry right now, just copying down what I wrote about it.

For me, few scenes I've read in many years can match the marvelous ending of Friedrich Duerrenmatt's *Der Richter und Sein Henker* (*The Judge and His Hangman*), recently filmed as *End of the Game*. The detective slowly eats himself to death as he reveals the trap he's set for the killer. Yeah, I know it's contrived; so are all my favorite Ellery Queens. And who gives a damn? What marvelous theater!

—George Warren

Texas Red

(A Frontier Chili)

2 slices bacon
2 pounds onions, chopped
2 cloves garlic, minced
2 pounds Anaheim chili peppers*
¼ cup plus 2 tablespoons butter, divided
2 pounds lean beef, cut into 2-inch cubes
4 cups chicken broth, fresh or canned
2 pounds tomatoes, peeled, seeded, and chopped
2 tablespoons tomato paste

¼ cup chili powder
1 tablespoon ground cumin
½ cup Mexican beer
2-3 tablespoons chopped cilantro (fresh coriander)
1 cup Monterey Jack cheese, shredded
Juice of 1 lime
4 chopped onions
Crackers
Safflower or corn oil, if necessary

Fry bacon until crisp. Drain, reserving fat. Measure 2 tablespoons of the fat into a large skillet. Add oil if drippings amount to less. Add onions and garlic,

* Two 9-ounce cans of chili peppers may be used if fresh are unavailable. To prepare fresh peppers, roast on fork over gas flame until skin is blistered. Place in plastic bag, close bag tightly with rubber band, and let partially steam in their own juice for ½ hour. Wearing rubber gloves, peel under running water, chop, and seed. For a mild chili, remove most of the seeds; for a hot one, leave more. The seeds dictate the heat.

and heat over low heat until onions are transparent. Remove from pan and set aside. Pour remaining fat or oil into same skillet (there should be approximately 2 tablespoons), and add the prepared Anaheim peppers (see note). Sauté until soft. Drain and add to onion mixture. In same skillet melt ¼ cup butter and sauté meat until brown. Drain off all but 2 to 3 tablespoons of the butter. Add onion-pepper mixture. Blend well. Add chicken broth to barely cover mixture. Cover and simmer until meat is tender, adding more broth if necessary. Cool to room temperature and refrigerate overnight. Next day, puree tomatoes in blender with the tomato paste. Heat remaining butter until bubbling. Add chili powder and cumin, and simmer about 1 minute. Heat the meat mixture and add tomato puree, chili, cumin, and beer. Stir in cilantro and simmer, uncovered, for 1 hour. Fold in cheese, and simmer 5 minutes. Stir in lime juice and serve hot with onions and crackers. Yield: 8 servings.

"Few of us gringos will be able to deal with unseeded chilis in all their infernal glory. Wash chili down with Mexican beer. If you can't get Mexican beer, you're living in the wrong town. If you can't move, Pabst's Andeker brand will serve as a substitute."

—George Warren

Beef and Claret Moriarty

4 pounds beef chuck, cut into ¾-inch cubes

2 cups claret

4 green onions, with tops, chopped

Pinch thyme

½ teaspoon dried basil

¼ cup margarine

½ pound small mushrooms, stems removed

1 cup cubed potatoes

1 bunch small carrots, scraped and halved if necessary

2 teaspoons salt

Pepper

1 beef bouillion cube, optional

5-ounce jar pitted green olives

12 ounces noodles

Place beef in large casserole. Cover with claret. Add chopped onion, thyme, and basil. Marinate overnight in refrigerator. Next day, remove meat from marinade. Reserve marinade. Dry meat with paper towels. Melt margarine in large skillet, and add meat and mushrooms. Sauté until slightly browned, and return to casserole. Add potatoes, carrots, salt, pepper and reserved marinade. Place covered casserole in 375° F. oven and bake for 3 to 3½ hours until meat is tender. If more liquid is needed, add water in which bouillon cube has been dissolved. Cook noodles according to package directions. Spoon meat mixture over noodles, and garnish with olives. Yield: 6 servings.

"For over 75 years this Beef-and-Claret dish was thought to have been created by Colonel Moriarty, younger brother to the infamous Professor who was Sherlock Holmes's arch foe. The Colonel was the only military man in the family. However, during World War II the original handwritten recipe was discovered in the pantry of a bombed-out cottage near Liverpool. . . ."

—Barbara Walton

Steak and Kidney Pudding

¾ pound beef, cubed
¾ pound beef kidney, cubed
½ cup flour
Salt and pepper
¼ pound mushrooms

2 large onions, thinly sliced
Water
Red wine, optional
Suet Crust (below)

Roll cubes of meat in flour seasoned with salt and pepper, making sure they are well coated. (The flour thickens the gravy, and there is no other seasoning in the pudding.) Wash the mushrooms, and halve or quarter them if they are large. Fill a 1½ quart casserole with successive layers of beef, mushrooms, kidney and onions, continuing until all ingredients are used. It is important to fill casserole to brim. Pour in water or wine, or mixture of both, until liquid appears between the cubes of meat. Top with suet crust. Cover with foil. Tie in place. Do not stretch too tight, as crust rises. Place casserole in large saucepan of boiling water. (The water should reach half way up sides of casserole.) Cover the larger pan with lid or foil. Simmer at least 4 hours. Add boiling water to large pan as necessary. Serve immediately. Yield: 4-5 servings.

Suet Crust:

5-6 ounces suet   1 teaspoon salt
  8 ounces self-rising flour   Water

Use ready-prepared suet, imported from England if available. Otherwise, purchase veal kidney fat from butcher and prepare at home. To do this, remove all skin and membrane possible and thinly slice. Finely chop (by hand or in blender). When suet is ready, mix flour and salt. Rub suet gradually into flour, discarding any remaining bits of skin. Continue rubbing until mixture has the consistency of breadcrumbs. Add just enough water to make a springy, elastic dough. Roll on floured board to make a circle to fit top of casserole, 1-inch or more thick. Yield: Crust for 1½-quart casserole.

"Simmering for at least four hours makes all the difference to the flavor. The pudding may be edible after two hours, but the true rich taste is lacking. It is almost impossible to spoil this dish by overcooking."

—Patricia Moyes

Stout-Hearted Menu

Table d'hate—price of main curse determines price of dinner

Shrimp Hitchcocktails   *Bitter Fruit (from the Weed of Crime)*
                        Vicious soise

Shish Kebob Bloch   *Eggs Benedict Arnold*
Roast Fugitive Pigeon   *Tom Walsh Rabbit*
                  Death Roe au Brrrr
Graham Greene Salad with Asey Mayonnaise   *Ron Goulartichokes*

Bail Bonbons   *Hawkshawcolate Ice Cream*
Brett Pudding Halliday   *Marple Cake*
Trent's Last Cheese   *David Fromage*

Sir Henry Merriv Ale   *Hampton Stone Ginger Beer*
Black Nick Velvet   *Charlie Chanpagne*

Fu Manchuing Gum is available at the cigar counter

Beef in Beer

2 pounds beef chuck, cubed
2 tablespoons butter or margarine
¼ teaspoon garlic powder, or 1
    minced clove garlic
Seasoned salt
2 bay leaves
1 teaspoon dried oregano

1 teaspoon dried marjoram, optional
1 quart dark beer or ale
Water
4 potatoes, peeled and quartered
2 cups cut string beans
1 large onion, quartered
2 cups sliced mushrooms

Brown beef in butter. While browning, sprinkle with garlic powder and seasoned salt. Transfer to 5-quart casserole or other pot with a tight cover. Add bay leaves, oregano, and marjoram. Pour in enough beer or ale to cover meat, adding water if necessary. Cover pot and cook 4 hours, or until tender, in 300° F. oven. Check often to see if beer is evaporating. Add more beer or water when necessary. Add vegetables and mushrooms to meat 1 hour before serving. Continue cooking until vegetables are tender, about 1 hour. Yield: 4 servings.

"I call this my play-it-by-ear dish. It's perfect for card games or for one of those days when there isn't enough time for a gourmet dinner. (Whatever that is.) I always plan on a minimum of four hours in the oven; the longer this one cooks, the better it tastes. Better still, prepare it a day ahead of time and reheat for several hours before serving. I serve this with garlic bread I prepare an hour before serving. Slice a loaf of French or Italian down the center, smear with butter and garlic, wrap in foil and place in oven about half an hour before serving. I also do a salad; usually tomatoes, endive and avocado with dressing. There'll be next to nothing left over for the next day!"

—George Baxt

I'm back reading through the ten-cent fiction magazines of the depression years, where private eyes were a dime a dozen. You meet private eyes in *Black Mask, Dime Detective, Detective Fiction Weekly, Crime Busters*, and dozens of other pulp paper magazines.

Though the pulps were an ephemeral art form, they contributed at least one permanent hero, the private eye, to our folklore. Tough, detached but sentimental, frequently broke and sometimes drunk, he's almost always honest. For most of the world still Humphrey Bogart as Sam Spade *is* the private eye. Carroll John Daly still seems to retain the distinction of being the first to write a hardboiled story about a private eye.

Race Williams was no Sherlock Holmes, no Nick Carter. Race Williams was a tough, straight-shooting, wise-talking, pragmatic urban cowboy. His world was a night world filled with speakeasies, gambling joints, penthouses, rundown hotels. Of his critics Race Williams said, "When you're hunting the top guy, you have to kick aside—or shoot aside—the gunmen he hires. You can't make hamburger without grinding up a little meat."

—Ron Goulart

Hamburgers Wittenberg

2 cloves garlic	½ teaspoon paprika
1 tablespoon dry mustard	3 tablespoons salad oil
¼ teaspoon salt	2 pounds ground beef
⅛ teaspoon pepper	12 hamburger rolls

With a mortar and pestle or wooden spoon in a wooden bowl crush garlic. Mix garlic and seasonings in wooden bowl. Blend into a paste. Shape beef into patties. Spread with garlic seasoning mixture. Broil over coals or in hot broiler. Yield: 12 sandwiches.

—Philip Wittenberg

The meat ball is just as frequently found in France as it is elsewhere. This is because finely chopped or ground meat is economical and versatile. A skilled shopper chooses the meat, then asks the butcher to grind it, rather than buying ready-ground meat from the tray, because that is likely to be second-rate meat. Ground meat is best when used on the day of purchase.

Small meatballs can be grilled, sautéd, dipped in batter and deep-fried, poached in bouillon (use the bouillon afterwards, for a lot of the flavor will be lost into it), or wrapped in very thin dough (that prevents the flavor from escaping) and poached in bouillon or steamed. They can be served with any of the various sauces, sour cream, or a puree of tomatoes sometimes called *coulis*. Such a puree is made by putting half a pound of roughly chopped tomatoes, a big dob of butter, seasoning, and a tablespoon of chopped onion in a covered saucepan over low heat. After 40 minutes, strain the puree and adjust seasoning. You may need a pinch of sugar. This tomato *coulis* is a useful all-round sauce for fish, meat, or poultry. It's very little trouble to prepare—apart from final straining because there is no need to skin the tomatoes.

NOTE: Don't quote me, but tomatoes slightly less than fresh can be used up in this way. If you add vinegar, sugar, pepper, and spices and let it cool down you'll have tomato catsup.

—Len Deighton

Bobotie

1 thick slice bread	1 teaspoon salt
1¼ cups milk	1 tablespoon sugar
2 medium onions, sliced	1 tablespoon vinegar
2 tablespoons butter	1 tart apple, diced
1 tablespoon curry powder	2 eggs
Pinch chili powder	Cinnamon
2 pounds ground beef	Salt and pepper

Soak bread in the milk. Sauté onions in butter until translucent. Add curry and chili until onions are light brown. Add meat, salt, sugar, vinegar, and diced apple. Stir, mixing well, until the meat is browned. Drain milk-soaked bread, reserving the milk. Mash bread with a fork, and add to meat mixture, blending well with 1 beaten egg. Beat second egg with milk drained from bread, and season with salt and pepper. Turn meat mixture into buttered casserole, pour the egg-and-milk mixture over it, and sprinkle with cinnamon. Stand casserole in a pan of water and bake, uncovered, for 30 to 40 minutes in a 350° F. oven. Yield: 4-6 portions.

"Serve this with brown rice, coleslaw, and tomato-and-onion salad—not forgetting the mango chutney, sliced banana, and grated coconut. My detective character, Lieutenant Tromp of Trekkersberg Murder Squad, refuels rather than eats and lives almost exclusively on take-away fare—the only sort of meal he can share with Zondi, his Zulu sergeant. But the Widow Fourie knows there is one dish (besides herself, one presumes) that Kramer finds irresistible: the delicious Cape Malay concoction known as *Bobotie* (pronounced bo-boo-tee). Bobotie is quick and easy to make, cheap, filling, and too good for there to be any leftovers.

—James McClure

Steak Tartar

2 pounds raw, finely chopped, fresh
   lean steak
2 raw eggs
1 teaspoon sugar or sugar substitute
2 tablespoons catsup
1 teaspoon mustard
1 tablespoon Worcestershire Sauce

Salt and pepper, to taste
  2 tablespoons grated Parmesan cheese
  1 Bermuda onion, finely cut
¼ cup breadcrumbs, optional
  5 mashed anchovies, optional
  1 tablespoon capers, optional

Combine all ingredients. Mix thoroughly. Serve with melba toast; or, to give a different taste, croissants.

—Lucy Freeman

Scotch Collops with Suet Dumplings

Collops:

1 pound best steak
3 tablespoons butter
2 medium-size onions, chopped
Salt and pepper, to taste

¾ cup beef stock
¼-½ cup fine breadcrumbs
Dumplings (below)

Remove fat from steak and mince steak. Melt butter and add onions. Cook onions until just transparent. Add steak and brown, stirring constantly. Season with salt and pepper. Pour in stock and simmer for 1 hour. Just before serving, stir in bread crumbs. Add dumplings and cook 5-10 minutes or until dumplings are done. Serve at once. Yield: 4 servings.

Dumplings:

4 ounces self-rising flour
2 ounces suet, finely shredded
Salt to taste

2 teaspoons fresh parsley, chopped
Water

Combine all ingredients except water. Add just enough water to make a firm dough. Roll into small balls. Cook with Scotch Collops. Yield: 4 servings.

"There is the story of the Irish laborer, faced for the first time by a plate of this steaming brown mush, who announced rebelliously: 'I tell you, them that chewed it can swallow it'. But don't be put off."

—Dorothy Dunnett

Bloody Brisket

2 tablespoons butter
5-6 pounds brisket of beef, fat trimmed and discarded
Garlic salt
Freshly ground pepper

2-3 large onions, sliced thinly
1 11-ounce can tomato paste
½ cup warm water
2 carrots, cut into small pieces
1 small bay leaf

Melt butter in cast iron or Teflon skillet. Brown brisket in butter. Sprinkle lightly with garlic salt and pepper. Put onions around meat and brown. Remove meat and spread tomato paste over entire surface. Sprinkle again with garlic salt. Add ½ cup warm water to browned onions in pan and simmer, scraping the bottom once or twice. Put half the onions, the carrots and all the liquid from the pan into the bottom of a deep, 10½-inch casserole dish. Put brisket into dish. Sprinkle remaining onions over top. Cover and bake in 300° F. oven 3½ hours or until fork tender. If gravy is too thick, add a bit of *hot* water and stir. Slice meat. Pour some of gravy over it, and serve. Yield: 6-8 servings.

"In one of my mystery novels there is mention of a delicious roast-beef-with-gravy prepared by the cook housekeeper of a Catholic priests' rectory. It was *this* recipe, of course, that she prepared!"

—Geraldine Kamrass

102

Fruited Brisket of Beef

2 envelopes onion soup mix, divided

4-5 pounds lean brisket of beef

3 tablespoons dark brown sugar

1 teaspoon cinnamon

¾ teaspoon ground ginger

Grated rind of 1 lemon

1 12-ounce can of beer

1 teaspoon freshly ground pepper

¼ cup honey

3 tablespoons orange marmalade

2 tablespoons lemon juice

3 tablespoons brandy

1 teaspoon Worcestershire Sauce

1 pound dried apricots

1 pound dried pitted prunes

Preheat oven to 350° F. Place a large sheet of heavy-duty foil in center of a large open roasting pan. Sprinkle one package of onion soup mix on bottom. Put brisket in center of foil and sprinkle second package of onion soup mix over meat. Close and seal foil. Bake for 2½ hours. Combine all remaining ingredients and allow to blend while meat is cooking. Remove meat from oven, carefully open and turn back foil. Pour apricot-prune mixture over meat and reseal. Return to oven and bake for additional 1½ hours or until tender. Remove meat and fruits from foil. Carve brisket and place on large platter. Surround with prunes and apricots. Serve remaining gravy separately. Yield: 6-8 servings.

—Pauline Bloom

Inspector Heimrich Cooks Steaks

He wasn't going anyplace except, after a while, out to the breezeway to get the charcoal going. It would be cold in the breezeway; outdoor cooking was for summer; for terraces, and patios, and picnics. But steaks should be cooked over charcoal. His wife was about to be overruled.

He put on a heavy coat and went out to the breezeway. Shivering only slightly, he poured charcoal briquettes into the bowl of the broiler and put the electric starter on the charcoal and poured more briquettes on top of it and plugged it in. He went, thankfully, back to the fire and his diminished drink. It was, certainly, cold out for outdoor cooking. But Susan had found a butcher who had, at intervals, prime beef, and only charcoal could do justice to his steaks.

Heimrich lingered over his second drink, giving the charcoal time. He got up once and propped the steak board in the fireplace to heat. When he finished the drink, he went to the kitchen door . . . and looked out through its glass panel. The charcoal glowed red. Electric starters are admirable. Much superior to lighter fluid, which often burns off, igniting only itself. Heimrich put his heavy coat on again, switched on the breezeway light and got the steaks. They were thick strip steaks, and not yet at room temperature, as recommended. Whatever "room temperature" is supposed to be.

He went out to the breezeway and smoothed the glowing charcoal level. He lowered the grill so that it was only three inches or so above the coals. He put the steaks on and they sizzled. He stood to the lee of the broiler so that the heat would blow toward him—not that, now, the wind was more than a breeze.

Fat dripped from the steaks and flared into flame on the charcoal and enveloped the steaks, which, contrary to legend, would do the steaks no harm. When he decided it was time, he flipped the two thick steaks over. He went back into the living room and got the steak board, which ought to be warm enough by now.

Outside again, he raised the grill until it was almost a foot above the fire. He took one of the fire-crusted steaks off the grill and laid it on the board. He and Susan liked their steaks rare. The kids had specified medium. He went back for the third drink, which he knew Susan would have ready.

"Must be cold out there," Susan said. "I could have done them in the oven. I do them quite well in the oven, dear."

Merton Heimrich said, "Mmm." He said, "Not too cold."

When he had half finished his drink, he went out and put the steak destined for rareness back on the grill. He went back and finished his drink, not hurrying with it. When he had finished it he went back to the breezeway and pushed a long-tined fork into one of the steaks. He flipped both of them over again. Yeah. He opened the door and said, "OK" to Susan, who was forking open baked potatoes. He carried the steaks to the kitchen, sliced them and sorted slices onto hot plates. The rare ones were rare; the medium ones medium. Well, medium rare.

—Richard Lockridge
(From *Dead Run*, a Heimrich case
with a winter background)

Chris Steinbrunner and I were dinner guests of Christina Legg. Since it was a fine summer day, cooled by a long and enthusiastic rainstorm earlier in the day, and she is fortunate enough to have a terrace high above the noise of New York City traffic and street screams, the main attraction of the menu was filet mignon, to be barbecued outdoors on a hibachi. As with most instances of good fellowship, time passed swiftly and it was dark when the steaks actually hit the grill.

When time for the first turn arrived, Tina flipped them over with a rare panache, marred only by the fact that one of the steaks, still sizzling, flew over the side of the terrace to an ignoble thud ten floors below. Quite prepared to acknowledge and accept the disaster, she suggested splitting two filets among three people—a sensible and practical solution.

"No!" thundered Chris. "Let's retrieve it!"

"Impossible!" we replied. "It's velvet black down there, and the garden is thick with bushes, trees and other vegetation."

"It'll be an adventure!" he countered, making for the door.

It never seemed more impossible than when we arrived and saw the veritable jungle from ground level. And everything was heavy with the afternoon's rain. We squinted. We groped. I mumbled. A quarter of an hour passed, with no hint of anything meaty and juicy to reward our by now not inconsiderable pains. Suddenly from the deep interior of a particularly lush bush, came a cry. "I smell it!" exulted Chris, who was by this time on his hands and knees in the dewy grass. A moment later he emerged from the blackness, triumphantly holding the elusive filet over his head.

Cleaned and cooked it became virtually indistinguishable from the others and was served up heroically.

The following note arrived at Miss Legg's apartment two days later:

I wuz casin yer gardin de odder nite when PLOP a hunk o meat smacked down from yer balcony. I thot here at last is a grate hot meel when dese two gents come and stole it, de bums! I cudda used the stake betterin dem! So Im down here on yer lawn, waitin, waitin, fer de next lucky drop!

—Otto Penzler

I am what we call in Britain a "meat and potatoes" man, which is another way of saying that I like good, plain English food. I really don't appreciate rich sauces or food which, in my mother's telling phrase, "has been mucked about."

I could probably keep going forever on bacon and eggs which is to my mind the finest meal in the world especially if it is served with a little piece of fried bread and fried tomato. It must be English or Danish bacon and not the stuff which passes for bacon in the U.S. or Canada, which I find almost inedible and which fries up to a consistency rather like potato crisps.

To my mind there isn't much to touch a good steak-and-kidney pudding or roast beef and roast potatoes with real Yorkshire pudding. With roast beef the best cut is a sirloin and it should be medium cooked, not rare. It should also be cut in very thin slices, not in chunks. The Yorkshire pudding is an art in itself, and I have never come across the real thing outside of Britain. The mixture seems to be the same but the results are wildly different. The secret of making good Yorkshire pudding is twofold. First, the mixture should be allowed to stand in the open air for at least an hour. Second, it should then be poured into a hot pan and cooked under the joint so that the juice from the meat drops into the pudding. The result will be a Yorkshire pudding fit for the gods.

Needless to say everything I have recommended is highly fattening; but then what good food isn't? Over the years I have lived on this sort of food and managed, with a struggle, to keep my weight down to reasonable limits.

—Ted Willis

EDITOR'S NOTE: Appended is a Yorkshire Pudding recipe. Understandably, it cannot match Lord Willis's. But, *faut de mieux*, it is highly satisfactory.

Rudy's Yorkshire Pudding

1 cup flour
1/2 teaspoon salt
2 eggs, well beaten

1/2 cup milk
1/2 cup water
Drippings from roast beef

Preheat oven to 400° F. Combine flour, salt, eggs, and milk. Stir briskly. Stir in water. Let the batter stand for an hour or so. Pour it into the hot drippings from a roast of beef. Bake for 20-25 minutes. Reduce heat to 325° F. and bake 15-20 minutes more, or until puffy and brown. Yield: 6–8 servings.

—Nancy Webb

Cassoulet Edgar

2 pounds dried navy beans	3 large tomatoes, cut in chunks
½ pound bacon	3 cloves garlic
½ pound salt pork	2 bay leaves
1 pound hot Italian sausage	Basil, to taste
1 pound sweet Italian sausage	Thyme, to taste
1 pound kielbasa (Polish sausage)	Salt and pepper to taste
5 pounds cooked turkey, beef and lamb, cubed	2 cups breadcrumbs
4-5 large onions, cut in chunks	

Soak beans in water for 12 to 24 hours. Drain and cover beans with fresh water 6 hours before assembling the cassoulet. Simmer for 1 hour. Set undrained beans aside. Cut bacon into bite-size pieces, lightly brown in a skillet and set aside, reserving drippings. Cube salt pork and brown in bacon fat. Drain. Cut sausage into bite-size pieces and brown on all sides in same skillet. Set aside. Brown onions in remaining fat. When golden, add tomatoes, garlic, bay leaves, basil, thyme, and salt and pepper. Simmer gently for ½ hour or until sauce is thick. Stir often. Drain beans and reserve liquid. Thoroughly mix beans and sauce. In ovenproof deep pot or large casserole place layers consisting of ⅓ of meat, bacon, salt pork and turkey. Add layer of ⅓ of bean-tomato mixture. Repeat until all ingredients are used, ending with beans. Pour in liquid drained from beans until it reaches the top layer of beans, adding water if necessary. Cover with 3 tablespoons breadcrumbs. Bake in 300° F. oven for approximately 4 hours. Every ½ hour, break up breadcrumb crust into bean-meat mixture and re-cover top with 3 more tablespoons crumbs. At final ½ hour of cooking time, cover casserole with crumbs but do not mix. Yield: 15-20 hungry servings.

"Part of the delight of this cold-weather dish comes from what precedes it. It's a meal you have to save up for. One week you roast a turkey, cube (bite-size) a pound or more of the leftovers and freeze them. The next week a beef roast might taste good. Do the same thing with a like amount of the leftovers and slap into the freezer. How about a roast leg of lamb the following week? Cube and freeze a like amount of what is left

108

Meats

(you'll have to force yourself not to eat all of it at the original sitting). Now you are ready to go any time you care to come up with the rest of the ingredients."

—Gary Madderom

Tamale Pie

¼ cup olive oil
1 onion, finely chopped
1 clove garlic, crushed
1 green pepper, finely chopped
1 pound ground beef
¼ pound sausage meat
½ pound mushrooms, sautéd
1 8-ounce can mushroom sauce
1 1-pound 4-ounce can Spanish-style tomato sauce

1 teaspoon chili powder or hot Hungarian paprika
1 teaspoon Worcestershire Sauce
1 teaspoon dried oregano
Salt and pepper
1 6-ounce can pitted black olives
½ cup grated sharp cheddar cheese
Cornmeal Mush (below)

Heat olive oil in large skillet. Sauté onion, garlic, and green pepper. Add beef and sausage and brown. Add next 7 ingredients and simmer for 1 hour. Add olives and cheese. Pour into casserole, top with cornmeal mush. Sprinkle with additional cheese if desired. Bake, uncovered, for 1 hour in 350° F. oven. Yield: 4 servings.

Cornmeal Mush:

3 cups water
1 teaspoon salt

1 cup cornmeal

Combine 3 cups cold water, 1 teaspoon salt, and 1 cup cornmeal. Cook, stirring to prevent sticking, for about 10 minutes after bubbles appear. The mush will be soft, but will stiffen during baking.

—Richard Martin Stern

Tamale Pie

3 onions, chopped
2 cloves garlic, minced
2 tablespoons cooking oil
1 pound ground sausage
1 pound ground round steak
2 tablespoons chili powder

1½ cups yellow cornmeal
1½ cups milk
1 can tomatoes
1 can cream-style corn
1 8-ounce can ripe olives, halved
    and seeded

Sauté onions and garlic in cooking oil. Add meats and chili powder. Simmer, stirring frequently, until meat is done, about 10 minutes. Combine remaining ingredients and cook over medium heat, stirring frequently, for 10 minutes. Mix first and second mixtures together. Pour into casserole and bake in 350° F. oven for 45 minutes. Yield: 6-8 servings.

—Thomas Tryon

Virgil Tibbs' Note on Barbecue Ribs

A memory I will never be able to erase from my mind is my early childhood in the Deep South. If I recall correctly, I was about five when my father explained to me, with considerable emotion in his voice, that we were a Negro family and therefore a great many people considered us to be ethnically inferior. It was a total shock to me. However, it did at once explain certain things that I had noticed, but that I had never been able to understand. I had once spoken, rather timidly, to a little girl who was lighter in skin than I was; she was snatched away just as she was telling me her name.

110

There is no need for me to review here the experiences I underwent, but times were changing, and as I grew up I could witness a drastic transformation. It came too late for my father, but I have seen tears of joy in my mother's eyes when, on television, she saw an Alabama football crowd that was jamming a huge stadium rise and cheer with a single great roar when a Negro player ran sixty-five yards for an Alabama touchdown.

Perhaps I should explain here that I dislike the sorting of people by color; if anyone were to refer to my partner, Bob Nakamura, as yellow, I would consider it unthinkable. Consequently I prefer the dignified word Negro rather than black. I recognize the fact that others may think differently and that is their privilege.

One thing that did make my boyhood endurable was the food my mother prepared. And when she made spareribs, I must confess that for just a little while I knew joy. Some people consider this an ethnic dish; it probably is, as is spaghetti which happens to be Chinese in origin. But this is beside the point. My mother has sent me her recipe for spareribs, which I am happy to share with Mystery Writers of America.

—John Ball

EDITOR'S NOTE: "Virgil R. Tibbs" is John Ball's popular character, a member of the Pasadena Police Department.

Spareribs Virgil Tibbs

1 package pork spareribs (4 sides of ribs)

1 cup catsup

3/4 cup water

1/2 cup chopped onion

1/4 cup chopped celery

2 heaping tablespoons brown sugar

1 tablespoon Worcestershire Sauce

2 tablespoons vinegar

2 tablespoons lemon juice

1/2 teaspoon dry mustard

1 clove garlic (or 1/4 teaspoon garlic powder)

1/2 teaspoon salt

1/2 teaspoon hickory smoke flavoring

Dash pepper

Gently parboil spareribs, about 45 minutes or until tender. Lay out the ribs on a cookie sheet. Combine all the remaining ingredients in saucepan, bringing them to a boil and simmering 5 minutes. Brush sauce over ribs. Place ribs under broiler and broil for 5 minutes on 1 side. Remove, turn ribs, brush second side with sauce, and broil second side until browned, checking carefully so they do not overcook. Serve. Yield: 4-6 servings.

—John Ball

The Nameless Lunch

4 medium-size potatoes
Salt
2 cloves garlic, minced

2 cups milk, approximately
8 strips pork belly

Preheat oven to 350° F. Peel potatoes and slice into very thin rounds. Arrange potatoes in buttered shallow pan that is large enough to hold all pork strips in 1 layer. Salt potatoes and sprinkle garlic over them. Add milk to cover. Cover pan with buttered foil or waxed paper and cook for 20 minutes. Remove paper or foil and cover potatoes with pork strips. Milk should be almost absorbed. Turn up oven to 375° F. and continue baking, uncovered, for approximately 25 minutes. When the potatoes are soft, the dish is done. The slight burned edges of some of the potatoes add to the flavor. Yield: 4 servings.

—Peter Dickinson

For thirty-odd years my mother's recipe for Gingersnap Sauce was the only dish I could cook, a circumstance that came about through dire emergency.

The year my first book was published I thought it appropriate for a writer to take a house in Connecticut for the summer. I also thought it proper to invite friends for weekend visits. My mother enjoyed cooking for the guests, who invariably rewarded her with lavish praise. For good reason. She was such an accomplished cook that she never allowed me to touch a measuring cup or pot. All I was allowed to learn to do with food was enjoy it.

One weekend a young man, who used to take me to fine restaurants in New York, was due to arrive Saturday morning. On Thursday Mama felt the first pains of sciatica. On Friday she was unable to leave her bed. To compound the crisis, the farmer's wife who came in twice a week to help with the housework, telephoned to say that she was ill and could not come that weekend.

Who had to cook the two dinners? Who but the domestic idiot who had in almost thirty years never boiled an egg! I set about the tasks with trembling hands and a faint heart. As each ingredient was added I carried the pot upstairs to Mama's bedroom so that she could judge consistency and taste. A dash of salt, she said, or a bit more vinegar, or three more gingersnaps to thicken the sauce. I can't remember the result. But I must have been successful for I have served this dish in New York, and Hollywood, and London, and the guests have always been enthusiastic.

—Vera Caspary

Tongue in Gingersnap Sauce

1 4-pound fresh beef tongue	2 cups stock in which tongue was cooked
1 bay leaf	
8-10 large gingersnaps, crumbled	½ cup raisins
1 cup brown sugar	½ cup blanched almonds
½ cup vinegar	1 lemon, sliced

Put tongue and bay leaf in a large pot. Add water to cover. Cook, covered, over low heat for 2½ hours, adding more water if necessary. Peel skin and remove bones from large end of tongue. Discard bay leaf. Mix gingersnaps, sugar, vinegar, and stock. Cook until smooth. Add raisins and almonds. Heat.

Slice tongue. Pour sauce over. Garnish with lemon slices. Yield: 6 servings.

NOTE: The sauce must have the sweet-sour taste of vinegar and sugar, and a strong flavor of ginger. If it becomes too thick, more stock or water can be added; if too thin, add crumbled gingersnaps. Best results are obtained by tasting and adding whatever ingredients are needed.

"Packaged tongue can be substituted for fresh but should be soaked in cold water overnight so that the salt and spices do not ruin the taste of the sauce. Best of all substitutes is beef boiled to tenderness. This dish may be heated in the sauce and served hot with mashed potatoes or noodles, or kept for a few hours in the refrigerator where the stock jells into a mold. The cold dish is a sensation on buffet tables."

—Vera Caspary

Squealer's Tongue

1 beef tongue, 2-3 pounds	4 tablespoons olive oil
4 medium-size onions, peeled	1 1-pound 13-ounce can tomato
1 large carrot	sauce
3 ribs celery, with leaves	2/3 cup water
6 sprigs parsley	1 1/2 tablespoons chili powder
8 peppercorns	1/2 cup catsup

Put tongue, two onions, carrot, some celery, parsley and peppercorns in a large pot and cover with boiling water. Simmer tongue uncovered until tender, about 3 hours. Remove pan from heat. Take out tongue and allow to cool just enough to handle comfortably. (It skins easily at this point, but not if you let it get cold.) Trim and skin tongue and return to the pot to cool completely in the cooking juices.

While tongue is cooking, chop the remaining two onions. Sauté in a pan with olive oil until tender. Add tomato sauce, water, chili powder and catsup. Simmer for 5 minutes, then set aside to cool.

When tongue has cooled, slice and cover with the sauce. Let sit for at least three hours. The tongue can be served at room temperature or refrigerated. Keep the leftovers refrigerated if there are any.

"When I was assigned to the American Embassy in Paris, my wife Pam and I would host picnics in the Bois de Boulogne for my Interpol Colleagues and their families. This simple dish, based on an old Yugoslav recipe Pam learned from my grandmother, always garnered raves. Squealer's tongue, a cop-sized portion of mashed or fried potatoes and an escarole salad with vinaigrette makes a nice bistro-style meal.

I prefer the Greek table wine Retsina or a Beaujolais with the dish, but Pam (who graduated from the Cordon Bleu cooking school during our stint in Paris and hints that my tastes in wine may be slightly pedestrian), recommends a Burgundy.

—Gerald Petievich

Tongue Diablo

5-6 pound pickled tongue   *Glaze (below)*
1 bay leaf

Wash tongue thoroughly 2 or 3 times. Cover with cold, unsalted water in a large soup kettle. Add bay leaf. Bring to a boil. Skim the surface 2 or 3 times, using a large slotted spoon. Lower heat and simmer, uncovered, for 2½ to 3 hours, adding more water if necessary. Tongue is done when tender. When cooked, take from kettle and remove skin. Put in large Dutch oven. Put Dutch oven over low heat. Pour glaze over tongue. Baste tongue steadily until it darkens and has a shiny, glazed surface. This process takes from 20 to 30 minutes. Any leftover glaze can be used as a sauce. Yield: 8 servings.

Glaze:

½ cup beer   *½ cup dark brown sugar*
½ cup red wine   *½ cup dark molasses*

Combine all ingredients and simmer over low flame until well blended. Yield: glaze for 1 beef tongue.

—Betty Parry

115

Pasta and Liver

1 large onion, chopped
2 cloves garlic, chopped
1 green pepper, chopped
3 tablespoons cooking oil, divided
1 1-pound 4-ounce can tomatoes
Pinch marjoram

Salt and pepper
1 pound beef liver, cut in 1-inch
   cubes
¼ cup flour
1 pound pasta (shells are the most
   attractive, though any spaghetti
   may be used)

Fry onion, garlic and green pepper in 2 tablespoons of oil. Add the tomatoes and seasonings. In remaining oil, fry liver that has been rolled in flour until well browned. Add to sauce. Cook until tender. Pour over pasta cooked according to package directions. Serve hot with green salad and crusty Italian bread.

—Philip Wittenberg

EDITOR'S NOTE: Counsel Emeritus of the Mystery Writers of America, Philip Wittenberg, has authored a definitive book on copyright law. His cases, many bizarre, have included the invalidating of Adolf Hitler's claim to American royalties on *Mein Kampf*—on the grounds that the book was protected only by Austrian copyright, a law of a country Hitler himself had later destroyed.

He was going to have a sandwich when he got hungry, then decided to cook one of his specials. He sautéd onions and green pepper, threw in a can of tomatoes, peas, and cut-up ham, and dished it over Minute Rice. He could do a lot with a can of tomatoes:

tomatoes and lima beans, tomatoes and corn. Brown some chicken or chuck roast first, put it back in the tomatoes and onions to simmer a while and dish it out over rice or noodles. Ryan loved it. Rita said everything he cooked tasted the same.

—Elmore Leonard
(From *Unknown Man No. 89*, Avon)

Roast Veal with Garniture

3 pounds rump or shoulder veal
2 tablespoons plus 1 teaspoon butter, divided
7 carrots, scraped and quartered, divided
1 medium yellow onion, quartered
⅓ cup dry white wine

1 cup chicken bouillon, divided
1 bay leaf
3 strips bacon
12 small white onions
Salt and pepper
1 teaspoon brown sugar

Brown veal thoroughly in 2 tablespoons butter, using an iron casserole. Add 1 carrot and the yellow onion. Pour the white wine and ⅓ cup of the bouillon over meat. Add bay leaf. Place 2 bacon strips over top of meat and roast, covered, in 300° F. oven for 1½ hours. Remove cover and continue roasting ½ hour. Remove from oven and slice. While meat is receiving its final roasting, sauté 1 strip bacon in 1 teaspoon butter. Add white onions and lightly brown. Add remaining carrots, salt, pepper, and brown sugar. When carrots start to brown, add remaining bouillon, cover and simmer until vegetables are tender. Discard bacon and surround veal slices with vegetables. Yield: 6 servings.

"The purist may quarrel with my calling this a roast instead of braised veal. We generally associate the word *braised* with a lesser quality of meat. In this case, one might picture a rangy young bullock becoming more Oedipal than edible. The veal I have in mind is tender and milk-fed; and by asking for a roast, I feel more assured of getting it. Having paid for it, I am not going to call it by any other name."

—Dorothy Salisbury Davis

Vitello Tonnato

7 canned anchovies, drained, divided
2 tablespoons butter, softened
3-4 pound leg of veal, boned
2 onions
6 cloves
1 bay leaf
Parsley
2 carrots, scraped and chopped
4 stalks celery, chopped
2 6-ounce cans tuna, drained

1 cup mayonnaise
1 tablespoon prepared mustard
Lemon juice, to taste
2 egg yolks
Olive oil
24 pickle slices
36 capers
1 lemon, sliced
12 additional anchovies, optional

Mash 3 anchovies with 2 or more tablespoons softened butter. Rub over veal. Place onions stuck with 3 cloves each in deep pan. Add herbs and vegetables. Place veal on top of vegetables. Cover with cold water and simmer 2½ to 3 hours or until tender. Drain. Let veal cool, then slice thin and arrange on large, flat platter. Cover and chill. Combine 4 anchovies, tuna, mayonnaise, mustard, lemon juice, egg yolks, and olive oil in blender. Blend until smooth. Completely cover veal slices with sauce. Cover and chill platter until very cold. Serve garnished with pickle slices, capers, lemon slices and additional anchovies if desired. Yield: 10-12 servings.

—Nancy Webb

EDITOR'S NOTE: Broth may be served for soup if desired.

118

Coniglio in Agrodolce

3½-pound rabbit, disjointed and cut
    into serving pieces
Marinade (below)
  2 tablespoons olive oil
  4 tablespoons butter
  4 slices salt pork, diced
  5 cloves garlic, diced or pressed
  ¼ cup flour
3-4 crumbled English brandy snaps
    or U.S. gingersnaps
Salt and pepper

⅔ cup chicken stock
2½ tablespoons dark brown sugar
  2 tablespoons water
  ½ cup brandy, cognac, or armagnac
  ½ cup red wine vinegar
  4 tablespoons chopped seedless white
    grapes
  2 tablespoons chopped ripe olives
  2 tablespoons chopped stuffed olives
  4 tablespoons pine nuts or unsalted
    pistachios

Marinade:

2 cups dry red wine
1 small onion, sliced
2 cloves
1 large sprig parsley
1 bay leaf
1 teaspoon thyme

1 teaspoon dried marjoram
4-5 crushed black peppercorns
3 crushed juniper berries
1 pinch bitter rue, optional
1 pinch sea salt, optional

Wash and clean rabbit. Combine all marinade ingredients. Bring to slow boil. Cool until just warm and pour over rabbit.

Marinate in refrigerator 2 to 3 hours or overnight. Heat oil, butter, salt pork, and garlic together in large casserole until garlic and pork brown. Take rabbit from marinade, dry with paper towels, dredge with flour and brandy-snaps. Add to casserole and sauté until brown. Strain marinade and pour over rabbit. Cook, covered, 20 to 25 minutes over moderate heat. Season with salt and pepper. Add chicken stock and put into 350° F. oven to finish cooking rabbit and thicken sauce. Combine sugar, water and brandy in a separate pan and cook, stirring, until golden and thickened. Add vinegar and stir. Add grapes and olives, and stir. Add nuts and stir until sauce thickens. Add sugar mixture to casserole, stir and scrape bottom of casserole until all is thickened. Yield: 4 servings.

"You can use this same recipe for chicken. I use a lot of garlic in my cooking to keep off Vampires, as any Mystery Writers of America member knows. My suggestions for accompanying this rich dish:

1. Spinach, cress, and raw sliced mushroom salad
2. A couple of bottles of good, dry Orvieto or Frascati
3. French or Italian garlic bread."

—Hugh Jones Parry

The first job I ever held as a boy of thirteen was in a neighborhood grocery store. In a small operation, everybody does everything. Thus I was not only stock boy, delivery boy, and cashier, but also a butcher. One day while I was working behind the meat counter, a lady came up and asked for a pound of sliced bologna. I got the bologna, put it in the slicing machine and went to work. It wasn't until I'd wrapped the lady's package and given it to her that I realized I was bleeding. I'd actually sliced off the tip of my index finger. There was no major surgery required. A Band-Aid took care of that.

This is the point at which my memory falters somewhat. I'm not quite sure what happened to the part of my finger I sliced off. But whenever that lady returned to the store, she always had *me* slice her bologna.

—Percy Spurlark Parker

Venison Ragout

3 pounds venison
1 cup vinegar
1½ cups water, divided
Salt
Freshly ground pepper
4-6 bay leaves
2 cups chopped celery

2 cups minced onions
Pinch rosemary
¼ cup flour
¼ cup melted butter
¼ cup red Burgundy wine
½ pint sour cream

Preheat oven to 350° F. Marinate venison overnight in vinegar, ½ cup water, salt, pepper and bay leaves. Drain venison. Place in casserole with celery, onion, and pinch of rosemary. Add remaining cup of water. Cover and braise in oven for 2 hours. Remove venison. Slice and keep warm. Strain stock. In a medium-size saucepan, combine flour and butter, stirring until smooth and lightly browned. Gradually add stock and cook, stirring constantly, until thickened. Stir in wine and sour cream. Warm through and remove from heat. Pour over venison and serve from chafing dish. Yield: 6 servings.

—Jean Francis Webb

Priscillianist Pork Chops

6 1-inch thick center-cut pork chops
Kitchen Bouquet or Chef's Magic
1 16-ounce can peach halves in heavy syrup

Grand Marnier (if the royalty cheque came in) or Triple Sec (if it didn't)

Trim the fat from chops and render trimmings in a skillet over medium-high heat.

Rub chops lightly with either Kitchen Bouquet or Chef's Magic. Add to skillet and brown. Reduce heat to medium. Add syrup from the peaches and a dash or splash of liqueur depending on whom you are entertaining. Add sufficient water to cover the bottom half of the chops. Cover and simmer for 15 minutes. Turn and simmer another 15 minutes being careful not to let skillet go dry.

Place a peach half (dome side up) on each chop and cover to heat for 3 to 4 minutes.

Remove chops from skillet and set aside on a heated serving dish. Stir the carmelized sauce left in skillet and pour over chops. Yield: 6 servings.

"I usually serve these with white rice because the sauce is its own rich gravy. Other side dishes depend on availability of fresh vegetables, salad makings, or my mood."

—Priscilla Ridgway

It was 1957. A friend named Earl Nisbet was going to Tahiti on a tramp steamer and wanted me to be his witness when he applied for a passport. On the way down to the passport office I realized I was sick of my job, had a little money saved up, and had no personal commitments. "Witness mine, too, Earl," I said.

We spent a year in Tahiti in a twenty-five-dollar-a-month house of split bamboo a few miles north of Papeete in the Arue district. It was so small that I wrote at the kitchen table, and when company was over we had to move the beds out on the veranda. Tahiti has always been a special place to me ever since. There I developed the writing habits which have lasted me a lifetime: to the typewriter early, aiming for seven hours a day, six days a week. While there I made my first short story sale (to *Manhunt*) and, with Earl's photos, my first article sale (to *True* about Tahiti).

Earl and I also went broke in Tahiti. Frequently. For weeks we would live on fish we speared ourselves, along with coconuts, and breadfruit, and limes, and green mangoes from our own yard, along with occasional grapefruit scrounged elsewhere. Then we discovered the Chinese store on the corner would extend us credit—up to ten dollars at a time. When we owed him more than that, we always rode our bikes by very fast, with our faces averted so we wouldn't hear his shouts for payment.

Out of what we could charge *à la Chinoise* (along with cocoa) grew Tahiti Goop. What went in was what we had. It became a staple of our diet. Even today my family and I still like it. Tropical it ain't. Good it is.

—Joe Gores

Tahiti Goop

1 cup dry white rice	*½ pound cheddar cheese, grated*
1 pound bully beef (corned beef)	*Salt*
1 8-ounce can whole-kernel corn, drained	*Coarsely ground black pepper*

Boil the rice according to package direction. About 2 minutes before the rice is finished, add corned beef broken into chunks, and can of corn. Stir in the cheese until it has melted. Salt and pepper to taste. Yield: 4 servings.

—Joe Gores

Poultry

My wife Ann and I travel, if not constantly then most of the time, not only on the lookout for backgrounds for new books but also for recipes from off-beat places.

We discovered *Chicken Chilindrón* in Zaragoza while we were researching *Colossus,* my novel about the Spanish painter Francisco Goya which sums up Spain for me as, in its own way, does the damn near arrogant taste of *Chicken Chilindrón.* Every time we get to feeling nostalgic about Spain, we cook it for ourselves. I hope you'll see why and get around to testing it.

—Stephen Marlowe

Chicken Chilandrón

1 thick slice Canadian or Danish bacon (or Serrano ham if available)
Olive oil
1 cup thinly sliced Spanish onion
3 medium sweet green peppers, cored, seeded and thinly sliced (or 1 small can red peppers drained, rinsed and sliced)
1 1-pound can Italian plum tomatoes, drained (reserve juice) and coarsely chopped
1 clove garlic, minced fine
1 cup chicken broth
½ teaspoon dried basil
¼ teaspoon dried thyme
Several dashes Worcestershire Sauce
Dash cayenne pepper or Tabasco, optional
Salt and pepper to taste
1 clove garlic, sliced
1 3-pound frying chicken (cut into serving pieces)
4 cups boiled rice

Dice bacon and sauté in skillet in small amount of oil until slightly crisp. With a slotted spoon, remove bacon from skillet and reserve. Add enough oil to skillet to make 2 tablespoons. Sauté onion slowly until transparent. Add peppers and continue to sauté until softened. Stir in tomatoes and sauté 1 minute longer. Add the minced garlic, broth, reserved tomato juice, basil, thyme, Worcestershire and optional cayenne or Tabasco. Season to taste with salt and pepper. Simmer slowly, uncovered, stirring occasionally, until liquid is reduced and sauce is fairly thick, about 40 minutes. Meanwhile, in another pan, heat 2 tablespoons oil and sliced garlic until brown. Discard garlic. Salt and pepper the chicken pieces and sauté on all sides until golden, approximately 5 minutes per side. Reserve chicken. Discard oil. Sprinkle chicken with reserved bacon. When sauce has thickened sufficiently, ladle it over chicken and bacon. Simmer covered until chicken is tender, about 40 minutes. Serve over rice. Yield: 4 servings.

—Stephen Marlowe

Chicken à la Ramses

2-3 pound frying chicken
4 tablespoons butter or fat
4 onions, sliced
3 sweet green peppers, diced
1 eggplant, diced
1 cup carrots, cut in strips

1 cup potatoes, diced
1 1-pound 4-ounce can tomatoes (or
   2 fresh tomatoes)
Salt, to taste
¼ teaspoon pepper
1 teaspoon cinnamon

Clean and wash chicken, cut into quarters or pieces. Melt 2 tablespoons butter in large pan. Then add in layers: onions, chicken, green pepper, eggplant, carrots, potatoes, and tomatoes. Season with salt, pepper and cinnamon. Cover tightly. Cook 10 minutes. Add 1 cup hot water, and remaining butter. Simmer until tender. Yield: 4 servings.

"This recipe has, of course, been modernized. Amelia Peabody Emerson would never have enjoyed such niceties as potatoes while in Egypt."

—Elizabeth Peters

There are some people who eat their meals with a haunted look, as though behind each shoulder stands a demon, one named Coronary and one named Obesity. But I like my food with a high-fat, high-starch content. I like, for instance, *Bauernschmaus*, which is hunks of pork and German sausage, or, if I feel like it, goose cooked in a bed of pickled cabbage and eaten with suet dumplings. Or I enjoy a leg of fat lamb pot roast on a bed of beans to absorb the juices, or—for posher gatherings—*Poulet au Gratin à la Savoyarde* (which is chicken in a cream and Gruyère and tarragon sauce). Last time I made this somebody was very, very late. The cream sauce cracked and everything was swimming about in a mush of yellow grease and curdled cream. While we were eating it, the lady who was late suddenly said in a tone of mingled astonishment and triumph, "Oh, I know what this is *supposed* to be! *Poulet au Gratin à la Savoyarde!*" One of those things you don't say to cooks.

—Peter Dickinson

Chicken and Wild Rice

2 10-ounce cans cream of mushroom
    soup, undiluted
2 envelopes dry onion soup mix
1 bouillon cube
½ pound uncooked wild rice

1 cup uncooked white rice
Salt and pepper
Milk
6 chicken pieces (breasts or thighs)

Preheat oven to 350° F. Mix mushroom soup with 1 envelope onion soup mix. Add bouillon cube, rices, salt and pepper and enough milk to moisten all ingredients. Place in large casserole, arranging chicken pieces on top. Sprinkle with remaining onion soup mix. Bake for 2 hours, or until chicken and rice are tender. Add additional milk during baking if rice appears dry. Yield: 6 servings.

—Marilyn Granbeck

She watched silently while he fried the chicken, and readied the rest of the meal. Within half an hour he said, "Dinner is served. Scat.

I'll bring it all out. That way if anything falls on the floor I won't have anyone to blame."

With the lights lowered and music sweetened, Hardy served chicken à la Kiev, spiced peaches and wild rice. They washed it down with Dom Perignon. Dessert was fresh strawberries and Cockburn port. While they drank their coffee and B and B, she said, "That was absolutely the best. You sure have some technique. . . ."

—Martin Meyers
(From *Spy and Die*)

Chicken Kiev

2 chicken breasts, cut in half, skinned and boned
4 tablespoons butter, divided in four, frozen
2 tablespoons dried chives
1 teaspoon garlic powder

Salt
Freshly ground pepper
¼ cup flour for dredging
2 eggs, lightly beaten
1 cup soft breadcrumbs
Oil for frying

With a mallet flatten each of the 4 pieces of chicken to ⅛-inch thickness. Take care not to tear. Place 1 tablespoon butter in center of each portion of chicken. Dust each piece of butter with ½ tablespoon dried chives and ¼ teaspoon garlic powder. Salt and pepper to taste. Fold sides of chicken closely over filling like an envelope. (It will stick without help.) Season flour with pepper. Dredge chicken in peppered flour, dip in beaten eggs, roll thoroughly in breadcrumbs and refrigerate for ½ hour. Fry each portion approximately 15 minutes, turning until all sides are brown. Place in warm oven until ready to serve. Yield: 2-4 servings.

—Martin Meyers

Poultry

A writer is a nesting bird who finds his raw material in anything that happens to be at hand while the nest is building, and weaves it into the basic fabric of twigs, mud, and moss.

If a writer has a fight with a red-haired publisher over the advance, his villain will have red hair. If he knows Ming porcelain, he'll put that exquisite piece of *famille rose* he can't afford to buy for himself on his lucky hero's desk and let the villain steal it. In writing he satisfies all unsatisfied desires and pays off many an ancient grudge.

Nothing is more hypocritical than the smug assertion that any resemblance to any person living or dead in this book is purely coincidental. Nothing can come out of the mind that has not gone into it. Stories, like dreams, are mirrors that distort reality but always reflect it.

—Helen McCloy

EDITOR'S NOTE: Cooking is another medium in which we often employ the raw material at hand.

Poulet à la Cuisine Bouleversée

1 broiler-fryer, cut into serving pieces	Lemon slices
Salt and pepper	Orange juice
Corn oil	Sherry
Basil or tarragon, to taste	Rice
Garlic powder	

Use thighs, legs, and breast of chicken. Sprinkle with salt and pepper. In a large skillet over medium-high heat, brown chicken lightly in just enough oil to prevent sticking. Lower heat. Sprinkle chicken with basil or tarragon and a pinch of garlic powder. Top each piece of chicken with lemon slices. Mix equal parts orange juice and sherry sufficient to cover chicken. Cover skillet and simmer gently until chicken is tender, about 40 minutes. Add more orange juice-sherry mixture if necessary. Remove to serving dish. If necessary, reduce sauce, simmering it to a gravy-like consistency and pour over chicken. Serve with rice. Yield: 3-4 servings.

"Several years ago, our kitchen was being redecorated. Thanksgiving found us without a usable oven or adequate working space, and in need of something festive enough for a family celebration. The result was *Poulet à la Cuisine Bouleversée.*"

—Margaret S. Hunt

Poulet à la Mexicaine

2 2½-pound chickens, cut into serving pieces	2-ounce jar sliced pimientos
Salt and coarsely ground black pepper	1 teaspoon ground cumin (comino) or more, to taste
3 tablespoons olive oil	3 cups hot chicken stock
1 onion, chopped	3 tablespoons flour
¼ teaspoon garlic powder	3 cups boiled rice

Sprinkle the chicken pieces with salt and pepper and brown in the oil in a deep cast iron frying pan. Add onion and garlic powder, and cook until the onions soften. Puree pimientos in a blender and pour over chicken. Sprinkle with cumin, then flour. Stir gently. Slowly but steadily add the chicken stock.

Stir. Simmer for 45 minutes, stirring occasionally. Serve over rice. Yield: 6 servings.

"My insurance investigator hero, Dave Brandstetter, likes good liquor, good music, and good food. Food seems to crop up in the events of most of my books. In *Troublemaker*, Doug Sawyer, the man Dave lives with, gets together Poulet à la Mexicaine. I fixed it one Christmas in my London flat to the acclaim of assorted crowned heads. It warmed up a typical cold, rainy London day."

—Joseph Hansen

Chicken Haycraft

1 *2½-pound chicken*
Water
Salt

2-3 bay leaves
1 clove garlic

Leave chicken whole or cut into serving pieces. Cover with water in pot and add seasonings. Simmer gently 2 to 3 hours or until meat falls from the bones. Remove all bones and skin as well as bay leaves and garlic clove. Place meat and broth in covered bowl in refrigerator. Chill overnight. Reheat and serve chicken hot with some of the broth, or serve cold as an aspic. Yield: 3-4 servings.

NOTE: Fordhook lima beans, covered in some of the broth, make a good accompaniment.

—Howard and Molly Costain Haycraft

A Few Thoughts on Dieting

Fred C. Fellows, the Chief of Police of Stockford, Connecticut, is a tall, big-boned man who carries a good deal of excess weight without showing it.

He knows he should shed some pounds. He talks about it and even makes gestures in that direction—like drinking his coffee black and punishing himself with other minor concessions. He never seriously approaches the problem, however, and the effect of Fred's reducing efforts is, I'm afraid, more psychological than physical.

I, myself, am neither as tall nor as heavy as Fred Fellows, nor need I shed as much poundage. Nevertheless, I do take a more systematic and optimistic approach to diet than Fred does. For instance, I ask myself the question, "Is it not possible to lose weight, yet dine on tasty dishes, dine heartily, and spend a minimum time in meal preparation?"

The answer to this question, I discover, is a resounding "Yes!" And as proof of the pudding, consider the following meal presented with all its calories and preparation steps listed:

1. Puncture skin of 1 chicken thigh (75 calories) to drain grease and pop into 375°-400° F. oven to bake 30 minutes or until brown. (Total 75 calories.)
2. Sauté ½ cup sliced mushrooms (50 calories) in 1 tablespoon of butter (100 calories) over low heat 10 to 15 minutes, or until dry and crisp. (This is delicate, so watch that they don't burn.) Freshen and revive mushrooms with 1 tablespoon white Chablis (5 calories). (Total 230 calories.)
3. While all this is going on, prepare a broccoli sauce by stirring ½ tablespoon reconstituted lemon juice (3 calories) into 1 tablespoon imitation mayonnaise (40 calories) until creamy. (Total 273 calories.)

4. Mix salad as follows: Break up 3 leaves of lettuce (9 calories) and combine with 1 slice diced Bermuda onion (3 calories), 1 small cut up tomato (25 calories), 1 crumbled slice of blue cheese, 1″ × 1″ × ¼″ (50 calories), and 1 tablespoon imitation mayonnaise (40 calories). (Total 400 calories.)
5. At 20-minute mark, drain grease from chicken thigh, add mushroom-wine—in joint juncture is best—and bake until done.
6. Cook 1 cup frozen broccoli spears (66 calories) according to directions on package. (Total 466 calories.)
7. As appetizer, prepare ½ 11-ounce can chilled consommé (25 calories) with 1 tablespoon sour cream (50 calories) as topping. (Total 541 calories.)
8. Serve chicken and broccoli (don't forget the broccoli sauce) with salad after dining on the consommé.
9. Skip dessert.

Since a six-foot male (which is what I am) will lose weight on 1,560 calories a day, it would be nice to bring in this meal at under 500 calories, or less than one-third of the quota. This can readily be done, without any loss of bulk, by cutting out one of the extras, like the mushrooms, or the blue cheese, or the broccoli sauce, or the appetizer. One such extra might be dispensed with. But deleting too many will make the meal pedestrian, which defeats the goal of tastiness.

If calories aren't too critical, and you want to "gourmet it up" a little (bad English, but one of my pet expressions), add a glass of white Chablis (75 calories) to the meal. If you do overindulge, look on the bright side. Remember that you can always eat mushroomless chicken, sauceless broccoli, and cheeseless salad 7.1559633 times the next day to make up for it.

—Hillary Waugh

Beckford Chicken

5 breasts of chicken, halved
Pepper
3-4 tablespoons butter

Bottle dry white wine (Chablis or sauterne)

If desired, bone and skin chicken breasts. Dry between paper towels. Pepper well. Brown breasts in butter on electric skillet set at 350° F. When

135

browned, reduce heat to 250° F. Cover chicken with wine. Cover skillet and cook 1 hour. Check occasionally, adding wine as it cooks away. Serve hot or cold. Yield: 6-10 servings.

NOTE: No salt is used. Wine provides the flavor.

"As you may know, the Eastern Shore of Maryland is famous for good chicken. This recipe is standard fare when the Ainsworths entertain."

—Norma Ainsworth

Some years ago a tale went the rounds of New York gourmet circles. Even gourmands were telling it. It concerned a hostess who had in her employ a great cook. Dinner invitations were greatly sought after but there was one difficulty. People were always begging for recipes and the cook, jealous of her skills, could never be persuaded to part with her secrets. At one dinner party a guest was unquenchably insistent. The hostess broke down and summoned the genius out of the kitchen. After the cook had been softened up by chorused praise, the hostess gathered her courage and asked.

"My friend here will never be happy again unless she has your recipe for your wonderful dessert. Would you let her have it?"

Much to everyone's astonishment, the cook consented. She began listing ingredients. "Two cups of flour, a half-pound of butter, a cup of sugar, a little water . . ."

"A little water?" the guest broke in. "How much water?"

The cook scowled in concentration. After some moments of deep thought, she smiled happily. She had the answer. "A mouthful," she said.

End of recipe. End of dinner. End of story.

—Aaron Marc Stein

Poultry

Baked Chicken with Tarragon

2 *young pullets, cut up*	3 *tablespoons butter*
Flour	½ *cup boiling water*
4 *teaspoons salt*	½ *cup dry vermouth, approximately*
¼ *teaspoon black pepper*	¼ *cup cognac*
2 *tablespoons dried tarragon*	4 *cups boiled rice*

Preheat oven to 400° F. Wash and dry the pieces of chicken. Dredge them in a mixture of flour, salt, pepper and 1 tablespoon of the tarragon. Arrange chicken in roasting pan and dot with half of the butter. Bake for 15 minutes. Reduce heat to 375° F. Melt remaining butter in a mixture of the hot water and ½ cup vermouth and steep the remaining tarragon in it. Baste chicken with this mixture and bake for 1 hour or more until tender and crusty brown. If more basting liquid is needed, use additional dry vermouth. Turn once during baking to brown undersides, then turn back to dry the tops. When ready to serve, remove chicken to a hot platter. Add enough boiling water to pan to make about ¼-inch of liquid. Deglaze the pan with the cognac, scraping all brown bits into the sauce. Cook over high heat to evaporate the alcohol. Serve sauce in sauce boat. Pass hot boiled rice. Yield: 4 servings.

"Some years ago when the great Point was still presiding over his kitchen, we went the few miles down the Rhone from Lyons to Vienne to lunch at the Pyramide. Point gave us a never-to-be-forgotten meal. My New York butcher, though French and sympathetic, could never supply me with a *poularde* from Brasse. But he does supply me with tender and flavorful chickens. I make no claim that this recipe produces the equivalent of the Point masterpiece, but it comes closer than any I've had from the kitchens of other French cooks."

—Aaron Marc Stein

Chicken Stovies

2 heaping tablespoons butter
1 3-pound chicken, cut into serving
   pieces
2½ pounds boiling potatoes, sliced
   into medium-thick rounds
2 large sliced onions

Salt and pepper, to taste
3 cups stock made from the giblets
   or canned chicken consommé, divided
3 tablespoons chopped parsley

Melt 1 tablespoon of butter in a Dutch oven or heavy, covered skillet and lightly brown chicken pieces on all sides. Remove the chicken. On the bottom of same skillet, place a layer of potatoes; then layer of onions; then layer of chicken. Season each layer to taste and dot with remaining butter. Continue until all the food is used, ending with a layer of potatoes on top. Pour in 2 cups of stock. Cover skillet with a layer of buttered waxed paper and then with the lid. Cook in a slow 275° F. oven for about 2½ hours, adding a little *warm* stock halfway through cooking time if the dish appears dry. Sprinkle with parsley 5 minutes before serving. Yield: 4-6 servings.

"According to a Scottish friend, the name of this dish is a corruption of the French word *étouffée:* to stew in a closed vessel. My husband and I first encountered stovies one gloomy night in northwestern Scotland. Our rented car's engine trouble had forced us to stop at an inn in a small village 20 miles short of our destination. The proprietor told us, with one of those dour Scotch-Dissenter looks, that he served no spirits. In the bleak little parlor, six or seven middle-aged English tourists conversed in the funereal whispers that the English deem proper for use in inn parlors. My husband and I felt more depressed with each passing moment.

"But in the small dining room, around seven o'clock, all was made right when the landlord's wife placed before us a chicken, potato and onion concoction. Even before we tasted it, the steam arising from the dish told us that her cooking method had preserved every essence of the bird. By means of shameless flattery, we extracted from her a promise to write out the recipe before we left in the morning. She did, and I have cooked Chicken Stovies many times since."

—Velda Johnston

Casserole Maison

2 turkey breasts or 4 chicken breasts, slightly salted
1 11-ounce can condensed cream of mushroom soup, undiluted, divided
¼ cup grated American cheese
Salt, optional
1 tablespoon grated goat's cheese
10 ounces mushrooms, sliced
2 tablespoons butter, divided
Green noodles, as desired
Water
1 can clear chicken broth (stock)
Swiss cheese, sliced

Steam (do not boil) turkey or chicken breasts until fork tender, about 2 hours. Drain off all liquid and combine it with ½ can of mushroom soup. Add American cheese while cooking liquid is still hot. Stir well. Taste and add salt if necessary. Allow to cool. Stir in 1 tablespoon of goat's cheese. (This gives a delicious but mysterious flavor.) Skin turkey or chicken breasts and cut into bite-sized pieces. Add to soup mixture. Refrigerate until needed. Sauté mushrooms in 1 tablespoon butter until tender. Remove from pan with slotted spoon. Boil noodles according to package directions in water to which the chicken broth has been added. Drain. Spread a thin layer of noodles on the bottom of a well-buttered open flat baking dish. Spread half the mushrooms over the noodles, then a layer of turkey or chicken. Repeat until all are used. Pour remaining soup over all. Top with slices of Swiss cheese. Bake in 350° F. oven for 1 hour. If Swiss cheese is not bubbling, place briefly under broiler before serving. Yield: 6 servings.

NOTE: The casserole may be refrigerated before cooking.

"This is really the best company casserole I've ever eaten. It may also be made with cooked lamb instead of poultry."

—Evelyn Berckman

Breast of Turkey

1 half turkey breast, 2 pounds
1 package stuffing
½ cup chicken broth
Melted butter or jelly

Preheat oven to 350° F. Bone and skin turkey. Butterfly it (pull it apart with fingers, spread it out like a butterfly and divide it up the middle).

139

Prepare stuffing according to package directions. Spread thickly over meat. Roll and tie with string. Roast for 1 hour, basting with chicken broth. Glaze with melted butter or jelly. Slice and serve. Yield: 4 servings.

—Jean L. Backus

Paris is different. The habitués of the Montparnasse and St. Germain cafes appreciate the ebb and flow of a writer's career, possibly because they have not been weaned on Henry Luce. They would not look at Writer X pityingly if he had fallen on fallow times. They would look at him with admiration.

"He is germinating," they would say. "It is the hardest part of a writer's life, and the most fruitful."

By contrast, shortly after my return to New York I was accosted somewhat belligerently by a fairly prolific writer of mysteries.

"What have you been working on?" he asked aggressively.

"Book," I mumbled. It had been a hard book to write.

The fairly prolific mystery writer pounced. "Haven't seen much of your stuff around," he said gleefully.

"Guess not."

"You used to really turn them out," he accused me.

He had me either way. I wondered if there is still an empty chair at the Montparnasse cafe where X and his friends hang out.

—Stephen Marlowe

Stuffed Duck Bordelaise

Stuffing:

2 tablespoons butter

4 tablespoons finely chopped shallots

Duck livers, chopped

1 tablespoon minced parsley

8 green olives, chopped

1/2 teaspoon sage

1/4 teaspoon dried, crushed thyme

Pinch grated nutmeg

Salt and pepper, to taste

4 slices white bread, finely diced

2 eggs

Melt butter in large saucepan, add shallots and simmer for 2 minutes. Add livers and simmer 2 minutes more. Add remaining ingredients except bread and egg. Remove from heat and add the bread, stirring with a rubber spatula. Stir in eggs 1 at a time, mixing well after each addition.

Roast Duck:

2 ducks (4½-5 pounds each)

Salt and pepper, to taste

4 tablespoons butter

2 carrots, scraped and coarsely chopped

1 pound mushrooms, sliced

2 stalks celery, coarsely chopped

1 bay leaf

Pinch rosemary

2 cups chicken stock

1 cup dry white wine

2 tablespoons Madeira wine

Several leaves braised lettuce, optional

Preheat oven to 350° F. Loosely stuff ducks and truss with kitchen string. Season stuffed ducks with salt and pepper. Brown them in butter on both sides over medium heat in flame-proof casserole or roaster. Add carrots, mushrooms, celery, seasonings, stock, and white wine. Cover and bake 1–1½ hours or until fork tender. Remove ducks and reduce pan juice to 2½ cups. Remove fat from juice, add Madeira and bring to a boil. Carve ducks. Arrange on large platter. Pass juice separately. Garnish with braised lettuce if desired. Yield: 6 servings.

—Patricia McGerr

Sweetheart Duck

5-6-pound duck
½ cup plus 2 tablespoons curaçao, divided
2 navel oranges
¼ cup brown sugar

½ cup fresh orange juice
2 tablespoons arrowroot
2 cups rich beef stock
3 tablespoons tomato puree
Pinch thyme

Preheat oven to 400° F. Rub duck inside and out with 2 tablespoons curaçao. Prick skin all over with a fork to ensure fat running off during roasting. Place duck in oven for about 1½ hours or until fork tender. Thinly peel skins from oranges and cut into julienne strips. Put strips, brown sugar and orange juice into a saucepan and slowly reduce to about 1½ cups. Set aside. Mix tomato puree, thyme and arrowroot with curaçao. Add to the beef stock and simmer for 2–3 minutes. Add orange syrup and simmer for another 5 minutes. (Taste carefully at this point to correct seasoning by adding more brown sugar or more curaçao. If sauce seems too thick, add a bit more beef stock.) Cut duck into 8 serving pieces and place in flameproof casserole. Pour sauce over duck and let simmer on low heat until duck is heated through. Yield: 4 servings.

"Serve this with potatoes that have been pureed with butter and cream. Don't waste your best wine with this dish. Opt for a robust local white, or splurge with a bottle of Kriter."

—Nan and Ivan Lyons

Old English Pigeon Pie

6 pigeons
6 strips bacon
2 cups bouillon, divided
2 cups Burgundy, divided
2 large mild onions, sliced fine

4 large pork sausages
Peas, carrots, string beans, or other vegetables, cooked in desired quantities, optional
Unbaked pie shell

Carve pigeons to remove breast meat. Discard the rest of the pigeons. Wrap each breast with strip of bacon, securing with toothpick. Place breasts in casserole and cover with half the bouillon and half the Burgundy. Cover

142

tightly and simmer in oven at lowest possible temperature (200° F. or less) for 6 to 10 hours. Pigeons are done when tender. Make sure stock does not cook away. Add more if necessary. Remove from oven. Remove breasts and put aside. Discard bacon. Wash and dry casserole and place layer of the sliced onions in it. Top with half the breasts. Repeat layers, and top with pork sausages. Combine remaining bouillon and wine, until food is covered by 1 inch of liquid. Cover casserole and cook for 1½ hours in 425° F. oven. Prepare vegetables, if using. Roll pastry thin to cover casserole. Remove casserole and add vegetables. Invert cup in center of casserole to support pastry. Top with pastry, pinching firmly around edge of casserole. Bake in hot (400°-450° F.) oven until pastry is browned, about 20 minutes. Yield: 4-6 servings.

"This dish has been prepared and eaten by inhabitants of the English countryside for many centuries. Our Anglo-Saxon ancestors enjoyed the flesh of the wild wood pigeon, or ring dove, since before the Norman invasion. The birds infest the rural areas, living on high-grade grain, berries, and clover only. They eschew all forms of food that have chemical preparations in them. From this it may be deduced that the flesh of the bird—a dry, dark red, strong-flavored meat—tastes today much as it did a thousand years ago, which is one hell of a sight more than can be said for any store-bought meat.

"Go out into the countryside with a twelve-gauge shotgun, take up a strategic position under a tree facing a field of cut wheat or clover, where the pigeon may be expected to land to feed, and wait for the prey. Spend three days thus, sipping from a thoughtfully provided hip flask to ward off the common cold, then trade the gun back in at the hardware store and buy six pigeons from the local poultry merchant. WARNING: Do not go down to Rockefeller Plaza and shoot six of the city's pigeons at point blank range. For one thing, this is unsporting; and for another, it upsets the N.Y.P.D.

"Serve your pigeon pie piping hot, two or three breasts per person, surrounded by the vegetables doused with the gravy from inside the pie. Help it down the hatch with another bottle of Burgundy. Retire to a deep armchair before a log fire."

—Frederick Forsyth

I have recently realized how large a part the eating of meals, good or bad, has played in the lives of characters in my novels and short stories.

To mention just a few: the *Königsjäger* Inn at Allstadt and the obscene breaded *Kalbslunge* upon which Herr Dirnkreuz gorged himself while he prepared to make Jim McCabe the offer he couldn't refuse. Or in a more sensual vein, the salmon mayonnaise and *Pfalzerwein* that Harry Benton and Magda ate at the table overlooking the Neckar after they had made the border crossing from the East. Or the bread and cheese and wine that David Brooks and Nicole ate at her villa in the Riviera when he had turned up there as a fugitive.

Then there are less pleasant meals: the last supper of Belarmino Galan at the cheap Spanish restaurant in Paris with two Caribbean killers or the drab and glutinous repast that Cassius Aurelius McPherson and Harry Blood pushed down their gullets at the Midcoast University Club. Or more ambiguous dinners like the one that brought Steve Bowman and Ann to eat *Sole cardinale* and *Poulet Normande* at the corrupt penthouse in Bradford Falls. Or, finally, the horrid fiasco at Chez Chaptal in front of the jury of the Companions of Lucullus, which cost Pierre Chaptal his gastronomic stars, his wife and his life.

Oh, there's a lot of action in food. Each of my scenes served both as a momentary false pause and as a prelude and signpost for coming action—love, death, ruin, flight.

Owning a small, really good restaurant has been one of my Walter Mitty dreams for twenty-five years. But I know it wouldn't work. First of all, as my wife points out, I am extravagant with raw materials. In my hands, lasagna, an inexpensive bourgeois Italian dish, costs out at the same amount as filet mignon; the same with

English veal and ham pie. Then, too, I am slow. I dice and chop and brown and mix and season for several hours. Finally, I am sloppy. I use up vast quantities of pots and pans and casseroles, of knives and blending tools. I spill things on counters. While I am preparing a dish, I am too caught up in the act of creation to clean as I progress. When the actual cooking begins, I am worn out. What I need is vegetable-chopping apprentices, assistant *sauciers*, pot boys, and scullions. These our household does not provide.

"What do you want me to cook for your birthday?" I once asked my eldest son.

"Snails. Then rabbit *agrodolce.*"

That's another reason why I don't cook regularly.

—James Cross

Rock Cornish Hens Financier à la James Cross

4 Rock Cornish game hens or pigeons	1 8-ounce jar pimiento-stuffed olives, chopped
1 pair sweetbreads	Thyme, sage, persillade, rock or sea salt, peppercorns, to taste
1 quart water	
1 tablespoon vinegar	4 hard-cooked eggs, diced
3-4 slices salt pork	1 cup flavored breadcrumbs or Swiss cereal
1 tablespoon butter	
1 tablespoon olive oil	1 cup chicken stock, divided
4-8 cloves garlic, pressed	1 cup dry white wine, divided
8 chicken livers, diced	
1 8-ounce can pitted black olives, chopped	

In medium saucepan simmer sweetbreads in water and vinegar for 15 minutes. Drain and rinse sweetbreads in cold water. Devein and dice. Reserve. Blanch salt pork for 2 minutes to remove excess salt. Dice. Put in large stovetop casserole, over medium heat, with butter, olive oil and garlic. When slightly browned, add game hens and brown well on all sides. Remove hens from casserole and set aside. Turn heat to low. Add chicken livers, olives, spices, eggs, sweetbreads and breadcrumbs to casserole. Brown slightly. Add ¼ cup each of chicken stock and white wine. Stir. Turn off heat. Cool and spoon into cavities of game hens. There will be stuffing left over. Add stock and wine to remaining stuffing, stirring with wooden spoon to make sauce. Simmer for ten to 15 minutes, stirring constantly. Replace hens in casserole and bake, uncovered, in 325° F. oven for 1 hour. Test by piercing with blunt fork. Juices should be clear and colorless. Serve hot. Pass sauce separately. Yield: 4 servings.

—Hugh Jones Parry

Vegetables

Po Chu-i's Bamboo Shoots

My man Paul Harris in the Gavin Black books has been inhibited about recipes ever since, in the earliest products, my wife absolutely stamped on my tendency to take up four pages describing a meal which she said, not unreasonably, played hell with suspense. Since then all Paul Harris ever does is grill a filet of prime Angus beef, and quickly.

However, bamboo shoots have a kind of relevance to Gavin Black. I came on the gastronome poet Po Chu-i through the Waley translations, actually just the day before receiving a request for a recipe. Since we are not allowed coincidence in our business, I can only take it that this was *meant*. Do you find in your private living that coincidence happens not just occasionally, but the whole time, so that in writing one is in fact falsifying reality by avoiding it? Half of my life has been made up of events which the reader would say rated the big raspberry—like the time in Manila when I saw my cousin, who I thought was on the other side of the world, climbing on the back of a truck and the truck starting to move. I ran after it shouting, but he never even saw me. To this day I have never found out what he was doing in Manila and why he was climbing into a truck, because I have never been able to find out what happened to him. Could I use this in a Black? Like hell. Anyway, who ever tries to find missing cousins?

Another time I had to work for a year on the University magazine in Edinburgh with a character who has since made a big success in life, but without my love to help him along. Indeed we could scarcely share a room and keep control of our nerves. It was a really outsize mutual antipathy. I went to London for a big change over a holiday period, got out of the train, left my bag in a station locker, got in the subway to Piccadilly, walked up the steps to the street and the first man I met on the pavement was this character whom I thought had gone to Norway. Use that in a Black? Joan Kahn would send me one of her deep analyses of story-line failure using one word . . . 'No.' And quite right, too.

But about Po Chu-i. Mr. Po might have been said to have been a failed top echelon civil servant who lacked career drive for pretty obvious reasons, like preferring to eat and drink and no ulcers. He did make it to become governor of a fairly unimportant province, his record there (by his own admission) so undistinguished that Peking moved him to an even more remote province where he described the population as resembling wild apes, saying he was pleased to meet anyone who was even remotely human. But here in Chung-Chou he *did* have bamboos.

I'd have got on with that guy 1,200 years ago. Indeed, maybe I was one of his buddies once. He had only four friends left when he died of drink and maybe a surfeit of bamboos."

—Oswald Wynd

Eating Bamboo Shoots

My new province is a land of bamboo groves:
Their shoots in spring fill the valleys and hills.
The mountain woodman cuts an armful of them
And brings them down to sell at the early market.
Things are cheap in proportion as they are common:
For two farthings I buy a whole bundle.
I put the shoots in a great earthen pot,
And heat them up along with boiling rice.
The purple skins broken—like an old brocade:
The white skin opened—like new pearls.
Now every day I eat them recklessly:
For a long time I have not touched meat.
All the time I was living at Lo-yang
They could not give me enough to suit my taste.
Now I have as many shoots as I please
For each breath of the south wind makes a new bamboo.

—Po Chu-i (A.D. 772–846)

Bamboo Shoots

1½ pounds canned or 3 pounds fresh   2 tablespoons butter
    bamboo shoots   White sauce, optional
Salted water
1 tablespoon vinegar

If canned shoots are used, discard liquor in can. Cut shoots into bite-size chunks. Bring shoots to a boil in salted water to which a tablespoon of vinegar has been added. Boil for 10 minutes. Drain. Briefly sauté in skillet with butter. Serve plain, or combine with white sauce if desired. Yield: 3-4 servings.

"In the Far East, like Mr. Po, I can eat bamboo shoots for every meal but breakfast and to hell with meat . . . Surely in the States there must be areas in which the giant bamboo grows, and possibly is uncropped? They have to be collected like mushrooms, preferably in the morning just after the new shoot (about the size of two fists put together) has shoved through the ground. Leave them even a couple of days and you're chewing at fencing. If you have the fresh article I recommend Mr. Po's recipe, which can scarcely be bettered, but if it must be the tinned stuff then . . ."

—Oswald Wynd

Leeky Pie

½ pound flour   1 pound leeks
Salt   ¼ pound bacon
4-6 ounces butter or lard   2 eggs
3-4 tablespoons cold water   Seasoning

Preheat oven to 350° F. Sift flour and add salt. Cut half of the butter into the flour with knives or pastry cutter until mixture is grainy. Cut remaining butter into mixture until pebble sized. Sprinkle with cold water. Mix dough with a fork or hands. When dough can be formed into a ball it can be rolled and half fitted into a 9-inch pie pan.

Boil or steam leeks until tender. Chop leeks into small pieces. Cut bacon into half-inch strips. Mix leeks in pie pan and season. Cover loosely with pastry, crimping edges over pie pan. Cut several slits in pie crust, and bake in oven until pastry is pale in color. Whisk eggs and pour through a slit made in pastry. Return to oven and cook for a further 15 to 20 minutes. Yield: 6-8 servings.

"Quite a number of my books are set in Cornwall, and as the characters naturally eat now and then it has been necessary to know something about the food they enjoy in those parts. The Cornish are inordinately fond of pastry and although some of their dishes may not benefit their waistlines they are frequently, as they would say, 'proper tasty.' I was intrigued by *Star-Gazy Pie*—which turned out to be a number of sad-looking pilchards gazing heavenwards (as the name implies) as they emerged from a crisp brown pastry. It was a small wonder that they had the look of suffering martyrs and to a non-Celtic palate were revolting in every way. *Star-Gazy* does, however, appear to be an acquired taste. I did discover this other dish for less squeamish stomachs, known in those parts as Leeky Pie. It should be tried for a light supper dish. It is easy, quick, and 'proper tasty.' "

—Victoria Holt

Ratatouille Provençale

⅓ *cup olive or safflower oil*
¾ *cup thinly sliced onions*
1 *medium to large eggplant, peeled and diced into chunks*

2 *large green peppers, sliced lengthwise*
2 *large tomatoes, sectioned*
Salt and pepper, to taste

Heat oil in a large frying pan or casserole and sauté onions until golden brown. Remove onions and combine half with half eggplant, peppers and tomatoes. (The tomatoes may be peeled and seeded if you're finicky, Dan Fortune isn't.) Make a layer in the frying pan, and salt and pepper the layer. Repeat for a second layer. Add a little more oil, cover tightly, and simmer over very low heat 45 minutes to an hour. Serve hot. Yield: 4-6 servings.

"Dan Fortune doesn't cook much in my books. As a single New Yorker he tended to eat in bars, restaurants and diners, so I rarely mention anything like a recipe. But Dan has now moved to California, is living in a house for the first time in his life, has started to do more cooking. About his favorite vegetable dish is his personal stripped-down version of *Ratatouille Provençale*. It's a real challenge for a one-armed man, but the result that is like a canvas from his favorite abstract expressionists is worth it."

—Michael Collins

Braised Lettuce

6 small lettuce hearts
Butter

Beef or veal stock

Blanch lettuce hearts in boiling water for 4 minutes. Remove from fire, drain and cool. Place in heavily buttered casserole. Dot with butter and pour in stock to barely cover the lettuce. Bake in 350° F. oven until most of the liquid is absorbed, basting frequently. Drain and serve hot with poultry or cold meats. Yield: 6 servings.

—Nancy Webb

Lima Beans Amber Dean

2 teaspoons salt
1 pound large dry limas, soaked overnight
¾ cup butter

¾ cup dark brown sugar
1 tablespoon dry mustard
1 tablespoon molasses
1 cup sour cream

Add salt to limas. Cook until just tender; do not overcook. Drain, saving liquid. Put beans in casserole. In a small saucepan heat 1 cup bean liquid. Add butter, sugar, mustard, and molasses. Stir until butter melts. Pour over

Vegetables

limas. Cover and bake 1 hour in 350° F. oven. Uncover for the last 15 minutes. Yield: 4-6 servings.

—Amber Dean

EDITOR'S NOTE: A fine budget-balancer if the check doesn't arrive.

Burgundy Onion Rings

4 large yellow onions, sliced and
  ringed
4 tablespoons butter

Salt and pepper
1 cup Burgundy

Sauté onion rings in butter until translucent. Sprinkle heavily with salt and pepper. Pour in Burgundy. Cover and steam onions until tender. Drain and serve hot with steak or roast beef. Yield: 4 servings.

—Joyce Kadryna

The Colonel's Delight

1 pound white onions
¼ cup margarine
3 eggs
¼ cup heavy cream

½ teaspoon nutmeg
Salt and pepper, to taste
1 strip lean bacon

Peel onions, and let them stand in cold, salted water to cover for 1 hour. Slice and sauté them in margarine until soft. Do not allow to brown. Cool. Preheat oven to 350° F. Beat eggs, and add cream. Season with nutmeg, salt and pepper. Mix with onions. Pour into a buttered ovenproof casserole. Slice bacon in tiny strips and lay on top. Bake 20 minutes or until custard is thick. Yield: 6 servings.

153

"The rumor that this delicious onion custard was wrung from a captured enemy quartermaster is not true, although first mention of the delicate dish was found in Colonel Moriarty's field diary of the Boer War."

—Barbara Walton

Table D'Hoch Menu

Coquilles St. Jacques Futrelles   Clams on the Half Shell Scott

Soupe de Jordan   Mushrooms à la Gregg

Some Berried Caesar Salad

Mixed Rolls with Beurre d'Étrangers au Train

Filet Mignon Eberhart with Father Brown Sauce

Deviled Kiddies à la Rosemary's Baby

Roulades de Morgue

Spiedini alla Hammett   Fish Robert Sauté with Shallots Armstrong

Bouillabaisse Canard   Chicken à la Rufus King

Salisbury'tec Davis with Fu Manchucroute

Filet #5, Joe Gores   Murdermost Fowl

Arthur Porgies Baked with Herbes Brean

Asparagus Vinmaigret   Carrots Julienne Symons

Baba av Rhum Davidson   Stollen Rubens

Daniel Webster Coffee   Christianna Brand Rawson Cake

May we suggest

a Steinbrunner of Shaffer beer

a Goldfinger of Bonded whisky

Catered by McDonalds—Ross, John D. and Ronald

Risotto with Peas and Ham

¾ cup butter
1 large onion, chopped
1¼ cups raw Carolina long grain
*   white rice*
Approximately 1½ quarts fresh or
*   frozen chicken or turkey stock,*
*   divided*
1 teaspoon dried basil

1 package frozen tiny peas
Salt and pepper
¼ cup heavy cream
½ cup or more small cubes of cooked
*   ham*
⅓ cup grated Parmesan cheese

In a large skillet melt butter over medium heat. Add onion and rice, and stir with a wooden spoon for at least 5 minutes. The object is to coat the rice thoroughly. It must not stick. The rice will begin to sizzle and pop, and butter will foam. Add about ¾ cup of stock and stir until rice has absorbed it. Repeat last step twice more, adding stock and stirring until it is absorbed. Add ¾ cup stock for a fourth time along with basil and still-frozen peas. Add another ¾ cup of stock. When liquid is absorbed, season with salt and pepper. Taste rice. If it is not plump and tender, add more stock and continue cooking until it is absorbed. Add heavy cream, ham, and cheese. Stir until piping hot, and serve immediately. Yield: 4 servings.

"Every cook who makes his own stock should have this risotto in his repertoire. The stock used should be fresh and well-seasoned. I use bay leaf, marjoram, thyme, juniper berries, peppercorns, and salt in addition to the usual chopped celery, onion, and carrot. After straining, cool the stock in the refrigerator and remove all fat from the surface. This risotto is an easy dish to make, but time-consuming. You must stay with it, stirring constantly, for about forty minutes. It's fun to make if you have a large kitchen, people to talk to, and a glass of wine in one hand."

—Fred Jarvis

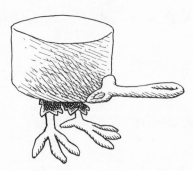

Risi e Bisi

(Rice and Peas, a Venetian Side Dish)

5 cups chicken broth or stock
2 tablespoons butter
½ cup chopped onions
2 cups fresh or thawed frozen green
    peas

1½ cups uncooked rice
½-1 cup ham, Italian or other, cut
    in half-inch pieces
½ cup grated Parmesan cheese

Use less ham if it's to be a side dish, more if it is a main dish for lunch.
Bring chicken stock to a boil in a saucepan while you sauté onions just until soft in butter in a skillet. If you are using fresh peas, add them now with ham, rice and onions to broth and simmer until rice is done. If you are using frozen thawed peas, add peas to the simmering mixture about 5 minutes before rice is done. Remove from heat. Stir in cheese. Serve immediately. Yield: 8-12 servings.

—Barbara D'Amato

Tom's Potato Pudding

5 pounds old potatoes
6 medium onions
6 eggs
2 teaspoons salt

2 teaspoons baking powder
8 tablespoons melted chicken fat or
    cooking oil
Pepper, to taste

Preheat oven to 375° F. Peel and grate potatoes and onions fine. Combine with all other ingredients. Butter custard cups or casserole lavishly. Heat in oven until very hot. Fill with pudding mixture. Bake for 1½ hours until dark golden brown. Yield: 12-20 servings.

—Charles M. Plotz

I don't cook at all. All I do is defrost, and the recipe for that is on the back of the package.

—Ira Levin

Potato Puffs

5 potatoes
1 large onion, diced
2 cloves garlic, minced
¼ cup chicken fat or butter, divided

2 beaten eggs
6 tablespoons matzo (or other) meal
Salt and freshly ground pepper, to taste

Peel potatoes and boil until tender. Sauté onion and garlic in 1 tablespoon of fat or butter until soft. Mash potatoes, add onion, garlic, remaining fat, eggs, meal, salt and pepper. Mix thoroughly. Form into balls, roll in additional meal, and bake on well-greased baking sheet for ½ hour in a 375° F. oven until golden brown. Yield: 4-6 servings.

—Pauline Bloom

Potato Pie

Pastry for 10-inch, double crust pie
4 large potatoes
Salt and pepper, to taste

5 tablespoons melted butter
1 pint heavy cream

Preheat oven to 425° F. Line pie pan with ½ of pastry. Peel and thinly slice potatoes. Drop slices in rapidly boiling water and cook for about 3 minutes.

Drain and dry thoroughly with paper towels. Line pie shell with layer of cooked potatoes. Sprinkle with salt and pepper and drizzle with melted butter. Repeat until pie shell is filled. Roll and cut remaining pastry into strips, and cover pie in lattice pattern. Put in oven until pastry starts to brown, about 10 minutes. Reduce heat to 350° F. and continue cooking. In about 15 minutes when pie is half cooked, remove from oven and pour in as much cream as potatoes will absorb through lattice openings. Return to oven to finish cooking for about 20 minutes or until potatoes are tender. Add more cream if necessary during cooking. Yield: 4-6 servings.

—Alexandra Roudybush

Kartoffelpuffer

1½ *pounds potatoes, peeled*   *Dash salt*
 1 *medium-size onion, grated*   *Lard for frying*
 2 *large eggs, beaten*   *Applesauce*
¾ *cup flour*   *Cranberry sauce*

Shred potatoes fairly fine. Mix thoroughly with grated onion. Beat in eggs, flour and salt. Melt lard in skillet. Pour in potato mixture by spoonfuls, flatten into thin pancakes. Brown on one side, turn and brown on other side. Drain on paper towels. Keep warm. Serve hot and pass cold applesauce topped with cranberry sauce. Yield: 4-6 servings.

"With a name like *Kartoffelpuffer*, what more do you want? This is used in Germany as a main dish, meatless and filling, semi-sweet, semi-savory. The rounder and thinner you can get your pancakes the better. You eat the *Kartoffelpuffer* with knife and fork, and you teaspoon out the applesauce. I ate them first off the autobahn above Würzburg, with a stunning view of that delectable city. They tasted fine. I've made them many times since."

—Ellis Peters

Spinach at Its Best

3 tablespoons olive oil
1 tablespoon minced onion
1 pound spinach, washed and
   drained

5-6 anchovies, chopped
Slivered almonds

Heat oil and add minced onion. Cook slowly until onion is light brown. Add spinach. Cover skillet and cook until just tender, 3 to 5 minutes. Chop fine. Add anchovies. Reheat if necessary and serve sprinkled with slivered almonds. Yield: 4 servings.

—Catherine Barth

Southern Medley

1 cup mashed cooked rutabagas
½ cup mashed cooked carrots
½ cup chopped cooked onions

4 slices bacon
2 tablespoons drippings
Salt and pepper

Combine vegetables. Fry bacon. Drain. Add the drippings to the vegetables, season, and crumble bacon on top.

—Eleanor Sullivan

When crime gets into the history books, something usually happens to twist it all out of recognition. Too often it is perfumed into

160

Vegetables

something sweeter and purer so that we don't really appreciate what a fine share crime has had in our glorious past.

Everybody knows the story of John Smith and the Indian maiden. But not many know what really happened, although the true account is contained in *The Papers of the Virginia Company* published by the Library of Congress. Here's how it all came about:

On a warm day in 1613, Samuel Argall, a captain employed by the Virginia Company of London, proprietors of the colony at Jamestown, was sitting in the cabin of his ship writing a report of his latest trading voyage up the James River. On arriving in Jamestown he had found the colony starving—not unusual in those days. The Governor asked him to sail up the river to barter with the Indians for food.

Peaceful negotiations at several Indian camps failed. These simple people seldom accumulated a greater surplus of food than they needed to get through the winter, so they had none to spare.

But at one camp, an attractive girl about twelve years old was pointed out to Argall as Pocahontas, daughter of the great chief Powhatan. Powhatan was supposed to be the most powerful ruler in Virginia. This made Pocahontas an emperor's daughter worth, in Argall's eyes, at least a king's ransom.

He had enough experience with Indians to know that they always were curious to see the white man's miracles. So he invited the girl to visit his ship. While she was looking at the strange furniture in the cabin, he pulled up anchor and sailed away to Jamestown "seized upon Pocohuntas" was the way he wrote it.

Delighted with his enterprise, the Governor sent a typical ransom message to Powhatan demanding six canoeloads of corn and two English prisoners held by the chief tribes. Powhatan promptly paid up, but like most kidnappers the men of Jamestown thought they had discovered an easy way to riches and raised their sights. They asked for more. Powhatan replied that he had paid as much as any girl was worth. If the white men did not agree, they could keep her; he had plenty more children in his tepee.

The Governor was stumped. He did not want the girl either. He tried to arrange to have her escape, but Pocahontas refused to cooperate. She liked it where she was. The life was easy compared to what she had known. Besides, she had met the most eligible young

161

man in the colony, John Rolfe. He in his turn was fascinated. Between them, they solved the Governor's problem by getting married. It was a romance which attracted attention on both sides of the Atlantic.

—David Loth

Salads

Trying to produce as good a book as you can should be as important to you as eating properly. (Sometimes writers find it hard to make enough money from their writing to eat properly. But the arts have never been an easy way of making a living and they probably never will be.) What you put in your mouth has an effect on you. What comes out of your head has an effect on you, too.

—Joan Kahn

I love salads. My idea of a real gourmet meal is a big plate—or small platter—with two or three halves of papaya—no lime juice, just a little salt—lots of fresh figs, apricots, little white peaches that the stores don't stock because today's super-marketeers think peaches should be big and yellow, and all kinds of plums except Santa Rosas, a mango very ripe, and (if I'm lucky enough to come upon them) a few *sapotes*. Heaven!

—Dorothy B. Hughes

Summertime Salad

Salad:

2 cups cubed, cooked chicken or 2
  cups canned tuna, drained and
  flaked
1 cup pineapple chunks
1 cup mandarin orange sections

½ cup seedless grapes, halved
¼ cup slivered almonds
Salad dressing (below)

Combine all ingredients and chill. Yield: 4-6 servings.

Dressing:

⅔ cup mayonnaise
 1 teaspoon curry powder, or to taste

3 tablespoons sour cream

Combine all ingredients and mix until thoroughly blended. Yield: dressing for salad for 4-6.

—Nancy Wynne

Serving dinner to the creator of Nero Wolfe takes nerve. Still, my wife and I were willing to try it. Our Beef Stroganoff passed muster. But (Rex) Stout drew the line at our sliced tomatoes.

"I can only eat so much, and this afternoon I picked a tomato from my garden and ate it right from the vine. No point in using up my capacities with a wood-pulp tomato from a New York supermarket."

Stout drew us out beyond our expectations. I waxed witty and incisive on the subject of paperback distribution, a feat as unlikely as being eloquent about turnips.

—D. R. Bensen

Salade Niçoise, Knebel-Ross

 5 *stalks celery, scraped and chopped*
15 *radishes, thinly sliced*
 1 *16-ounce can French string beans, drained, or 2 cups fresh string beans, blanched*
 3 *hard-boiled eggs, chilled and thinly sliced*
 2 *small (or 1 large) boiled potatoes, peeled, cooled, and thinly sliced*

6-8 *scallions, washed and thinly sliced*
12 *pitted black olives*
12 *green olives with pimiento*
 2 *tomatoes, sliced into eighths*
 1 *6½-ounce can white tuna, drained*
 1 *2½-ounce can anchovies*
 ¼ *cup olive oil*
 ⅛ *cup wine vinegar*
Salad greens, optional

Gently toss all ingredients except salad greens together. Serve plain or with greens. Yield: 4 servings.

—Fletcher Knebel

Salade Russe à la Française

Everything about this recipe is simple except the seasoning.

The dish consists of a mixture of six vegetables: potatoes, carrots, beets, peas, flageolet beans, and string beans. They should be presented in equal amounts by volume, once those that have to be diced are reduced to that condition. (The flageolet beans may be replaced by lima beans, provided these are fresh and small.)

Each vegetable is to be cooked and seasoned separately, so as to retain its characteristic taste—no point in the salad if the mixture has a uniform flavor of undifferentiated starch. Thus, the potatoes and beets should be marinated in vinegar after boiling, and the peas and carrots given a little added sugar. *No baking soda* must be found on the premises, let alone in the finished product.

Depending on one's taste, several herbs may go into the marinating or dressing of each vegetable, but not indiscriminately in all: thus, tarragon in the string beans, dill weed in the potatoes, etc. The beets and potatoes receive a regular oil-and-vinegar dressing till well soaked.

The final step consists in making mayonnaise, preferably by hand, and mixing it with all the vegetables together *except* the beets. An oblong dish is thus heaped with a rounded form, into which the pieces of red beet are inserted in such a way as not to color the whole mass. Thin trails of mayonnaise may be added crosswise for looks. Some even add small pieces of truffle or black olives for a truly Late Roman Empire assault on the palate. Serve partly chilled but not cold. Yield depends upon the amount prepared.

—Jacques Barzun

Italian Salad

1 clove garlic
1 head romaine, chilled
8 anchovy fillets, chopped
½ cup croutons
1 tomato, peeled and cut into wedges

Capers, to taste
3 tablespoons grated Parmesan or
   Romano cheese
Italian dressing

Rub wooden salad bowl with garlic. Discard clove. Line salad bowl with romaine torn into bite-size pieces. Add remaining ingredients in order. Toss lightly. Yield: 4 servings.

—Helen Wells

Korean Salad

Salad:

1 bag fresh spinach, washed, drained,
   and chilled
1 8-ounce can bean sprouts, drained,
   or 1 cup fresh bean sprouts,
   blanched

1 6-ounce can water chestnuts, sliced
2 hard-cooked eggs, chopped
5 strips bacon, cooked and crumbled
Salad dressing (below)

Combine all salad ingredients, add dressing, and serve at once. Yield: 6 servings.

Dressing:

1 cup salad oil
¾ cup sugar
¼ cup vinegar
⅓ cup catsup

1 onion, grated
2 teaspoons Worcestershire Sauce
Salt, to taste

168

For dressing, combine all ingredients in blender. Mix well. Pour over Korean salad just before serving. Yield: 2⅛ cups.

—Joyce Kadryna

All-Purpose Salad

Salad:

Have ready a bowlful of chopped contents of icebox or larder. These may include: Diced cheese, hard-boiled egg, celery, cabbage, nuts, chicken or chicken liver, cold pork, raisins, fennel, pineapple, small young raw turnips, carrots, apples, raw cauliflower, green peppers, olives, bits of prunes—in a word, *anything firm and chewy.*

Blender Mayonnaise:

1 egg
1¼ cups oil (preferably olive),
   divided
1 teaspoon salt
Dash white pepper

1 teaspoon ground mustard
Dash curry powder
3 tablespoons lemon juice

In blender combine egg, ¼ cup oil, salt, pepper, mustard and curry until thoroughly blended. Putting blender on lowest speed, remove cover and slowly add ½ cup oil. While continuing to blend, add lemon juice. When mixture is thoroughly blended, slowly add ½ cup oil and blend until thick. Yield: 1¾ cups.

At the last moment, sprinkle the leftovers with a little dill seed and combine with mayonnaise. Serve with crusty bread and white wine.

—Joan Aiken

Green Goddess Salad Dressing

1 2-ounce can anchovies, chopped
3 tablespoons chopped chives
1 tablespoon lemon juice
3 tablespoons red wine vinegar (pref-
    erably garlic)
½ tablespoon tarragon

1 cup sour cream
1 cup mayonnaise
½ cup chopped parsley
¼ teaspoon medium ground pepper
½ teaspoon salt

Combine ingredients in blender for 30 seconds, or until thoroughly mixed. Chill. Yield: 2 cups.

—J. J. Lamb

EDITOR'S NOTE: This dressing was introduced in the Palm Court of the earthquake-surviving Palace Hotel in San Francisco.

Herbed Cherry Tomatoes

¼ cup minced parsley
¼ cup salad oil
3 tablespoons vinegar
½ teaspoon dried basil
½ teaspoon dried oregano

½ teaspoon salt
½ teaspoon sugar
1 pint cherry tomatoes, halved
Lettuce leaves

Mix first 7 ingredients in a quart jar. Add tomatoes and cover. Refrigerate for at least 3 hours, turning occasionally. When ready to serve, remove tomatoes with slotted spoon. Serve on lettuce. Yield: 4-6 servings.

—Marilyn Granbeck

Mushroom-Cheese Salad

Salad:

1 head iceberg lettuce	3 endives
1 head romaine	1 pound sliced raw mushrooms

Separate leaves of greens. Wash, dry, and chill all ingredients. Remove from refrigerator and toss with cheese dressing.

Dressing:

1 4-ounce package blue cheese	Salt
4 tablespoons wine vinegar	Onion powder
1 cup salad oil	1 teaspoon dried parsley
Garlic powder	

Mash cheese until crumbly. Add vinegar and oil. Stir to blend. Add seasonings to taste. Refrigerate. Stir well before using. Yield: 2½ cups.

—Dorothea Gildar

Bloody Mary Aspic

Aspic:

3 envelopes unflavored gelatin	2 tablespoons Worcestershire Sauce
1 46-ounce can tomato juice, divided	Tabasco, to taste
1 tablespoon dried instant onion flakes or 3 tablespoons finely chopped onions	Salt, to taste
	Garlic powder, to taste
	4-5 stalks celery, chopped
1 tablespoon dried oregano	

For basic aspic, empty 3 packets unflavored gelatin into large saucepan. Add enough tomato juice to cover. Let gelatin soften. When it is spongy, add enough tomato juice to liquify. Heat, stirring frequently, until gelatin dissolves. Do not boil. Remove from heat. Add onion and oregano, stir and set aside. When gelatin mixture is cool, add remaining tomato juice, seasonings and chopped celery. Pour into oiled 6-cup mold and chill. Unmold and serve with lemon or curried mayonnaise. Yield: 6-8 servings.

SUGGESTIONS:

For a luncheon dish add to above:

Thin cucumber slices
½-1 pound bay shrimp

1 ripe avocado, peeled, pitted, and sliced

Line a fluted mold with alternating avocado slices and large cooked, shelled shrimp. (A fish-shaped mold may be lined with thin cucumber slices to resemble fish scales.) In lining the mold, the basic aspic mixture can be used as a holding agent. Lay vegetables in mold, or stand shrimp and avocado slices against sides of mold and add a few tablespoons of the gelatin. Refrigerate until firm, then add remaining aspic mixture. Chill and unmold.

Lemon Mayonnaise:

1 cup mayonnaise
1 tablespoon lemon juice

Pinch dill weed

Mix together. Yield: 1 cup.

Curried Mayonnaise:

1 cup mayonnaise

½ teaspoon curry powder

Mix together. Yield: 1 cup.

—Charles Larson

Caesar Dressing

1 rounded tablespoon dry mustard
1½ cups olive oil
½ cup white vinegar
Juice of 1½ lemons
1-inch anchovy paste from tube
Seasoned pepper
1 tablespoon soy sauce

½ teaspoon Worcestershire Sauce
Dash of Tabasco
1 egg, beaten slightly
1 clove garlic, minced
½ teaspoon salt
3 ounces blue cheese

Combine all ingredients and blend until smooth. Yield: 2½ cups.

—Richard Martin Stern

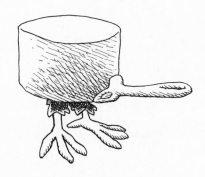

Desserts

Along about the middle of the dessert at every Awards Dinner comes the moment when the lights go dim, a silence falls on the multitude, and a figure mounts the podium to stand before the array of Edgars and Ravens to bring the group to order.

"Who's *that?*" someone asks.

"You said Bob Hope would be emcee," a voice protests in the dark.

"Where's my dessert?"

And the figure on the podium . . .

Well, *somebody* has to be Awards Chairman, to be that strange and awesome combination of discernment and integrity responsible for the committees that decide what mystery novel is best, what mystery short story is best, and so on.

The Awards Chairman has a largely unsung job which begins actually at the end of Awards Banquet A and climaxes at Awards Banquet B. He begins lining up his committee in April. By the time the committee heads are chosen, the arduous task of logistics begins; sending the books and short stories around to all the committee members for judging.

With the motion picture committee, special showings are arranged. The television committee tries to catch the shows live on the tube, but are given special showings when they ask for them. Mostly the judging is smooth sailing, with the decisions all locked in several weeks before the date of the Banquet.

—Edward D. Hoch

176

Desserts

Writers' Respite Cookies

¼ cup butter
¾ cup brown sugar
1 large egg
1 teaspoon vanilla extract
⅔ cup flour

¼ teaspoon salt
1 teaspoon baking powder
½ cup chopped pecans or walnuts
1 cup coarsely chopped dates

Preheat oven to 350° F. In medium saucepan, melt butter and add brown sugar. Stir until combined. Beat in egg and vanilla extract. Sift together dry ingredients, mixing briskly. Stir in. Fold in nuts and dates. Spread in lightly buttered 9″ × 9″ pan and bake for 25 minutes. Cool and cut into bars. Yield: 6-12 servings.

VARIATIONS:

For nut-date mixture, substitute ½ cup chopped nuts or 1 cup chocolate pieces—add ½ teaspoon cinnamon and ¼ teaspoon nutmeg to dry ingredients before sifting—use 1 teaspoon coffee (liquid) in place of vanilla extract and add ½ cup raisins—substitute ½ cup dates and ½ cup walnuts for 1 cup dates.

"These can be made, or eaten, in between extended periods of inspired creativity or rewriting drudgery."

—Geraldine Kamrass

Father Crumlish's Christmas Cookies

3 tablespoons butter
½ cup sugar
½ cup heavy cream
⅓ cup sifted flour
1¼ cups very finely chopped blanched
    almonds

¾ cup very finely chopped candied
    fruit and peels
¼ teaspoon ground cloves
¼ teaspoon ground nutmeg
¼ teaspoon ground cinnamon
½ cup melted chocolate, optional

Preheat oven to 350° F. Combine butter, sugar and cream in a saucepan and bring to a boil. Remove from the heat immediately. Stir in other

177

ingredients to form a batter. Drop batter by spoonfuls onto a greased baking sheet, spacing them about 3 inches apart. Bake 10 minutes or until cookies begin to brown around the edges. Cool, and then remove to a flat surface. If desired, while cookies are still warm, drizzle melted chocolate over tops. Yield: About 24 cookies.

"These cookies are the climax of 'Father Crumlish Celebrates Christmas,' a story appearing in *Ellery Queen's Mystery Magazine*."

—Alice Scanlon Reach

Aunt Ferne's Seven-Layer Cookies

½ cup butter or margarine
1 cup graham cracker crumbs
1 cup coconut
1 6-ounce package chocolate chips

1 small package butterscotch chips
1 15-ounce can sweetened condensed milk
1½ cups chopped nuts

Preheat oven to 350° F. Melt butter in a 9″ × 13″ pan. In order, sprinkle the remaining ingredients evenly over butter. Do not mix. Bake for 30 minutes. Cool and cut. Yield: 100 plus 1-inch squares.

"My Aunt Ferne makes the best cookies in the world."

—Barbara Michaels

Thin Sugar Cookies

2 eggs, beaten
1 tablespoon milk
1 teaspoon vanilla extract
2½ cups flour
3 teaspoons baking powder

¼ teaspoon salt
¼ teaspoon nutmeg
½ cup butter
1 cup sugar
Sugar for garnish

Combine eggs, milk and vanilla extract. Sift flour, baking powder, salt and nutmeg together. Cream butter and sugar together. Add liquid and flour

178

mixtures, alternately, to butter mixture. As the last of the flour mixture is added, it may be easier to blend with hands. Chill dough for several hours or overnight. Preheat oven to 350° F. Roll dough on floured board until very thin. Cut into shapes with cookie cutters. Reroll scraps and cut with cookie cutters. Place cut dough on greased cookie sheet. Sprinkle with sugar. Bake for 10 to 15 minutes or until delicately brown. Watch carefully to prevent over-browning. Remove from cookie sheet and store in tightly covered tin or jar. These may be frozen. Yield: 4-6 dozen cookies, depending on size.

—Lenore Glen Offord

Macaroons

½ pound ground almonds or filberts　　　*¼ cup egg white, approximately*
1 cup sugar
Pinch salt

Preheat oven to 325° F. Butter two cookie sheets. Mix ground nuts, sugar and salt in a bowl until well blended. Add egg whites slowly, a little at a time, and rub well into dry mixture until all of it is moistened and adheres in a solid mass. Make certain that you have no unmoistened nuts and sugar in the bowl. The mixture should be moist and sticky to the touch. When it seems right, try to form it with your fingers into solidly packed spheres about 1 inch in diameter. If the spheres crumble, add a bit more egg white and try again. As soon as they form successfully, form all dough into spheres and set on the cookie sheets about an inch and a half apart. Bake 20 minutes. Remove from oven and let stand on cookie sheets to cool. A gentle nudge with the blade of a dinner knife will loosen them from the cookie sheets. When cooled, store in refrigerator in tightly closed coffee tins. Bring them out half an hour before serving to let the macaroons come to room temperature. Yield: Approximately 30 macaroons.

Years ago, when these macaroons were first made by my family, the recipe called for the whites of three eggs. Since then, eggs—like basketball players—have been larger and three egg whites are far too much. Therefore, judge the quantity of egg white needed by observation and feel.

179

"These keep well. But no one ever has the self-control to test out just *how* long."

—Aaron Marc Stein

Linzer Torte

½ cup butter
1 cup superfine sugar
1 egg
1 tablespoon unsweetened cocoa
1 teaspoon allspice

⅛ cup grated almonds
2 tablespoons cinnamon
2 cups flour
Raspberry jam or preserves

Preheat oven to 370° F. Cream together butter and sugar. Add remaining ingredients except jam. Mix well, and knead until thoroughly blended. Form into a ball. Wrap in waxed paper. Refrigerate overnight. Butter and flour 2 6-½" × 9" × ¾" pans. Cut off pieces of dough and work between palms of hands to soften. Press onto bottoms of pans until approximately ¼- to ⅜-inch thickness of dough covers entire area. Press dough up sides of pans to same thickness. Cover dough completely with layer of raspberry jam approximately ¼ inch thick. Roll remaining dough between palms to make long, narrow strips. Crisscross over jam in lattice pattern. Bake in oven for 40 minutes. Let cool in pans and cut each torte into 12 pieces, cutting through the cross-strips if possible. Yield: 24 pieces.

"You must go a long way to find a great Linzer Torte. Some years ago, when involved in the settlement of the estate of an ancient aunt, among her papers I came on a brown and brittle sheet written over in green ink. Bringing to it all the skills I had acquired doing Japanese cryptanalysis during World War II, I deciphered it and discovered I had a recipe for Linzer Torte."

—Miriam-Ann Hagen

Jan Armstrong's Harvey Wallbanger Cake

Cake:

1 package orange cake mix
1 4-ounce package instant vanilla
   pudding mix
½ cup cooking oil
4 eggs

¼ cup water
¼ cup vodka
¼ cup orange juice
¼ cup Galliano

Preheat oven to 350° F. Blend all ingredients in a large bowl. Beat with electric mixer at medium speed for 2 minutes. Bake in buttered and floured 10-inch tube or Bundt pan for 45 to 55 minutes until center springs back when touched lightly. Frost. Yield: 8 servings.

Frosting:

2 tablespoons vodka
2 tablespoons orange juice
2 tablespoons Galliano

1½ cups confectioners' sugar, approximately

Combine vodka, orange juice and Galliano. Add confectioners' sugar to desired consistency (about 1 cup). Poke holes into warm cake with fork. Pour frosting over cake and sprinkle with powdered sugar.

—Joan Kahn

Coffee Cake

3 envelopes of dry yeast
¾ cup lukewarm water
1½ cups plus 1 teaspoon sugar, divided
5½ cups flour
1½ cups lightly salted butter

¾ cup milk
2 eggs, beaten
¼ teaspoon salt
2 cups chopped pecans or walnuts
¼ cup sugar
½ teaspoon cinnamon

Sprinkle yeast and 1 teaspoon sugar on water and stir until blended. Set aside and allow to proof, about 10 minutes. Mixture will have expanded and look puffy. Sift flour into a large bowl and make a depression at the center. Pour yeast-water mixture into depression and sprinkle flour from sides of bowl over the liquid until it is covered completely with a light layer of flour. Let stand. Combine butter and milk in saucepan and heat on low until butter is melted. Do not let milk boil. Set saucepan aside to cool slightly. While waiting for milk to cool, add sugar, eggs, and salt to flour. Mix with a wooden spoon until well blended. Mixture will be rather dry and grainy. Add milk and butter mixture. Stir and beat with wooden spoon until dough holds together in a single mass and comes clean from side of bowl. (This takes long and hard beating.) This should be done in the evening after dinner. Dip a tea towel in warm water and ring out well. Cover bowl with towel. Set to rise overnight in a warm spot. Next morning, mix chopped nuts, ¼ cup sugar, and cinnamon in a small bowl. Punch down dough. Butter 2 Bundt pans. Put one fourth of the dough in each pan and sprinkle each with nut mixture. Top each with half the remaining dough. Set in lowest heat oven (250-300° F.) until double in bulk. Turn heat to 375° F. and bake approximately 1 hour or until top is golden brown and toothpick inserted in center comes out clean. Yield: 2 coffee cakes.

—Hampton Stone

Royal Shortcake Fans

½ cup brown sugar   ¾ cup butter, very cold
2 cups flour

Preheat oven to 350° F. Mix sugar and flour together well. Cut butter in chunks and blend into flour mixture with a pastry blender or 2 knives until mixture is crumbly. Pat resulting dough in 8-inch round pan. Bake 25 minutes or until lightly browned. While still hot, cut into 8 fanshaped pieces. Yield: 8 servings.

—Alexandra Roudybush

Desserts

Frederica's Blitz Kuchen

2 cups flour	3 eggs
3 teaspoons baking powder	1 cup milk
1/2 cup butter	1/2 teaspoon cinnamon
1 teaspoon vanilla extract	2 tablespoons chopped walnuts or
1 cup sugar, divided	almonds

Preheat oven to 350° F. Sift together flour and baking powder. Cream butter, vanilla extract, and ¾ cup sugar until fluffy. Add eggs one at a time, beating well after each addition. Add dry ingredients gradually, alternating with milk. Turn batter into well-buttered 9″ × 9″ × 2″ cake pan. Sprinkle with mixture of cinnamon, ¼ cup sugar and nuts. Bake for 25 minutes or until toothpick inserted in center comes out clean. Yield: 6-8 servings.

"When Cherry Ames's youthful great-grandmother Frederica fled to the United States from Germany in 1855 to avoid religious persecution, she came in a sailing boat which took months to get here. She brought with her many music scores, ankle-length aprons edged with lace she and her mother had made, and her recipe for *Blitz Kuchen* (Quick Cake).

—Helen Wells

Grandma's Rolled Fruit Cake

1/2 pint of tea	1 teaspoon ground cinnamon
1/2 cup butter	1 teaspoon ground cloves
5 ounces brown sugar	10 ounces plain flour
6 ounces currants	2 level teaspoons baking soda
6 ounces sultanas	1 large egg
1 teaspoon ground nutmeg	

Preheat oven to 350° F. Put tea, butter, sugar, fruit, and spices in a saucepan. Simmer for 20 minutes. Cool, then beat in the flour, baking soda, and egg. Pour into greased loaf pan and bake for 1¼ hours, or until a skewer comes out clean. The cake will stay fresh in a tin for a week. Yield: 1 loaf cake.

—Ellis Peters

A really good book on true crime is, in my opinion, the top of the heap and transcends any good piece of detective fiction. Here is the reason. A piece of fiction is only as wide and as deep as the one mind that creates it—which I admit is sometimes plenty wide and deep. But an account of a real crime, if thoroughly and imaginatively understood, is as wide and as deep as all the lives involved plus the social milieu behind it. That's a large order—and rarely filled.

—Lillian de la Torre

Mystery Cake

1 cup flour
1 cup sugar
1 egg
1 teaspoon baking powder
½ teaspoon salt

1 1-pound 4-ounce can fruit cocktail, drained
½ cup brown sugar
½ cup chopped walnuts
Whipped cream or whipped topping, optional

Mix first 6 ingredients. Pour into greased 8" × 8" pan. Sprinkle top with brown sugar and walnuts. Bake in 350° F. oven for 45 minutes. Cool. Cut into squares. Top with whipped cream or whipped topping if desired. Yield: 6-8 servings.

"This lovely, crunchy-topped cake is a mystery for two reasons. One: When people taste it, they usually say, 'This is delicious. What's in it?'

Desserts

And two: It's a mystery how something that is so easy to make can taste so good."

—Clayton Matthews

Sour Cream Pound Cake

2¾ cups sugar
1 cup butter or margarine
6 eggs
3 cups sifted flour
½ teaspoon salt
¼ teaspoon baking soda

1 cup dairy sour cream
½ teaspoon lemon extract
½ teaspoon orange extract
½ teaspoon vanilla extract
Confectioners' sugar, optional

Preheat oven to 350° F. In a mixing bowl, cream together sugar and butter until light and fluffy. Add eggs, one at a time, beating well after each addition. Sift together flour, salt, and baking soda. Add to creamed mixture alternately with sour cream, beating after each addition. Add extracts. Beat well. Pour batter into greased and floured 10-inch tube pan. Bake for 1½ hours or until toothpick inserted in center comes out clean. Cool in pan 15 minutes. Remove from pan. When cool, sprinkle with confectioners' sugar if desired. Yield: 6-8 servings.

—Percy Spurlark Parker

Hungarian Sponge Cake

6 eggs, separated
1 cup sugar, divided
2 tablespoons lemon juice

1 cup flour
Preserves, optional

Preheat oven to 375° F. Beat egg whites until stiff but not dry. Beat in ½ cup of the sugar. With same beater, beat yolks, and lemon juice until thick and lemon-colored. Fold gently into egg whites. Mix flour with remaining

185

sugar and fold gradually into egg mixture, scraping down sides of bowl occasionally. Pour into tube pan. Bake for 35 minutes or until a light finger touch leaves no depression. Invert and allow to cool before removing from pan. (If necessary, loosen edges with spatula.) Spread with favorite preserves if desired. Yield: 1 cake.

"If you want to freeze part of the cake, you can do so if it is wrapped without icing or other additives. It is just as good when used at another time, defrosted at room temperature."

—Dorothea Gildar

Miz Julie's Authentic Lemon Chess Pie

Pie Crust:

2 cups flour
1/2 teaspoon salt
1 cup lard

1/2 cup ice water, temperature is essential

Mix flour and salt. Work in lard and then add ice water. By all means use your hands. Pay no attention to people who say you'll ruin a piecrust if you touch it. This is flummery, as Nero Wolfe would say. Really get in there and have a great sensual experience, like a kid making mud pies. Roll out dough and line 9-inch pie plates (or freeze leftover dough—it'll keep forever). The uglier your piecrust, the more authentic. Small children actually run *away* from my pies.

Pie Filling:

3/4 cup butter
1 cup sugar
5 eggs, separated

Juice of 3 lemons
Rind of 2 lemons, grated

Preheat oven to 325° F. Cream butter and sugar. Beat in egg yolks. Add lemon juice and rind. Beat egg whites and fold them in. Bake 30 minutes or until pie turns a lovely light brown. Yield: 1 9-inch pie.

"If it weren't for the non-vegetarian crust (vegetable shortening can be substituted), you could feed this to the most finicky food faddist—it's so seriously lemony your guests may pucker up."

—Julie Smith

Nathan Heller's German Chocolate Pie

3 egg whites
1/8 teaspoon salt
1/4 teaspoon cream of tartar
1 teaspoon vanilla extract
1 cup sugar
1/2 cup finely chopped walnuts or
   pecans

1 bar German sweet chocolate
3 tablespoons water
1 teaspoon vanilla extract
1 cup heavy cream

Preheat oven to 275° F. Beat the egg whites with salt, cream of tartar and vanilla extract until foamy. Add sugar, two tablespoons at a time, beating well into stiff peaks. Gently fold in the nuts. Spoon into a lightly greased 8-inch pie pan and form a nest-like shell, building up sides to ½ inch. Bake for 50 to 55 minutes. Cool. Stir chocolate in the water over low heat. Cool until thickened. Whip the cream, adding the vanilla extract. Fold the whipped cream into the chocolate mixture. Pile into the pie shell and chill two hours. Eat and die! Yield: 1 8-inch pie.

"This is my detective Nathan Heller's favorite pigout food; he's been known to eat the whole damn thing, particularly after a depressing case."

—Max Allan Collins

Chocolate Pie Supreme

Crust:

2 squares semisweet chocolate
2 tablespoons butter
2 tablespoons hot water

²/₃ cup confectioners' sugar
1¹/₂ cups ground almonds or flaked coconut

    Melt chocolate and butter in top of double boiler. Remove from heat. Mix hot water and sugar. Stir into chocolate mixture. Add almonds or coconut and mix well. Butter *well* a 9-inch pie pan and press mixture along sides and over bottom evenly. Chill for 1 hour or until hard.

Filling:

1 envelope unflavored gelatin
1¹/₃ cups milk, divided
1 cup sugar, divided
¹/₂ teaspoon salt
2 teaspoons instant coffee grains

3 squares semisweet chocolate
3 eggs, separated
1 teaspoon vanilla or almond extract
Pinch cream of tartar
¹/₂ cup heavy cream

    Sprinkle gelatin over ¹/₃ cup of milk and set aside for 5 minutes to soften. Combine gelatin mixture, ¹/₂ cup of sugar, salt, remaining milk, and coffee in double boiler. Add chocolate and cook over hot water until chocolate and gelatin are melted. Remove from heat and stir until mixture is blended. Beat egg yolks slightly. Gradually add about ¹/₄ cup chocolate mixture to yolks. Pour into chocolate mixture gradually, stirring constantly. Cook over hot water or double boiler for 5 minutes or until mixture thickens. Pour into bowl. Add vanilla or almond extract. Chill until mixture begins to jell and mounds slightly when gently heaped with a spoon. Beat egg whites with cream of tartar until stiff but not dry. Fold into chocolate mixture. Whip cream until thick and glossy and fold in also. Pour into piecrust and refrigerate until firm. Yield: 1 9-inch pie.

—Alexandra Roudybush

188

Glazed Raspberry Pie

3 cups fresh raspberries
½ cup cold water
2½ tablespoons cornstarch or arrow-
    root
1 cup sugar

1 tablespoon lemon juice
Pinch of salt
Baked 9-inch pastry shell
Sweetened whipped cream

Crush one cup of the raspberries and mix with water, cornstarch, sugar, lemon juice, and salt. Cook over low to medium heat until mixture thickens (about 15 minutes). Cool. Spread half of this glaze on the pastry shell. Fill with the remaining two cups of berries (use even more if you like), and spread the rest of the glaze over them. Serve with whipped cream. Yield: 1 9-inch pie.

"The glaze can be made with strawberries. The taste will virtually be unchanged."

—Kay Nolte Smith

Lime Pie

2 tablespoons butter, softened
4 eggs, separated
1 15-ounce can sweetened condensed
    milk

Sugar, to taste
½ cup fresh lime juice
¼ teaspoon vanilla extract
1 9-inch baked piecrust

Preheat oven to 300° F. Cream together butter and egg yolks. Beat in condensed milk until creamy. Beat in sugar and lime juice. Beat egg whites until stiff. Stir 3-4 tablespoons whites into yolk mixture. Flavor remaining whites with vanilla extract. Pour yolk mixture into pie shell. Spread whites over all. Bake until meringue is golden. Cool. Yield: 1 9-inch pie.

—Frances Crane

189

Sly Pie

1½ cups stale cake
1 16-ounce can apricot halves
1 banana
¼ cup rum or sherry

1 package raspberry-flavored gelatin
1 9-inch graham cracker crust
1 package instant vanilla pudding

Break cake into bite-size pieces. Place in medium-size mixing bowl. Drain apricots, reserving juice. Chop and add apricots to cake. Slice banana and add to cake. Drizzle rum over cake. Dissolve gelatin, using 1 cup boiling water. Measure apricot juice and add enough cold water to make 1 cup. Add to gelatin. Place in refrigerator until almost set. Pour over cake mixture. Mix gently and spoon into baked crust. Mix pudding according to package directions and pour over pie. Refrigerate until firm. Yield: 1 9-inch pie.

—Jean Darling

Impossible Pie

4 medium eggs
2 cups milk
1 teaspoon vanilla extract
½ cup all-purpose flour

1 teaspoon baking powder
¼ cup butter, softened
¾ cup sugar
1 cup coconut

Preheat oven to 350° F. Mix all ingredients in blender and bake in ungreased 10″ pie pan for 45 minutes. Yield: 1 10-inch pie.

"One mystery I have never solved. Do I write about food because I'm hungry, or do I get hungry because I'm writing about food? Come to think of it, I don't think I've ever written about any dish I myself am not particularly fond of. More than one 3:00 A.M., I can be found down in the kitchen concocting a glorious sardine sandwich or scrambling eggs with just a touch of grated cheese. Eating is very important to writing, it seems to me. On the other hand, writing can be pretty important to eating, can't it?"

—Kage Booton

EDITOR'S NOTE: This pie forms its own crust.

Grandmother's Fudge Pie

2 eggs, beaten until light
1 cup sugar
4 tablespoons unsweetened cocoa
1 teaspoon salt

1 teaspoon vanilla extract
½ cup flour
1 cup chopped nuts
½ cup melted butter

Preheat oven to 375° F. Combine eggs with sugar and cocoa. Add salt, vanilla extract, flour, and nuts. Then add melted butter. Bake in a 9-inch pie pan for 20 minutes. Do not allow pie filling to get hard on top. Yield: 1 9-inch pie.

—Michele Slung

Funeral Pie

Pie:

1 cup seedless raisins
2 cups water
4 tablespoons flour
1½ cups sugar
1 egg, well beaten

3 tablespoons lemon juice
2 teaspoons grated lemon rind
Pinch of salt
1 unbaked 9-inch piecrust
Crumb Topping (below)

Soak raisins for 3 hours in 2 cups of water. Mix flour, sugar, and egg together. Add lemon juice, rind, salt, raisins, and liquid. Cook over hot water in a double boiler for 15 minutes, stirring occasionally. Cool and pour into piecrust. Add crumb topping and bake about 30 minutes or until browned in a preheated 425° F. oven. Yield: 8 servings.

Crumb Topping:

¼ cup butter, very cold
½ cup packed brown sugar

⅓ cup all-purpose flour, sifted
¼ teaspoon cinnamon

Blend together with a fork or pastry blender.

"In Pennsylvania Dutch country, the best food is served after a funeral. My first encounter with 'Funeral Pie' was in 1951 at an old farmhouse off a dirt road—high up on Haycock Mountain, Bucks County. There was no electricity in the house where the funeral was held. It was a candlelight viewing, followed by a lantern-light burial in the woods. After the graveside ritual everyone returned to the house to console the widow and partake of the delicious German food."

—Doris B. Henry

There are writers who I feel are walkers, even if in fact they can hardly make it to the corner drug store for aspirin. Sherlock Holmes may have hopped a hansom cab now and then. But I will eat my adjectives (which I should like to get rid of in any case) if Conan Doyle was not a walker.

A walker is an observer and more, a thoughtful observer.

When I walk I wear an old reversible with pockets. In one I carry a small purse and in the other a book. With the shoes of a school mistress and my hair like a battered bird's nest, I am inviolable.

Nevertheless, I keep more to the curb than I used to, and don't poke around much in hallways—only enough to catch a whiff of what's cooking.

—Dorothy Salisbury Davis

192

Pecan Pie

1 9-inch pie shell, unbaked	1 teaspoon vanilla extract
2 cups pecans, chopped	1/4 teaspoon salt
1/4 cup butter	3 eggs
1 cup brown sugar	Whipped cream, optional
1/2 cup light corn syrup or molasses	

Preheat oven to 350° F. Prepare a pie shell. Line with chopped pecans. Cream butter and sugar. Combine with corn syrup, vanilla extract and salt, mixing until well blended. One at a time, beat in 3 eggs. Fill the pecan-lined pie shell. Bake for about 1 hour—until a silver knife inserted into the filling emerges clean. Serve warm or cold. Top with whipped cream if desired. Yield: 1 9-inch pie.

"I was about to start my third plantation novel, *Tintagel*. This time I knew I could not go through another long session of plantation writing without an occasional pecan pie in the oven. How could I write about the gourmet delights of New Orleans and Savannah without such sustenance? My daughter Susie, who even at 14 was the family baker, insisted she would find the perfect recipe for pecan pie. She did. With her customary charm she wheedled this one from an Irish chef in a delightful restaurant a few miles *south* of Salem, New York—near the Vermont border."

—Julie Ellis

Acumenu

Dread Herrings
or
Odessa File Gumbo

Pot Pot Pie   *Ross Turkey Macdonald (with fix in)*
Woman in White Sauce   *Banaceken Fricassee*
Preserved Creaking Dormouse on Mr. Motoast   *Hijacketrabbit Stew*
E. Eggs Ferrars   *Crime Club Steak*

Above main dishes served with choice of

Melancholiflower   *Vile Asperges*
Pommes de Terror   *Moriartichokes*

The Watercress Salad has had to be removed from the
menu as it showed signs of tapeworm infestation and bugs.

Robbery Shortcake   *The Spanish Cake Mystery*
The Cake of the Journeying Boy   *Huyghens Pound Kek*

Ask the Waiter for our Whine List
Special Children's Beverage: *Hawaii Five-Ovaltine topped*
with Owen Marshallmallows

Guests who prefer to observe the proceedings from the bar
may avail themselves of the Nicolas Freelunch.

Mystery Pie

 3 egg whites
½ teaspoon baking powder
 1 cup sugar
14 Ritz crackers
⅔ cup chopped walnuts
 1 teaspoon vanilla extract

½ pint heavy cream
1-3 tablespoons confectioners' sugar,
    optional
½ teaspoon vanilla extract,
    optional

Preheat oven to 350° F. Beat egg whites until stiff. Add baking powder and sugar. Beat. In another bowl, crumble crackers until powdery. Add nuts. Add this to first mixture. Add vanilla extract. Mix. Pour into a greased 8- or 9-inch pie plate. Bake for ½ hour. Cool. Whip cream. Add confectioners' sugar and vanilla extract, if desired, and spread over top. Chill. Yield: 4-6 servings.

"This really deserves its name, Mystery Pie. I got it from an aunt, Theresa Morse, who is a super and most particular cook. Originally, she was rather disdainful of a dessert with a base of commercial crackers. But when the friends who had recommended it served it to her, it was delicious. I have used it often. It's fun to hear the guesses my guests come up with—an amazing assortment of ingredients that aren't in it! Most frequent guess is old-fashioned pecan pie, and there's nary a pecan. Aside from its interest as a mystery, I've never served anything people have found tastier."

—Norma Schier

Chocolate Cream Cheese Cake

Cake:

1½ cups flour	1 cup water
1 cup sugar	½ cup oil
¼ cup unsweetened cocoa	1 tablespoon vinegar
1 teaspoon baking soda	1 teaspoon vanilla extract
½ teaspoon salt	

Topping:

1 3-ounce package cream cheese	Pinch salt
1 unbeaten egg	1 6-ounce bag chocolate chips
½ cup sugar	

Preheat oven to 350° F. For cake, blend together all ingredients. The batter will be thin. Pour into 8-inch greased cake pan. For topping, combine cheese, egg, sugar, and salt and beat until well blended. Stir in chips. Drop the topping by spoonfuls over cake, then spread evenly. Bake for 50 to 60 minutes. Yield: 6 servings.

"This is like nothing you have ever tasted!"

—Pauline Bloom

Mother Murphy's Mysterious Cheesecake

1 package yellow cake mix (mixed as directed on box)	4 eggs
	¾ teaspoon vanilla extract
2 pounds whole milk ricotta cheese	Powdered sugar
¾ cup sugar	

Preheat oven to 350° F. Pour prepared cake batter into a 13″ × 9″ greased and floured baking pan. In a separate bowl mix ricotta and sugar. Beat in one egg at a time. Add vanilla extract. After beating the cheese mixture, pour over prepared cake batter. Bake for 1 hour. Chill for 1 hour. When cool sprinkle with powdered sugar. Yield: 1 cake.

"During baking, the cheese mixture disappears into the center of the cake, leaving no trace on the surface. To find it, sleuths will have to slice the evidence. But beware—once this cake makes an appearance on your table, it will vanish!"

—Molly Cochran

Cooking by Ouija Board

At one time Addie lived in the big house with her brother Jack and Margaret, his wife. But when she became an author, they built her a cottage in the back yard. It wasn't that they objected to writing as such. It was her collaborator, Weejee (Addie's understanding of how the letters O-U-I-J-A were pronounced), who bugged them. A Ouija board is used by people to contact the spirit world. It shows a half moon alphabet crowning a smaller half moon of numerals, with YES at one end and NO at the other. The planchette, in this case a plywood hand with fingers extended, moves from letter to letter until the answer to a question is spelled out.

Besides this association with Weejee, she affected bead curtains, fan-backed chairs, hassocks, incense, Chinese robes, hookahs and beaded eyelashes. She also painted abstracts on black velvet. More to the point, Weegee painted abstracts on black velvet through Addie. She was going to exhibit these works in the lobby of the Wilshire Ebell Theater as soon as her next income check arrived. This time, however, only "Ouija" would appear on the bottom right-hand-corner of the paintings. Addie had learned her lesson the hard way. Recently she'd placed her own name as coauthor on the cover of the slender volume of poems on which they'd collaborated. When Weejee found out about her presumption, an argument ensued in which Weejee's planchette lost one of its five little legs.

Several months later solitude had healed lonely Weejee's feelings, and the two friends began writing a book with the working title *Recipes from Beyond*.

It was at this point Mamma and I Trailwayed back to Hollywood. After five years with *Our Gang* comedies and almost two years headlining in Vaudeville, we were stony broke despite my good salary in those tax-free days. Since I could remember, Mamma had been conducting a one-woman campaign to remove all America's fortune-tellers from Mr. Roosevelt's dole queues by setting them up for life in modest luxury. She was hard pressed to scrape together enough of my earnings to pay for our bus tickets. Happily, we didn't have to worry about eating. Loft's Candy Store on Broadway was running a loss leader sale on fudge and Mamma stocked up. She bought a dozen little pans; half chocolate, my favorite; the other half vanilla, her favorite. This fudge was the mainstay of our diet during the five days it took us to cross from New York to California.

Only once during the trip did regret at having blown our bankroll put a frown on Mamma's pretty face. This was when we couldn't afford to stop over to have our fortunes told by some Gypsy who had slipped past Mamma's largesse. Most catholic in her tastes, my parent invested in tea leaves, palmistry, astrology, and crystal balls as well as in diverse and little-known religions. Myself, I read the Tarot cards.

Back home again in Hollywood it wasn't long before we had to face up to the fact that ten-year-old children were out of style moviewise. So Mamma decided to get rid of me for a few weeks. Nothing exhilarated her more than getting rid of me. The only excuse for our association in the first place was the success I had enjoyed. Now my career had hit a snag, best lumber me on assorted friends—none of whom had any connection with the movie business. I was dropped off at Jack and Margaret's.

Being a pariah (ex-child star) leprous with has-beenery, I beelined for the back yard and Addie as soon as Mamma deposited me at the house. Addie and Weejee took me to their hearts. Addie fed me candied pineapple and, at Ouija's suggestion, put me to work taking dictation on their cookbook. Every day we'd sit from dawn to dusk, Addie with fingers perched on a rapidly moving planchette and singing out the letters in a high soprano, I penciling into a blue-ruled notebook.

As time passed and the recipes multiplied, Addie's curiosity grew in direct ratio; she was dying to test a few, particularly the sweet ones. One day, in casual fashion, she happened to mention this desire to Weejee, who promptly flew off the handle. Recriminations degenerated from a nasty bout of name-calling into an out-and-out tantrum. At last, Weejee refused point-blank to move the planchette.

Addie stormed into the bathroom with me in tow and slammed the door. She jammed a handful of candied pineapple into my mouth with promises of a limitless supply if I kept silent no matter what happened. I agreed.

Smiling sweetly, Addie begged Weejee's pardon—pressing the planchette tight against her heart. When her temperamental coauthor was sufficiently lulled to hazard a grudging YES when asked if Addie were forgiven, she plonked a box over the board—planchette and all. After covering the lot with a Spanish shawl, the woman piled a stack of books on top so Weejee couldn't get out. As an afterthought, she tucked cushions in around the sides. "To make sure the nosey thing doesn't eavesdrop," she explained to me.

It's unfortunate the full ingredients of the chosen dish escape me. Suffice it to say it was unusual. Throughout the preparations, my job was to keep the Victrola wound up and playing Ouija's composition for harp and fiddle, which Addie had recorded at great expense. Ordinary mortals didn't make records in those days. But Addie was no ordinary mortal. She'd hired musicians and facilities, and the recording was made. To date Ouija was unaware the musical work was on a disk, which was why Addie felt so secure in daring Ouija's wrath. Such was her friend's conceit that hearing the composition played would drive away all thoughts of anger—so Addie thought.

When at last the dish was ready, candles burning and incense smoking from a little Buddha's bellybutton, Addie danced around the table sprinkling rose leaves, coconut, peppercorns, and candied violets onto "Ambrosiatic Dream" (which was the name of the dish selected for testing). Addie adored exotic desserts, the sweeter the better. And no matter how much she indulged herself, she remained reed slim.

By this time I was every bit as eager to try this marvel as was she. Without bothering with such niceties as plates, she spooned a heap into my mouth; then she spooned one into hers. That one bite stuck our jaws tight shut. It was only after what seemed hours of leaning over the sink, pouring hot water over our teeth, that the crumbly mass softened enough for a finger to gouge it out.

Addie was beside herself. She was of the firm conviction that her friend had altered the recipe behind her back. She studied the blue-lined notebook at length, but found there was no writing other than mine. Even so, it was all I could do to keep her from beating Ouija to death. It was only later, while putting away things in the kitchen, that she noticed her mistake. That morning she had been mending a statuette of Nefertiti's broken neck with Plaster of Paris, and it was this she had dumped into the mixing bowl mistaking it for cornstarch.

All contrition, Addie unveiled Ouija. But once more the planchette refused to budge. It fell to me to act as go-between. Perched upon Addie's knee with her arms reaching round me in order to get her fingers on the planchette, she hissed into my shoulder blades what I was supposed to say to Weejee. This ploy was supposed to fool her friend into thinking that my hands were operating the planchette and not hers.

Next morning, Mamma arrived to take me away. But just the other day, on South Ann Street, I ran into Weejee—sorry, Ouija. Funny, isn't it, to look into a window way over here in Dublin and see my childhood friend, leg missing and all? You'll be glad to know we have come to an agreement. We are about to resume work on *Recipes from Beyond*. I bought my son a pencil and a blue-lined notebook. As soon as I mail out this story, I'll place my fingers on the little planchette and we'll begin again.

—Jean Darling

EDITOR'S NOTE: Although now a successful writer of mystery short stories, Jean Darling has had showings of her watercolors in Johannesburg, raised a son, and toured the world with her husband Kajar the Magician's magic show. Her very early years were spent in Hollywood as the leading lady of the Our Gang comedies.

Hot Apple Compote, Orient Express

6 large tart apples
1½ tablespoons butter
1 cup sugar
½ teaspoon cinnamon
⅓ teaspoon nutmeg

½ cup heavy cream
1 cup chopped walnuts or hazelnuts, optional
1 pint heavy cream, optional

Preheat oven to 350° F. Wash, core and slice apples and arrange in a shallow baking dish. Dot with butter. Mix together sugar, cinnamon, nutmeg, and cream. Pour over apples. Bake ½ hour. Serve warm. Pass a bowl of chopped nuts for sprinkling, and a pitcher of extra cream. Yield: 6 servings.

"A few years ago I took the famed Orient Express night train from Trieste to Belgrade in the dead of winter. Darkness fell fast; snow seeped in around the window frames; and chill air seemed to rise up even through the worn, spotted carpets. I wrote a short story called "The Sound of Murder" about that night. Not because I actually saw or heard something sinister, but perhaps I did. In the dining car, warming our hands over cups of barley soup, we noted a nearby table of four silent, swarthy men in dark hats and overcoats which they never removed. They simply ate and stared intently at each passenger who entered or left the diner.

"I remember that for dessert we had an excellent hot apple compote. A week later, I read in the *Rome Daily American* that a businessman-agent had been thrown to his death on a night trip of the Orient Express. As to the apple compote and the mystery men in the black overcoats, all four ate it with relish. They seemed to like it very much. Or—did they just need their strength?"

—William P. McGivern

Bananas Flambé à la Irving Schwartz, Bourbon Street

3 good-size, ripe bananas
½ pound dark brown sugar
½ cup butter
2-3 ounces banana liqueur

½ teaspoon cinnamon
2 tablespoons light rum
French vanilla ice cream

Peel bananas and slice into quarters lengthwise. Cut into ½-inch lengths. Have the sugar and bananas handy in separate dishes. Melt butter in large chafing dish. When fully melted, shake in sugar gradually and stir until mixture is a smooth, thick paste. Add a generous dollop banana liqueur. Heat and stir until smooth and hot. Stir in bananas. Add cinnamon. Continue heating until bananas are cooked. Spoon over well-rounded scoops of ice cream in stemware. Splash a little rum all across the top and quickly ignite. Yield: 8-10 servings.

"This is a nifty company dessert because you can prepare and serve it with great flourish right at the table. And it is virtually fool-proof. I've done it lots of times."

—Stanley Cohen

Banana Fright

4-6 ripe bananas
Cinnamon or ginger, to taste

Pinch of salt

Mash the ingredients together at room temperature. Put into glass molds and place in freezer half an hour before serving. Top with more cinnamon. The bananas are sweet enough that no sugar needs to be added. Yield: 4-6 servings.

"If you're low on funds and in a hurry, here's a dessert that will cover both exigencies and still impress your guests. As La Rochefoucald said, 'The devious mind hides behind a simple facade.'

"This concoction, slightly heated in a double boiler, makes a nice poultice for gun wounds."

—Barbara Norville

202

Desserts

Caramelized Peaches

4 large ripe peaches　　　　　　　*Brown sugar*
1 cup heavy cream

Peel, pit, and slice peaches. Drain in colander, saving juice for other use. Place sliced peaches in baking dish. Whip cream until very stiff and cover peaches completely. Sprinkle with brown sugar about ½-inch-thick, covering all the cream. Chill overnight in refrigerator. Immediately before serving, brown quickly in very hot broiler to melt sugar. Serve at once. Yield: 4 servings.

—Michael Gilbert

EDITOR'S NOTE: Dipping the peaches in boiling water for 30 seconds makes the peel easier to remove.

Spiced Peaches

4 large peaches　　　　　　　*8 cloves*
1 teaspoon cinnamon　　　　　*Water to cover*
¼ teaspoon ginger　　　　　　*½ teaspoon sugar, optional*

Peel, pit, and slice peaches. Add spices and sugar, if desired. Cook, uncovered, in a saucepan until liquid is syrupy. Remove cloves before serving. Yield: 2-4 servings.

"The Meyers' private detective, Patrick Hardy, is appetite incarnate and constantly panting after food and women. Books featuring him also feature both. He is not as discriminating as Nero Wolfe (who is?) when it comes to food. Hardy might prepare a delicious gourmet meal, eat it with great appreciation, and follow it in an hour with a salami-and-catsup sandwich. Hardy is a slimmed down 325-pounder, constantly eating and constantly exercising to melt the fat. He lives alone with a black poodle named Sherlock Holmes."

—Martin Meyers

Simple Pears Microwave

1 *Bosc pear per serving*   *Curry powder*

Wash ripe pear and halve. Core. Dust lightly with curry powder and place in a glass dish. For a single pear, microwave one minute, turn and microwave another minute. Since I always do this a pear at a time, I'm not sure what the exact time for microwaving more than one pear but I would suggest the standard microwave arrangement of the halved fruit in a circle, then three minutes and three minutes. Fork test.

"This is an extremely low-calorie dessert or breakfast and goes well with plain yogurt, vanilla ice cream, or whipped cream, though of course the diet's out the window with the last two."

—Tabitha King

Istria Fritters

2 *cups dry white wine*   *Pinch salt*
4 *cups flour*   *1¾ cups confectioners' sugar, divided*
5 *teaspoons baking powder*   *¾ cup maraschino liqueur*
¾ *teaspoon ground cloves*   *Grated rind of 1 orange or lemon*
1 *teaspoon nutmeg*   *1¾ cups oil for frying*
Pinch cinnamon

Heat wine. Sift all dry ingredients, except sugar, together and add to wine. Mix in liqueur. Stir in grated rind, 1½ cups sugar, reserving ¼ cup for later use. Beat with electric mixer for full ½ hour. Let mixture stand at room temperature for 2 hours. Heat oil to 375° F. Fry fritters by dropping spoonfuls of batter into hot oil. When golden, remove from oil and drain on paper towels. Sprinkle with reserved sugar and serve hot. Yield: 10-12 servings.

"Here is something that I picked up in Yugoslavia—a delight to the palate and death to the waistline. If you want to kid your friends into believing that you can speak Serbo-Croatian, these are *Istarske Fritule*. Gorging yourself on fritters like these is fine occasionally."

—Rona Randall

Desserts

What do British crime writers eat, and how do they cook it? Here is my modest (and fairly typical) diet.

Breakfast

Two rounds of toasted bread, lightly browned, with plenty of margarine. One pint of tea brewed in a pot. No tea bags, but loose tea over which is poured boiling water, then let "stand" for two or three minutes. Pour into cups and add a little milk and sugar.

Lunch

Usually just a sandwich (English-size) and another pint of tea.

Dinner

Normally a good-size piece of steak cooked medium rare, and French fries (the English call them chips). A vegetable, often garden-fresh peas. The French fries are cooked in a pan about six inches deep until they are golden brown and firm outside with a soft inside. Tea.

This diet is not fattening and contains plenty of nutrition. The steak, of course, provides plenty of iron—which is good for writers because it provides that necessary energy.

—Peter Riley

Crepe Hangers

Crepes:

1   cup all-purpose flour
2   large eggs
5   ounces milk
2   tablespoons sugar
²/₃ teaspoon lemon extract or 2
      teaspoons lemon juice

¹/₃ teaspoon orange or vanilla ex-
      tract
1-2 tablespoons water
Sweet butter

Combine first 4 ingredients, mixing until smooth. Add extracts. Refrigerate overnight. (If batter has thickened too much, add water. It should be the consistency of heavy cream.) Melt walnut-size piece of sweet butter in a 6-inch cast-iron skillet. Heat until a drop of water spatters instantly. Pour tablespoon of batter in bottom of pan very thinly. Turn when crepe is golden. Cook 30 seconds on other side. Place each crepe on wax paper. Do not allow them to touch each other. These crepes may be frozen. Yield: 18 crepes.

Sauce:

6   tablespoons sweet butter
1   teaspoon sugar
Juice of 1 large orange

2   ounces Cointreau or Triple Sec
2   ounces brandy

Melt the butter in large skillet. Dissolve sugar in butter, and add orange juice. Fold each crepe into quarters and heat in butter to warm. In small pan, warm liqueurs and pour over crepes. Ignite and bring to the table blazing. (The dining lights should be out.) Serve 3 crepes per person, spooning the sauce over all crepes. Yield: sauce for 18 crepes.

—George deLucenay Leon

Desserts

Orange Bread Pudding

2 oranges
½ cup sugar
¼ cup water
3 cups milk

1½ cups diced stale bread
2 eggs, slightly beaten
⅓ teaspoon salt
½ cup raisins

Preheat oven to 350° F. Remove outer skin of one of the oranges. Cut in slivers and boil in syrup made by combining the sugar and water until the syrup spins a small thread (230° F. on a candy thermometer). Remove peel to a china plate. Add milk to syrup and scald, stirring constantly, until syrup is completely dissolved. Pour over diced bread and let stand for 10 minutes. Combine eggs and salt and stir into bread mixture. Add raisins, grated rind of remaining orange, and candied peel. Mix well and pour into a greased loaf pan. Set in pan of hot water and bake for 1 hour or until a silver knife inserted near center comes out clean. Yield: 4 servings.

—Lillian de la Torre

Bread Pudding Flambé

4 cups stale bread
1½ cups applesauce
4 tablespoons dark brown sugar
½ teaspoon cinnamon
2 dashes allspice

¼ cup sherry
10 pitted prunes, cut up
⅛ teaspoon nutmeg
Pinch salt
¼ cup brandy or rum

Preheat oven to 400° F. Break bread into small pieces. Add all remaining ingredients except brandy or rum and mix well. Heavily butter a casserole and pack mixture into it, tamping down thoroughly. Smooth top evenly. Bake 30 to 40 minutes until top is crusty and brown. Invert onto serving platter. Heat brandy or rum in a small saucepan. Pour over hot pudding. Quickly ignite it. Let flame die. Slice and serve pudding. Yield: 6 servings.

"Around my corner there is a pastry shop so French that it is barely bilingual. I was there one day when a man asked for an angel cake. While he

207

and the girl serving him were struggling to bridge the linguistic chasm, the baker came storming from his ovens to fix the would-be customer with an enraged eye.

" *'Monsieur,'* he thundered, 'I have never baked an angel cake. I do not bake an angel cake. I shall never bake an angel cake. Good night, *Monsieur.'*

"He remains steadfast, but unfortunately too many other people have been taken off cholesterol. Although they soon come to hate angel cake, they are unable to shun that rubbery sweet. I invented this pudding in an effort to give such unfortunates something more interesting when they come to dinner. Since it has gone equally well with the omnivores among the guests, we serve it regardless of diet."

—Aaron Marc Stein

The Last Meal

One of the meetings of the Society of Connoisseurs in Murder was devoted to famous Last Meals. Each member was called upon to relate a true story of a repast which, for at least one participant, might be called terminal.

To the uninitiated this might seem a lugubrious occasion. But no. Each new fatality was greeted with cheers or catcalls depending upon the felicity of the storyteller, the imagination of the culinary display, or the uniqueness of the fatal instrument.

Death, so reported, is not to everyone's taste.

Thinking that the subject of last meals might make interesting reading, I once broached the subject to an editor of what I deemed the appropriate gourmet magazine. The man was so plainly appalled by the very idea that the subject has since, until now, lain fallow.

Desserts

From the tales told at that meeting I have culled a few samples—just enough, I hope, to make the editor regret his summary rejection.

In introducing the subject, the chairman of the meeting referred briefly to that torrid morning of August 4, 1892, when Andrew Borden sat down to a breakfast of hot mutton soup, a fearsome offering in that heat. Borden survived that dish, but never the many blows from an axe (later immortalized in rhyme) which smashed his skull a few hours later.

Murderers rarely get credit even for the virtues they possess. It is good to report, then, that John Washburn, an otherwise dull and brutish fellow, facing hanging for the murder of a Cincinnati shopkeeper in 1836, did not lose his sense of humor. To a professor of anatomy he sold his body for fifty dollars and bought a fine black broadcloth suit for his execution and had ten dollars left over. On his last morning, while the prison chaplain prayed for him, he stole the parson's watch and put it in his own pocket—where it remained during the hanging. On the scaffold his last gesture for the large crowd which turned out to see his execution was to eat the remaining ten dollar bill, a new kind of last meal.

For sheer persistence some award is due Mrs. Lena Miller, who dispatched her husband in Covington, Pennsylvania, in July 1866. Let us hear her tell of her difficulties in finding the right concoction to put an end to him:

> I first tried to poison him with tea made from laurel leaves and the filings of a brass buckle. Then with the quicksilver off the back of a looking glass. Then I gave him doses from a bottle of laudanum which I got from Dr. Potter for cramp. Then some indigo. Then one day, going after the cows, I killed a small green grass snake which I boiled and gave to him in coffee. None of these had the least effect on him—did not even make him sick.

After such an imaginative beginning it is regrettable that, despairing of results, she turned to that old standby rat poison and quickly dispatched him—and was as quickly discovered.

It is for just such a case as Mrs. Miller's that I have had for some time now among my unwritten books one prospectively entitled *A Garden Book for Poisoners*. To avoid the necessity of shopping about for a pinch of poison and later being identified as the purchaser, the recommended solution is raising it in your own garden. That others have thought of this solution I have but to cite one case.

Mary McConkey, in County Monoghan, Ireland, cooked up a mess of greens which she fed to her husband who complained, as well he might, that "they had a wild, bad taste." Mr. McConkey proffered some of them to a neighbor who was dining with them and made the prophetic remark that they would be a novelty to him. The neighbor survived, although barely, but McConkey perished three hours after the meal in painful spasms.

The noxious dish was identified as made from a common garden plant *Aconitum napellus* or monkshood, although in Ireland it is referred to as blue rocket. A member of the buttercup family, it is described by Blyth as "rich in poisonous alkaloids." This tall, attractive plant can be found in many a garden border, although it has had a long and fatal history due to the root which contains the poisonous principle. This root has often been mistaken for horseradish. Here certainly one would have the backing of the conservationists. Down with manufactured chemicals! Up with natural remedies like *Aconitum napellus!*

The last meal we will take will be in San Francisco, in San Quentin more precisely, where Theo Durrant was scheduled to die for the murder of two girls in the belfry of the Emmanuel Baptist Church in 1898. While the hangman himself kept to a liquid diet to brace himself for the task ahead, Durrant put down a solid meal of beefsteak, potatoes, eggs, ham, and toast, hardly the gourmet's choice which the condemned are supposed to eat—at least in fiction. But it is not this repast which is notable, but one which came just after the execution was over.

Durrant's body had been brought to a room where his parents waited. A strange couple who had behaved oddly throughout the ordeal of the trial, they stayed in character. An attending prisoner asked if they would like some tea. "Thank you, I would," the mother replied. An enormous tray containing a generous sampling of the prison fare was brought in and set on a table three feet from the open casket. If the waiter who had procured the repast had concern for his guests' appetite, he was reassured when he heard Mrs. Durrant say, "Papa, I'll take some more of that roast."

—Thomas H. McDade

Deadly Bread Pudding

4 tablespoons butter, softened,
divided
4 slices bread
4 eggs
½ cup sugar

2 cups milk, scalded
1 teaspoon vanilla extract
1 teaspoon cinnamon
Whipped cream, optional

Preheat oven to 300° F. Butter bread with 2 tablespoons butter and cut into cubes. Beat eggs with sugar, gradually beating in scalded milk. Add bread cubes, 2 tablespoons butter, vanilla extract, and cinnamon. Blend well. Put into buttered 1½-quart baking dish. Put baking dish in a pan of boiling water and bake pudding 1 hour, or until knife inserted near center comes out clean. Cool and serve with a dollop of whipped cream. Yield: 4 servings.

"This delicious pudding is light and custardy. It will violate your will-power. It is absolutely deadly to the waistline."

—Patricia Matthews

To his surprise, he (Henry Tibbett) found that he was extremely hungry. From the hot plate, one of his favorite steak and kidney pies smiled up at him, steaming and succulent, flanked by fresh green beans tossed in butter and a fluffy mound of *pommes mousseline*. On the side table an iced Gooseberry Fool stood beside a bowl of whipped cream. Henry decided to postpone the domestic peace talk until after dinner. As he ate voraciously, his chief emotion was pity for Emmy. She was missing an excellent meal.

—Patricia Moyes
(From *Johnny Under Ground*)

Gooseberry Fool

1 quart gooseberries
Water
Sugar, to taste

1 pint heavy cream, whipped
Additional heavy cream

Trim and cook gooseberries in water and sugar until tender. Process in blender or force through fine sieve. Combine with whipped cream. Chill. Serve very cold and pass additional cream. Yield: 4-6 servings.

"This also may be made with rhubarb or raspberries (instead of gooseberries). A very traditional English dish which I find goes down well with my American friends."

—Patrica Moyes

Brandy Chocolate Mousse

1 6-ounce package semisweet chocolate
  chips
2 egg yolks

1 pint light cream
Brandy
1 tablespoon instant coffee

Put chips and egg yolks in blender. Blend until smooth. Add hot (not boiling) cream to mixture. Blend until smooth. Add brandy to taste, and instant coffee. Reblend until all is smooth. Chill.

—Thomas Chastain

My mother, Doris Miles Disney, was a terrific cook. But as anecdotes go I can think of only one that was even slightly amusing regarding her mysteries and the kitchen.

She was interviewed on a TV talk show in Connecticut. At the end of the show their format was to ask the guest a fairly easy question *à la* quiz show. Mother answered it with no trouble, while I chewed my nails and hung on. When she learned that she'd just won a cookbook, she looked up over her glasses and said (to my embarrassment) "But I already have too many cookbooks!"

—Elizabeth Disney Laing

Orange Dessert

2 tablespoons butter	2 tablespoons flour
⅔ cup sugar	1 cup milk
2 egg yolks, unbeaten	2 egg whites
¼ 6-ounce can frozen orange juice concentrate, undiluted	Whipped cream
	Maraschino cherries

Preheat oven to 375° F. Cream butter, add sugar gradually, and cream thoroughly. Add egg yolks. Beat well. Add orange juice, then flour. Add milk gradually, blending well. Beat egg whites until stiff but not dry. Fold them into orange mixture. Spoon into greased custard cups, or baking dish. Place in pan of hot water (filled to about ½ inch) and bake for about 30-35 minutes. Test for doneness by inserting a knife near the edge of custard. If knife

213

comes out clean, the custard will be solid all the way through when cooled. Chill. Unmold and serve with whipped cream, garnished with cherries. Yield: 4-5 servings.

—Doris Miles Disney

Philippa Carr's Own Syllabub

2 egg whites
½ pint heavy cream
1 tablespoon superfine sugar

1 package gingerbread cookies
1 glass sherry

Beat egg whites until stiff. Beat cream until stiff, adding sugar during beating. Fold together and pile on top of biscuits soaked in sherry. Yield: 3-4 servings. (The yield is, frankly, a Colonial's guess.)

"In the Tudor and Stuart periods with which I have frequently been concerned, people's eating habits were slightly different from those of today. Apart from venison and suckling pigs, gargantuan joints of beef and mutton were consumed. Tables always 'groaned' under the weight of the food. At a house party to entertain a King or Queen one reads that 1,200 chickens, 333 geese, and 237 pigeons were consumed as extras. It is always pleasant when writing of such foods to try them out; and as it would be quite impossible to cope with all those pigeons and capons, to say nothing of 2,500 eggs and 430 pounds of butter which were used on one royal occasion, I have turned to the ever present and delicious syllabub. I have varied mine from the earlier version, and this one is really delicious."

—Philippa Carr

The Mystery of the Missing Salamander

I was glad when I was asked to contribute to the Mystery Writers of America cookbook because it gave me an excuse to reread one of my favorite detective stories, *My Foe Outstretch'd Beneath the Tree*, by V. C. Clinton-Baddeley.

Like all his delightful stories, this one digresses every now and then to include a literary allusion, a wry observation, or a bit of folk lore. Of these digressions the one that I found most fascinating was a recipe for *Crème Brûlée*. It has nothing to do with the ingenious plot of the story, but it adds a nicely calculated touch to the character of the detective, Dr. R. V. Davie. He is an aristocrat in the forgotten, Greek sense of the word; someone who wants the best quality in everything.

For *Crème Brûlée* is the King of Custards as *Château d'Yquem* is the King of Sauternes, not to be confused with *Crème Caramel* or any other custard, baked or boiled.

The moment I read the recipe I realized that it needed translation from English into American idiom. I had lived in England at various times, so that I knew that a "grill" is a broiler, "double cream" is heavy cream, a "double saucepan" is a double boiler, "caster sugar" is powdered or confectioners' sugar. But what was a "salamander"?

To me the word meant only a mythical lizard who could live unscathed in fire mentioned by Paracelsus. Consulting Webster, I found that a salamander is also a woman "who excites and foments passion without yielding to it," or "any of various articles used in connection with fire as: A culinary utensil with a plate, or disk, heated and held over pastry, etc., to brown it."

According to Clinton-Baddeley's recipe, Webster is wrong. A metal salamander is not to be "held over" a *Crème Brûlée* in order to brown it. It is to be applied to the surface of the *crème* directly in order to melt the sugar topping, and the result is not brown but "a sheet of golden ice." During the few moments when the salamander is applied, the *crème* is packed in ice, which no doubt makes this result possible.

Mr. Clinton-Baddeley warns the reader that a salamander "is not normally found in the modern kitchen." He suggests the use of a grill (broiler) instead. I did not believe that any broiler could produce the same effect as a salamander, so I set out to find a salamander for myself.

I began with Hammacher Schlemmer and another New York shop, one that specializes in French kitchen equipment. In both places I drew a total blank. During the weeks that followed, I made many inquiries among friends and haunted shops dealing with the rare, the old, and the imported. More blanks.

As a last resort I wrote to Mr. Craig Claiborne of the *New York Times* asking if he could tell me where to find a salamander on this side of the Atlantic. He kindly took the trouble to reply in detail. He said that salamanders are widely used in kitchens throughout America, that he has had one or another in his own kitchen for years, and that they are made by all makers of professional ranges.

I then got the address of a Boston distributor of professional ranges from Jordan Marsh and went down to their showroom on Purchase Street.

A very kind man, who was in charge, took great pains to show me several ranges with what he called salamanders attached. As gently as I could, I broke the news to him that these attachments were what I called broilers. When I told him that I wanted a metal salamander that could be heated and applied by hand to the surface of a custard, he said that he had never heard of such a thing.

I had made the same mistake in writing to Mr. Claiborne. I had not specified a metal salamander and he, too, had naturally assumed that I meant a salamander broiler.

As I did not have the nerve to bother Mr. Claiborne again, I decided to try making a *Crème Brûlée* with a broiler. Immediately I struck another snag. The recipe said: "Place the dish in a tray—the toaster is convenient because it is deep and has a handle."

Obviously, Mr. Clinton-Baddeley and I did not mean the same thing when we said toaster. My only toaster is an electric one without any handle. Apparently he was referring to a deep tray with a handle used for toasting bread or muffins over a flame.

I decided to use two Corningware baking dishes as a substitute, a large one for the tray or toaster and a small one for the *crème* itself with room for ice between the two as the recipe suggested. The *crème* was delicious, but, as I had anticipated, the golden ice did not form without the metal salamander. It was just caramel.

So I am still looking for a metal salamander.

If any reader of this book should travel abroad in England or France and have the luck to come across a shop where the true metal salamander is sold, I would be most grateful if he, or she, would send me the address of that shop. Then I could enjoy *Crème Brûlée* in my old age and leave the metal salamander to my heirs, an irreplaceable heirloom, worth its weight in gold.

—Helen McCloy

Crème Brûlée

6 egg yolks	½ pint heavy cream
½ cup sugar, approximately, divided	Whipped cream, optional

Beat egg yolks lightly with ¼ cup of the sugar. In top of a double boiler, over hot water, heat heavy cream to boiling point. Add a few spoonfuls of hot cream to egg yolk mixture, stirring constantly until adding half of the cream. Mix in remaining cream. Cook in top of double boiler over simmering water. Do not let top pan touch water. Stir constantly until custard has thickened. Pour into shallow oven-proof dish and allow to cool. Cover custard with even layer of remaining sugar. Pack dish into a large container filled with ice and chill in refrigerator. Heat broiler until very hot. Place custard close to broiler unit just long enough to melt sugar and turn it a light golden brown. *Do not allow sugar to turn dark.* Remove from heat at once. Garnish with whipped cream if desired. Yield: 4-6 servings.

"The (final) operation is so quick that with the aid of the ice the cream is not affected at all by this violent treatment. The moment the sugar cools it forms a sheet of golden ice over the cream and the deed is done. If the sugar becomes too dark it will also become too hard to bite—a disaster frequently encountered in restaurants. There are eighteenth-century recipes for this confection, so the claim that it was invented by a nineteenth-century chef of Trinity College, Cambridge, is manifestly false. But I do think it was probably rediscovered by Trinity. Today all Oxford and Cambridge colleges make a specialty of this miraculous pudding."

—Helen McCloy
(Recipe printed in an appendix to
My Foe Outstretch'd Beneath the Tree
by V. C. Clinton-Baddeley (Victor Gollancz, Ltd./Morrow, 1968)

Bill and I (the married mystery-writing team of Bill and Audrey Kelley Roos, writing as "Kelley Roos") knock off from the plotting and writing in the summer. He works his organic garden, and I do a catering service.

Recently one of my customers asked if I would make a Beef in Burgundy Casserole and an Iced Lemon Soufflé with Strawberry-Kirsch sauce for her to take to Connecticut for a small dinner party. I said but of course. She picked it up in the morning, and I saw her off.

For dinner Bill and I were having hamburgers, simple fare but enhanced by a Spicy Old Fashioned Tomato Catsup I had just made from Bill's organically grown tomatoes. Only it turned out to be Strawberry-Kirsch Sauce.

I keep wondering about that dinner party and how Iced Lemon Soufflé would taste smothered in Spicy Old Fashioned Catsup. I haven't heard from my customer since. I'll probably never know.

—Kelley Roos

218

Iced Lemon Soufflé

1 envelope gelatin
2 tablespoons water
Grated rind of 4 lemons
½ cup lemon juice

¾ cup sugar
1 cup (7 or 8) egg whites
1 cup heavy cream, whipped
Strawberry-Kirsch Sauce (below)

In small saucepan, soften gelatin in water. Add lemon rind, juice, and sugar. Stir over low heat until gelatin is dissolved. Chill to syrupy consistency. Beat egg whites until stiff but not too dry. Fold whites into lemon-gelatin mixture. Mix thoroughly. Fold in whipped cream. Rinse mold with cold water. Pour in lemon mixture and chill until firm. Serve with Strawberry-Kirsch Sauce. Yield: 4-6 servings.

Strawberry-Kirsch Sauce:

1 10-ounce package frozen strawberries

¼ cup sugar
2 tablespoons kirsch

Partially defrost berries. Put in blender, add sugar and blend for 20 seconds. Add kirsch. Chill.

—Kelley Roos

My Sister's Dessert

2 cups boiling water
2 4-ounce packages lemon gelatin
2 7-ounce bottles lemon and lime
   carbonated beverage
¼ cup lemon juice or juice of 2
   lemons

1 teaspoon or more grated lemon rind
1 pint heavy cream, whipped
Few drops yellow food coloring
Frozen strawberries or raspberries,
   partially thawed

Pour boiling water over gelatin powder and dissolve. Stir in lemon and lime beverage, lemon juice, and rind. Chill until *almost* firm. Fold cream into

219

gelatin mixture. Add yellow food coloring and blend thoroughly. Chill until set. Just before serving, top with nearly thawed frozen strawberries or raspberries. Yield: 4-6 servings.

—Dorothy Uhnak

Mignon's Dessert

"Take glasses like beer glasses; the lower part smaller than the upper part, which may branch out like a tulip. Fill the lower part, the narrow part, with any fresh small fruit; white grapes, strawberries, anything that looks good in the market. Fill the crevices with powdered sugar. Peel fresh peaches. Put fresh peach half on top of small fruits, then add white port to cover. Seal each glass with foil and put in fridge until time to serve. You'll need long spoons like iced tea spoons for this—although guests usually, indeed always, finish simply by lifting the glass and drinking.

—Mignon G. Eberhart

A fine one to contribute a recipe—I who am always on a weight-reducing diet! Well, intending to be on one. It got so bad that I went to a hypnotist.

"You are getting sleepier and sleepier," he said, not even bothering to wave his watch in front of my eyes—perhaps because he wore it on his wrist and his arm got tired. "Your eyes are beginning to close, your head falls forward . . ."

He seemed so convinced about it, poor chap, that (anything to please) I shut my eyes and slumped my chin on my chest, which anyway came pretty well up to it—that's why I was there. It must all have been enormously effective, for he wasted no more time but lit out on a fantasy of his own.

"There is a loooong table laid out in front of you," he said, "spread out with all sorts of things to eat." I opened one eye, but no such luck! It was all in the mind. *He* had no doubts at all, however. "Up at the left hand of this table," he said, "are all the wrong things for you to eat. The cream," he said, "and the cakes," he said, "and a great box of chocolates," he said, "and butter, and bacon, and potatoes, and rice, and spaghetti . . ."

I wiped surreptitiously at one drooling corner of my mouth, but he was too much carried away to notice.

"And down at the right end," he said, "are all the proper things to eat. The salads, and the—er—the lean meat, and the white fish, and the—er—the—" He was fast running out of proper things to eat. "The green vegetables," he insisted, grabbing at them, "and certain fruits . . ."

He lingered over the certain fruits, subtracting any that one could possibly wish to include in a regular diet. But time was running out. He snapped sharply with his fingers and I without difficulty awoke. "Well," he said, leaning back triumphantly in his large armchair. "How do you feel?"

"Exhausted," I said.

"Exhausted?" he said.

"Worn out," I said.

"But you can't be," he said. "You've just been lying back there, immobile."

"Don't you believe it," I said. "I've been dashing up to the left end of that table and dashing back to the other end with the cream and the cakes—dashing back for that huge box of chocolates—staggering under a load of potatoes, and rice, and pasta. And you didn't notice that there was a can of olive oil there for the mayonnaise. I didn't have time for the bacon, but I'm not all that keen on bacon. I've put the melon back," I said, "and swapped with the strawberries, as I've got all that cream. And I've got rid of most of the greens. Oh, and I forgot, I just managed to save the butter."

He got up from his chair in a stately sort of way, sat down at his desk, and made out a very large bill.

"My fee," he said, "we will take as the cover charge. But as for the rest—"

I paid up without a murmur. After all, without putting on an ounce of weight I'd lived through a jolly good meal.

—Christianna Brand

222

Phoney Rum-Raisin Sundae

3/4 cup black or golden raisins   1/2 cup orange juice
1 cup brown sugar   1 quart vanilla ice cream

Combine all ingredients except ice cream in a saucepan and heat for 2 or 3 minutes until raisins are plump and sugar is melted. Cool. Pour over ice cream. Yield: sauce for 1 quart ice cream.

Phoney Orange-Nut Sundae:

6 tablespoons orange marmalade   1 quart vanilla ice cream
3 tablespoons orange juice   1/2 cup all-bran, cut into small pieces

Mix first 2 ingredients. Pour sauce over ice cream and top with bran (which tastes like nuts).

—Catherine Barth

Steve and Jayne's Chocolate Mousse

4 eggs, separated   1/4 cup glazed orange peel, diced finely
3/4 cup finely granulated sugar   Pinch salt
1/4 cup orange liqueur   Lightly whipped heavy cream,
6 ounces or squares semisweet baking   sweetened with 1 tablespoon granu-
  chocolate   lated sugar
4 tablespoons strong coffee
3/4 cup unsalted butter or margarine,
  softened

Beat egg yolks and the 3/4 cup of sugar together until thick, pale yellow and forming a slowly dissolving ribbon off spoon. Beat in liqueur. Set 3-quart porcelain mixing bowl over pan of not quite simmering water, and continue beating for 3 or 4 minutes until mixture is foamy and too hot for finger touch. Beat over basin of cold water for 3 or 4 minutes until mixture again forms a ribbon, or mayonnaise consistency.

223

Melt chocolate with coffee over hot water. Remove and beat in butter slowly, to make a smooth cream. Gradually beat chocolate mixture into egg yolks and sugar, then beat in orange peel. Beat egg whites and salt until soft peaks form. Stir ¼ of egg whites into chocolate mixture and fold in remaining ¾. Turn into dessert petit pots or a serving dish. Refrigerate minimum of two hours, preferably overnight. Dollop mousse with desired amount of whipped cream.

—Steve Allen

Specialties

Recipes from Ghosts

The old recipe book in which I found the following recipes was among a number of ancient books which were sold from an old house near Tewkesbury. It has clearly been used a lot. It is bound in thin white parchment, the pages are thick and ivory colored, and the first owner has taken the trouble to number each page in the top corner. Expert opinion considered that it might not have been opened since the eighteen eighties; and as we are very nearly once again in the eighties, it could possibly be nearly three-hundred years since one contributor has written the date below his or her name—1715. But the "7" is only a guess because it is written: ꝗ.

The earliest writing may have been done with a quill. All the letters with tails, like G and D, are marvelously written; long tails frisk up and down, perfectly even, backwards over or under the word with great artistry. Later the writing becomes more sober, with a low church rectitude, as in fact do the recipes.

From Mrs. Bidgood

A sauce for carp and several other sorts of boiled fish—easily made and very good.

"Chop three anchovies, take one very large onion or two small ones cut into four quarters but not peeled, one large spoonful of vinegar, and a quarter of a pint of water. Boil all together till the anchovies are dissolved then strain off and thicken with butter having flour worked into it."

Specialties

From Lady Gambie

Jelly:

"Take two calves feet and half a pint of hartshorn shavings, boil these in a gallon of water till it comes to five pints, then strain it through a sieve and let it stand till quite cold. Skim off the fat and warm the jelly, take a pint of lemon and orange juice, a pint of mountain wine, a pint of fine sugar, the whites of twelve eggs, beat a little; mix these altogether and putting it into your jelly with the rinds of two lemons, let it boil about a quarter of an hour, then strain it through sieve until quite fine."

From Lady Beauchamp

To Make a Brioche:

"These are a squashy kind of buns, exquisitely edible when made in France. Take 1½ pounds flour, ½ pound butter, pinch of salt, ¼ pint cream, 6 eggs, and 2 spoonfuls of yeast. Mix together carefully and bake one hour.

"But as most cooks could neither read nor write, who would take the trouble to go into the kitchen and dictate to them?"

—Joan Fleming

Spaghetti Bolognese

1 onion	*1½ cups water*
1½ tablespoons butter	*½ teaspoon salt*
4 tablespoons chopped green pepper	*1 pound spaghetti*
¼ cup chopped mushrooms	*1 tablespoon olive oil*
½ pound chopped beef chuck	*½ cup freshly grated Parmesan*
1 6-ounce can tomato paste	*cheese*

Slice onion very thin and cook in butter until wilted. Add green pepper, mushrooms, and chuck. Cook, stirring constantly, until meat is a delicate brown. Add tomato paste, water, and salt. Mix well. Simmer 20 minutes. In a separate vessel cook spaghetti in salted water to which olive oil has been added. When tender, drain. Serve on hot platter with sauce poured over it. Sprinkle with freshly grated Parmesan cheese. Yield: 4 servings.

"My mother, and how mistakenly, assumed that like herself I would need to know nothing about cooking beyond having an educated palate. A genius out in the kitchen would do the rest. It has now been many years since there has been such a genius in my kitchen. The last incumbent took daily delivery of a fifth of whiskey and served dinner as though on one roller skate. Since then, not having learned to cook at Mama's knee, I have had to substitute whatever knee has come along.

"This Sauce Bolognese I learned in Torcello, where the Locanda Cipriani concocts the most superbly refined versions of Italian cooking."

—Miriam-Ann Hagen

Cherry Ames's Illinois Spaghetti

½ pound spaghetti, cooked
Salt and cayenne pepper, to taste
1 clove garlic, finely minced
1 16-ounce can chicken gravy

1 1-pound 4-ounce can peeled tomatoes
Grated sharp cheese

Place layer of spaghetti in baking dish. Sprinkle with salt, cayenne, and garlic. Add part of chicken gravy and part of tomatoes (including juice). Top with layer of cheese. Repeat until all ingredients are used, ending with cheese. Bake, uncovered, in 350° F. oven for 1 hour. Stir occasionally with table knife. Serve when brown and crusty. Yield: 4-6 servings.

"My character Cherry Ames is always involved in a mystery. But it's no mystery why the Ames family picnics, held along the banks of the Wabash River or even in their own yard, are always a success."

—Helen Wells

Macaroni Marietta

4 cups shell macaroni	Salt and pepper
8 slices dry whole wheat bread	1/4 teaspoon celery seed
1 pound sharp cheddar cheese	2 tablespoons prepared mustard
1 green pepper	4 eggs, beaten
1 3-ounce jar pimientos	2 2/3 cups milk
1 bunch parsley	Bacon, crumbled

Cook macaroni in salted water until tender. Drain and cool. Grind together and add bread, cheese, green pepper, pimientos, and parsley. Add seasonings, eggs, and milk. Mix well. Sprinkle over top with bacon. Pour into 2 2-quart casseroles or 1 4-quart casserole. Bake in 300° F. oven 1 hour, or until cheese is hot and melted. Yield: 12 servings.

"This makes a fine picnic dish, for it holds heat well."

—Amber Dean

Pizza Mafiosa

1/4 envelope dry yeast	Three or more of the following: sliced
1/2 teaspoon sugar	cheese, ham, tomatoes, olives,
1/2 cup lukewarm water	frankfurters, salami, anchovies,
1 cup flour	cooked fish, chopped cooked pota-
Cold water	toes, cooked mushrooms, or chopped
1 tablespoon tomato paste	onions

Mix yeast and sugar into water. Set aside for 5 minutes to proof. Add to flour and begin kneading, adding more water as necessary. Knead constantly until dough is elastic and easy to handle, adding more flour if necessary. Form into a ball and cover with clean cloth. Let stand in warm place for about 1 hour or until approximately double in size. Pat dough into desired shape (pizza does not *have* to be round). Preheat oven to 500° F. Place pizzas on greased baking sheet. Brush with tomato paste. Add selection of cheese, meats, fish, and vegetables. Bake pizza for approximately 8 to 10 minutes. Serve hot. Yield: 1 serving.

"This is a forgiving dish. None of the times or heats are really critical. These are for godfathers trying to control a mob of young hoodlums. And why not square or triangular pizzas? If you trust them, let each customer shape his own and add the ingredients of his choice. If you fear that any ingredient may dry out in the cooking time, either make sure it's under a slice of cheese or add it to the pizza halfway through the cooking. If there may be a problem of identifying the pizzas once cooked, suggest they shape slices of ham or anchovy, or arrange olives to make a sign or their initials."

—Gavin Lyall

The Most Terrible Sauce Ever Created by the Hand of Man

(A Non-Recipe)

Now and then, a writer needs a *terrible* recipe, for plot purposes.

In a *Playboy* story called "The Chef's Story" it became the task of my hero, a young sauce chef in a small but renowned French provincial restaurant, to create "the most terrible sauce ever created by the hand of man."

The reason was that the restaurant had a constant but unbearably boorish customer named M. Maugron. The restaurant's proprietor wished to be rid of Maugron as a patron, but could never muster the nerve to throw the man out forever.

This night, Maugron had come in drunk as usual, with three loud

230

and vulgar drunken women as companions. He had ordered filet steaks, and insisted that a *new* sauce be created to be served with the meat. Moreover, the sauce must be named, in his honor, "Sauce Maugron."

When the chef heard about this request, he had to be physically restrained by the proprietor from charging into the dining room and attacking Maugron with a cleaver.

My hero, an eighteen-year-old sauce chef, suddenly had an idea— he himself would invent this Sauce Maugron, and it would be the most terrible sauce ever created by the hand of man. It was to be so dreadful that when Maugron tasted it he would fly into a rage and stalk out—never to return.

The chef finally agreed, but only on the condition that nothing foul or rotten or distasteful would be used in the sauce. The young sauce chef promised that "Sauce Maugron" would be a compilation of good ingredients, frightfully combined. He would repeat all the mistakes he had ever made and compound them.

He put two cups of good olive oil into a hot skillet, and chopped up four cloves of garlic and two onions, and threw them in and let them char. He chopped two tomatoes and tossed them in and let them frizzle in the boiling fat. He then dumped in a cup of flour and stirred it just a little, until it formed into small hard lumps. He then added a half cup of salt, a pinch of white pepper, a tablespoon of curry powder, and just a touch of ginger. To this boiling oily mess he then added three egg yolks, stirred the mixture once, and let it curdle.

Seeing what resulted, the chef went into his office and slammed the door and started gulping cognac.

Feeling that his sauce still needed *something,* the young chef wandered around the kitchen and found half a cup of caramel sauce, a few strawberries, a half-bottle of sweet relish, and some pickled herring. All these went into the sauce, which was still bubbling under an inch of oil. To increase the liquid content, the young apprentice added half a cup of excellent champagne vinegar. To counteract the acidity, he added half a cup of brown sugar.

He then let the sauce reduce for a few minutes, brought out a silver sauceboat and a coarse sieve, and strained the sauce into the boat—leaving most of the charred and lumpy ingredients behind. For a garnish atop the finished sauce, he added a can of chopped anchovies, five chopped maraschino cherries, and six diced marshmallows, which began to melt in the hot sauce. Over all, he sprinkled some finely chopped chives.

"Here it is," he said, as he presented the sauce to the proprietor. "The most terrible sauce ever created by the hand of man."

"Have you tasted it?" the proprietor asked.

The young chef shook his head. "I may be an idiot, but I'm not a fool."

The proprietor picked up a spoon and tasted the sauce. He stood and shuddered for almost thirty seconds.

"I congratulate you, young man. Any good chef can make a good sauce. It takes a *genius* to make one as obnoxious as this."

This story does not have an obvious ending. M. Maugron does *not* like this sauce. But therein lies the story.

—Warner Law

Super Italian Tomato Sauce

1 26-ounce can pureed tomatoes
1 12-ounce can tomato paste
3 bay leaves
¼ cup California red wine
3 tablespoons sugar

Pinch salt
Generous sprinkling oregano, rose-mary, garlic powder
Dash or two freshly ground pepper, leaf thyme, parsley flakes, onion salt

Combine all ingredients in 3-quart pan. Simmer for 2 hours over low heat. Every 5 or 10 minutes stir ingredients to insure that sauce does not stick or burn. Remove bay leaves. Yield: 2 quarts of sauce.

—William Rivera

Spaghetti and Polpetti

Polpetti (Meatballs):

3 slices stale white bread
1 pound ground beef
3 eggs, slightly beaten
3 tablespoons grated Romano cheese

1 clove garlic
Salt and pepper
Flour
Cooking oil

Soak bread in water to cover for 5 minutes. Squeeze dry. Mix thoroughly with all remaining ingredients except flour and cooking oil. Form into egg-sized balls, roll in flour and fry in oil until golden brown. (Reserve oil for spaghetti sauce.) Yield: 4-6 servings.

Spaghetti con Salsa Semplice de Pomodoro:

Oil (from meatball pan)
2 tablespoons olive oil
2 cloves garlic, halved
2 11-ounce cans tomato puree
1 bay leaf
Salt and pepper, to taste

1/2 teaspoon dried oregano
1/2 teaspoon sugar
 1 pound spaghetti
Grated Parmesan or Romano cheese
Red wine

Heat oil from meatball pan. Add olive oil and next 6 ingredients. Simmer 1 hour, stirring frequently. Remove bay leaf and garlic. Add meatballs. Cook spaghetti according to package directions. Pour sauce over all and pass cheese. Yield: 4-6 servings.

"My wife Marty is a collaborator in most everything I write, although I sign my name singularly. We are often collaborators in cooking as well. For many years we kept searching for a meatball and spaghetti dish that satisfied us completely.

"This dish we struck upon a long time ago, but have added to it until I think it has become a personal creation—and one we guarantee, having made it so many times. I made use of it in a suspense novelette for *Good Housekeeping* titled *Forest Fire*."

—James McKimmey

233

Clam Sauce for Linguini

¼ cup olive oil or butter (or a combination of the two)
2 large cloves garlic, finely chopped (or 1 medium clove, if you're not as much of a garlic lover as I am)
2 tablespoons flour
2 cups clam juice (water added to liquid from canned clams, or straight bottled clam juice)

1½ teaspoons dried thyme leaves
Salt and pepper, to taste
2 8-ounce cans minced clams
Linguini for two servings (prepared according to package)

Heat oil/butter, add garlic and cook over low heat for 1 minute. Do not allow garlic to brown or crisp. With a wire whisk stir in flour. Add clam juice while continuing to stir. Add remaining ingredients (except clams and linguini) and simmer 10 minutes. Add clams and continue heating 2 minutes. Serve over cooked linguini. Yield: 2 servings (or 4 servings as side dish).

"Serve with French bread or sourdough and white wine."

—Aaron Elkins

Cosa Nostra Pasta

2 pounds hot Italian sausage
1 cup olive oil
2 large onions, chopped into 1-inch chunks
1 tablespoon Chinese Garlic Chili paste
Seasoning: salt, a few red pepper flakes, oregano
1 large sweet red pepper, chopped into 1-inch chunks

1 large sweet green pepper, chopped into 1-inch chunks
1 pound mushrooms, chopped into 1-inch chunks
1 pound pasta springs (or medium shells)
6 or more sizeable cloves fresh garlic, minced
1 6-ounce can tomato paste

Remove skin from sausages and shred them into pieces a bit bigger than .45 slugs. In a large skillet or Dutch oven let oil get well hot, then drop in to

234

frizzle. When sausages are hot, turning brown, drop in the onions and add the Chinese garlic chili paste, oregano, red pepper flakes, and salt to taste. When the onions are turning limp, toss in the sweet peppers and mushrooms. If hungry, have water for the pasta already boiling. (Always add a dollop of oil to the water—this applies to any pasta.) Add a pinch of salt.

With the sauce well simmering, and before peppers and sausages go soft, add garlic and tomato paste. Let simmer no more than five minutes once garlic is in. When the pasta is *al dente*, drain it in a colander. Toss the sauce with the springs. Top it with grated Parmesan cheese. Yield: 6 servings.

"What isn't eaten refrigerate and skillet-refrizzle tomorrow. Mama mia!
"I invented this while writing my first novel, *The Family Man*, which dealt with a crooked killer policeman, politics, eating, and the Cosa Nostra."

—Milt Machlin

Main Dish for When the Mafiosa Come to Dinner

½ cup chopped onions
2 tablespoons olive oil
2 cups whole-pack Italian tomatoes,
  undrained, chopped, or peel, seed,
  and chop fresh plum tomatoes
4 tablespoons tomato paste
1 teaspoon sugar

½ teaspoon salt
Fresh crushed black pepper, to taste
  2 teaspoons fresh basil, if you can
    get it
6-8 Italian hot sausages
Parmesan or Romano cheese, optional

Cook the onions in the olive oil over medium heat for several minutes, until soft but not browned. Add remaining ingredients except sausages and simmer twenty minutes. If you like a smooth sauce, press through food mill or blend in blender. For a medium-chunky sauce, put half the sauce through a blender, then add to the rest. If you like a really chunky sauce, leave it as is. Put sausage in sauce and simmer about half an hour, or until sausage is thoroughly cooked. Serve over any pasta, but it looks especially nice on mostaccioli or penne. Serve freshly grated or shredded Parmesan or Romano cheese. Yield: 6-8 servings.

—Barbara D'Amato

Angie's Basic Recipe for Spaghetti Sauce

1 onion, finely chopped	*1 teaspoon oregano*
1 large clove garlic, chopped	*1 6-ounce can tomato paste*
2 tablespoons oil	*¼ teaspoon sugar*
2½ cups peeled canned tomatoes	*Salt and pepper, to taste*
1 tablespoon parsley	*½ teaspoon dried basil*

Fry onion and garlic in oil until soft but not brown. Add remaining ingredients and simmer for about 1½ hours. Yield: 1 quart of sauce.

—Hilda Cushing

"Cyanide of potassium," he explained.

Angie shivered. "Won't he taste it?"

"It won't matter. Just put it in something he likes and the first mouthful will do it."

"He loves spaghetti," she mused. "I could mix it with the sauce."

Angie always made the spaghetti sauce early in the morning because it was better if it stood awhile. It was her own cherished recipe, with lots of garlic and oregano.

—Hilda Cushing
(From "The Poison Plate
Special" as it appeared in
Alfred Hitchcock's Mystery Magazine)

236

Soubise Sauce

  1 pound white onions
¼ cup butter
1½ cups Bechamel Sauce (below)
Salt and pepper, to taste

⅛ teaspoon nutmeg
½ teaspoon sugar
½ cup heavy cream, scalded
  2 tablespoons butter

Peel and finely chop onions. Blanch in salted water and drain. Melt ¼ cup butter in a heavy casserole with a lid. Add onions to butter and cook, covered, over very low heat until onions are translucent but not brown. Shake the pan occasionally to prevent sticking. Stir in Bechamel sauce and seasonings. Place dish, covered, in 350° F. oven for 30 minutes. Stir occasionally. Remove from oven and mix in blender or force through fine sieve until smooth. Return to casserole and reheat. Stir in cream and butter. Serve at once with meat or fish. Yield: 2 cups sauce, approximately.

"This recipe is attributed to Madame de Maintenon, an attribution which may be apocryphal. On a more plebeian level, her sauce raises the humble hamburger to royal rank. Delicious when served with cold roast beef."

Bechamel Sauce:

  2 tablespoons butter
  2 tablespoons flour
1½ cups milk

1 onion, finely chopped
1 small bay leaf

Melt butter in saucepan at low heat. Add and blend in flour stirring constantly for 4 minutes. Slowly stir in milk. Add onions and bay leaf. Stir with wooden spoon or wire whisk until thick.

—Jean Francis Webb

Topping for Vegetables

½ cup milk
2 eggs, beaten
1 tablespoon dry mustard

Salt and pepper, to taste
4 ounces cheddar cheese, grated
Cooked vegetables, well drained

Preheat oven to 375° F. Combine milk and eggs. Combine mustard, salt and pepper. Pour a little of the milk-egg mixture into the seasonings and blend until smooth. Combine two mixtures. Whisk in cheese. Pour over contents of baking dish filled with serving of cooked vegetables. Bake for 30 to 35 minutes, or until top is delicately browned.

"This topping can be used over almost any mixture of meat and vegetables, or as a flan filling, atop fried onions, or whatever one fancied that day. Given aubergines (eggplant) in the underneath part, one could even call this Moussaka. What I've done with this covering in my time would fill a book, and it usually succeeds. Beware of too much liquid in the mixture underneath. It makes a lovely pie consistency if it isn't too moist."

—Edith Pargeter

Ashoka's Repast

Before the Emperor Ashoka became a Buddhist he was, it is said, addicted to Peacock and Venison Curry. On one of the several Ashoka pillars scattered around India and Afghanistan there is a list of animals slaughtered for the royal kitchen. Peacock and deer predominate.

While the royals and semi-royals ate game birds and the venison of Barasing (Kashmir stag) or other deer, the non-royals partook of lamb and chicken. The prevalent idea seemed to be to combine red meat with white meat in a gravy called *josh* (juice). Thus one has Fasjenjosh (pheasant juice), Roghanjosh (lamb juice), and so on.

—M. Robert Joshi

Ashoka's Repast

12 ounces yogurt
1/8 cup oil (almond, apricot, walnut or safflower)
1/2 lime, juice and peel
1/2 teaspoon grated fresh ginger
1/2 cup fresh coriander (Chinese parsley), bruised
1/2 cup fresh mint leaves, bruised
1/2 teaspoon saffron
2 pounds boned poultry (pheasant, Cornish hen, duck, quail, or chicken)
2 pounds boned meat (lamb, top round, or venison)

1/2 cup sweet butter
1 large onion, chopped
1 large green apple, peeled and chopped
1 large fresh pear, peeled and chopped
1 teaspoon curry powder
1 teaspoon cardamom powder
1 teaspoon cumin powder
1 teaspoon garlic powder
1/2 teaspoon powdered cloves
1/2 teaspoon ground cinnamon
1 cup chopped nuts
2 cups boiled rice

Combine yogurt, oil, lime juice, peel, and spices. Mix in meats and marinate in refrigerator overnight. Next day melt butter very slowly. When foam and bubbles have subsided, skim off clarified butter and put into 6-quart enamel pot, discarding residue. Sauté onion in clarified butter until lightly browned. Add chopped fruits and stir until softened. Add spices, meats, marinade and chopped nuts. Remove and discard lime rind. Cover and simmer over very low heat for 5 to 6 hours, adding water if necessary. Cook rice according to package directions. Serve meat mixture over boiled rice. Yield: 6-8 servings.

"And of course you must have caviar relish (caviar, chopped onion, and a pinch of sumak). And Jasmine tea."

—M. Robert Joshi

A Bachelor Learns to Cook

I find that men of my generation—I'm in my mid-forties—usually know how to cook a minimum meal and are often quite adept at some particular area of cooking. Yet my father and father-in-law can hardly boil an egg. (But they can spell it.) All sorts of reasons, a lot of them to do with working wives, but another that hasn't been much mentioned: Before the Second World War most young men leaving home—still as bachelors—moved into apartments where the landlady provided breakfast and dinner as part of the overall deal. After the war that faded out, and you simply rented an apartment with cooking facilities built in.

I started cooking when I first came to London, sharing a flat with two old school friends who had arrived a year before. We kept impeccable accounts in the sense that every penny got split three ways but cooked lousily—the usual tinned and dried foods (we didn't have a refrigerator). The only thing I can remember being proud of was my onion gravy, and I now can't remember how to do it. The landlady went abroad for the winter, leaving her apple trees un-picked, so we collected the lot and put them through the wringer in an attempt to make cider, and we threw a Christmas party on the results. Luckily (I was a journalist at the time) I got sent abroad just before the party and so didn't have to drink as much of it as my colleagues and guests.

I married a year later and began to acquire an appreciation of food (being a schoolboy in wartime Britain didn't impress you with the idea that eating could be one of life's pleasures) and of my wife's cooking (based on her trips to the continent before we'd met). I started cooking for myself again when I quit as a journalist and started writing fiction full time, which meant working at home. So I either went down to the pub for a beer and a sandwich, or opened a tin, or ate something frozen or dried. Trying one of the new-fangled Indian and Chinese TV meals, I decided that it could be improved if I added a little something. And so the process started. From adding a something, I added two somethings, then three, replaced an element and so on until there was no need for the basic TV meal at all. (I didn't do this every lunchtime, of course. There were still plenty of beer-and-sandwich ones.)

By tacit agreement, I stuck to Indian and Chinese meals (which I was now doing for my wife as well) rather than get into arguments about how to prepare a classic French or British dish. Now, much of that agreement has worn away and she doesn't mind whatever I try to cook. On Mediterranean holidays we've found a pleasant pattern whereby my wife takes the children to the beach (which I loathe) while I potter at a typewriter and prepare their lunch.

At home, the tradition is that I cook a full meal once a week, usually Friday, and occasional dinner parties. Generally I still stick to Chinese or Indian, with the occasional barbecue and what might be called "Mediterranean" dishes: paellas, rissottos, pastas—children's food, perhaps, rather than the subtle French stuff which Katharine does so well. It's probably been useful in maturing our children's eating habits. The thrill of eating something Daddy has cooked can overcome their instinctive refusal of something new. Not many nine-year-olds know as many eastern dishes as does ours (with the obvious exception of eastern nine-year-olds).

I find cooking is a good plotting activity. I can't figure out plots behind a desk, but in a kitchen I can move about, boiling up a little of that, chopping a little of the other, muttering to myself, "If I do the chicken with almonds I'll need a strong-tasting vegetable dish. . . . Suppose the woman was the arms salesman's daughter, not wife, that would make the relationship with Harry more interesting. . . . I'm sure I copied out a recipe for a fish soup. . . . Try it if you want to, chum, but this gun'll shoot through a brick wall. . . . That bloody woman's used up all the paprika again. . . ." This drives our two cats barmy. They don't mind me talking to *them*, but when I'm giving the word to Banquo's ghost, they back into the corners making little chittering noises which probably translate as "Where are the boys in the white coats?"

241

Like most men, I came to cooking the wrong way round. I never learnt the basics at my mother's knee. I'm only just learning that good cooking starts in the marketplace, not on the stove.

—Gavin Lyall

Sukara-Maddava

⅛ cup mustard or sesame oil	1 teaspoon grated fresh ginger
1 teaspoon mustard seeds	2 teaspoons fresh lime juice
1 teaspoon sesame seeds	5-6 cloves garlic, crushed
½ teaspoon turmeric	½ cup grated fresh coconut
2 pounds wild boar or lean pork, cubed	1 cup chopped onion
	1½ cups water
2 large cans truffles, or 2 pounds fresh mushrooms	Salt and cayenne pepper to taste
	2 cups boiled rice

Heat oil until very hot. Add seeds. When seeds stop popping, add turmeric. Stir. Do not allow to burn. Add meat and brown thoroughly. Stir in all remaining ingredients. Cover and simmer over very low heat for 2 to 3 hours or until meat is tender and well done, adding more water if necessary. Cook rice according to package directions. Serve meat over rice. Yield: 6 servings.

"There is a lively debate among the Buddhists about what the Knowledge-able ate at the house of Cunda, the smith of Pava in eastern India, the day before he died. The whole thing revolves around the translation of the Pali words *Sukara-Maddava*. They can be translated to mean 'sweetness of choice meat of boar' or to mean just 'sweet truffles.' Most of Sidhartha's disciples of today are vegetarians. They would rather believe that their master ate truffles. On the other hand, there is no reason to doubt that Buddha did indeed eat a dish of wild boar. The Enlightened would never have insulted his host by declining his hospitality. Ecumenical as I am, I go for the combination of boar and truffles when I can afford them, or think I can. WARNING: The All-Knowing One died of dysentery!"

—M. Robert Joshi

Specialties

Corn Bread Dressing for Fowl

1 *favorite recipe corn bread, unsweet-*
   ened
1 *cup chopped celery*
2 *medium onions, chopped*
Pinch sage

Pinch thyme
Salt
Freshly ground pepper
2 *eggs*

Crumble entire corn bread in large mixing bowl until quite fine. Add remaining ingredients and mix thoroughly. Use to stuff turkey or chicken, roast as usual. Yield: stuffing for small turkey or large chicken. (Dressing may be doubled for larger bird.)

"From a skillet-happy Texan, here is something that isn't fried. If any dressing is leftover, it can be baked separately (for half an hour or so). Onto the extra batch of dressing, spoon a bit of the drippings from the cooking turkey or chicken. This 'extra,' cold or hot, is delicious the next day sliced like a pie or in strips. I have never seen it go begging. Even the French love it, and they are inclined to think that corn is strictly *pour les bêtes*.

—Patricia Highsmith

My Mother's Stuffing

1 *large loaf day-old white bread*
3 *teaspoons poultry seasoning*
1 *large onion*
Cooking oil

1 *pound sausage meat*
Salt and pepper, to taste
2 *eggs*

Break up bread into ragged pieces, crust included, and put into a large bowl. Sprinkle liberally with poultry seasoning. Slice onion very fine and brown in just enough cooking oil so that onion does not stick to pan. Add sausage meat to onions, mashing into granules as it thoroughly browns. (Do not discard any of the fat from the cooking meat.) Lightly beat eggs, then add to the torn-up bread. When onion-sausage mixture is thoroughly cooked, pour from skillet directly into the bread and egg, including all fat. Mix very thoroughly. Tamp down so that it all fits into a bowl. Cover with plastic wrap

243

or aluminum foil and store in refrigerator overnight. Yield: stuffing for one 15-18 pound turkey.

"NEVER store stuffing in an uncooked turkey!"

—Dorothy Uhnak

Calf's Foot Jelly à la Ister

2 calves' feet or 1 beef foot	*1 clove garlic, minced*
Water	*4-6 eggs*
Salt and pepper, to taste	

Have butcher cut feet into several pieces. Clean thoroughly. Place in large soup kettle and cover with 3-4 inches of cold water. Bring to a boil and cook briskly for 1 hour, adding hot water if needed. Season to taste with salt, pepper, and garlic. Reduce heat and simmer for 8 hours. Twenty minutes before meat is done, add eggs in their shells. After 20 minutes, remove from heat. Remove meat and eggs, reserving broth. Peel eggs and chop coarsely. Cover and place in refrigerator. Allow meat to cool until easily handled. Remove all meat and gristle from bones. Pour broth through sieve. (Make sure all small bones are discarded.) Replace meat in broth and boil until broth has thickened. Do not add water. When reduced add chopped eggs and turn into large mold or bowl. Chill overnight or until firm. (Skim off fat and use as a spread for bread or crackers, if desired.) When jelly is firm, slice and serve garnished if desired. Yield: 10 or more servings.

EDITOR'S NOTE: The Davidson way of expressing this makes better reading:

"Go to a butcher shop in an ethnic neighborhood and buy a couple of calves' feet or else a cow's foot or beef foot as it may be called. In any case, have the butcher cut it into several pieces for you. They should be clean of crud, and crap, and hair, and fur, and fuzz. If not so, clean it. Place in a large pot with a lot of water, bring to a boil awhile, say an hour, then reduce to a low boil or simmer. If you can keep a kettle going on the next burner to replenish the water as it cooks down, good. If not, replenish with cold but this slows down the cooking process. Season to taste? Of course, season to taste.

244

Go easy on the salt, you can always put the salt in but you can never take it out. Add pepper. Anybody who dislikes it isn't going to like this dish anyway. The Rumanians call it *Pitchah*. The hell with them. Okay. Add a *lot* of garlic, minced garlic if you got it, and, of course, real live garlic if you've got *that* and aren't afraid of it. It is said to keep off the Black Death and if it also keeps off the lady next door—then the hell with *her*, too. It is like lamb in that it is impossible to add too much garlic. The ancient Greeks tried to and they failed. Where are we? Oh, yes. The cow trotters are to berl for eight hours, just like they belonged to a union. So . . . a few hours before the end, put several eggs in their shells into the pot. What? It's already eight hours? Well, turn off the flame and take the pot off the stove. What are you WAITING for? Remove the eggs and let cold water run on them. Remove the trotters and if any flesh or gristle remains, remove same from the bones and cut up all the flesh and gristle and gunk and gooey. Put it back in the pot, which—by the way, ha! ha!—I forgot to say you should have eventually let cook down without adding water. Till the soup or liquid has gotten very sticky, see? Make sure *all* the bones are taken out. Be looking for small ones. Throw 'em all away. Shell eggs and cut in pieces. Place in soup. Or in bottom of mold. A big bowl, maybe. Let cool. Then put in fridge. Next day, skim off fat and discard (or save and use. Up to you). Slice jelly and eat. Yum yum. Enjoy!"

—Avram Davidson

Lovell's Pure Natural Granola

6 cups rolled oats	1/2 cup cooking oil
1 cup coconut	1/2 cup honey
1 cup wheat germ	1/3 cup water
1/2 cup shelled sunflower seeds	1 1/2 teaspoons salt
1/2 cup crushed peanuts	1 1/2 teaspoons vanilla extract

Preheat oven to 325° F. Combine first 5 ingredients. Combine last 5 ingredients. Blend both together. Spread mixture on 2 greased cookie sheets. Bake for 20 minutes, stirring frequently. Cool thoroughly and store in air-tight container. Serve as with any dry cereal. For variation, add raisins, dates, or dried fruit before baking. Yield: 8-12 servings.

"Readers of *Ellery Queen's Mystery Magazine* are familiar with the con man team of Lovell and Lang, whose adventures have appeared in that magazine over the past several years. Lovell, the inside man, is an artist of very great if somewhat limited talent in that he can successfully forge the work of any painter living or dead. He is also, in the words of his partner Harry Lang, 'a nut about the food he eats.' It was the blender Lovell used for his high-protein milk shake that provided Harry with the gimmick he needed for a last-minute switch of one of Lovell's forgeries in 'Only Bet on a Sure Thing.' All of their adventures have made some reference to Lovell's preference for natural foods."

—Robert E. Eckels

Singin' Hennies

½ pound plain flour (2 cups)
1 teaspoon baking powder
¼ teaspoon salt
2 ounces butter or fat (lard or other shortening)

1 ounce sugar
½ cup currants
Milk

Sieve flour, baking powder and salt. Rub in butter to produce quite coarse crumblike pieces. Add sugar, currants and enough milk to make a dough. Flour hands and make one ¼-inch thick round (or two smaller ones) and place on a *hot* greased griddle until brown (about seven minutes). Then turn and cook on other side. Butter while hot and serve with or without honey, cut into four parts. Yield: 4 servings.

"*Griddle* is spelled *girdle* in my grandmother's cookbook, written in her fine Italian hand. These were favorites for high tea when I was a child. With a bowl of soup, they make a filling, nourishing and inexpensive supper today."

—Alexandra Roudybush

Carleton Carpenter Solves the
Perfect Pancake Puzzle

The Plot: Air tight
The Pay-Off: Air light
The Characters: 4 good eggs, 2 cups buttermilk, 1 cup flour, 1 teaspoon baking soda, 1 teaspoon baking powder, a dash of salt and ½ cup oil.
Clues: Mix everything in a good-sized pitcher with non-lethal wooden spoon and be stingy when dolloping onto a hot griddle. No riddle. No mystery. Pure magic.

These really are super!

—Carleton Carpenter

Muffins and a Ghost

When we were transferred to a town in West Texas in 1970, we bought a rambling old house. It had begun life as a standard two-bedroom, one-bath home, but rooms had been added on until it sprawled over most of the lot with 11 rooms and four baths. It had no

247

particular floor plan, just rooms opening into other rooms with doorways hit or miss so that two people could wander through the house at the same time without running into each other. We had been in the house just a short time when a peculiar thing happened. We had just gone to bed, after checking to make sure the children were asleep. And I distinctly saw a child—a little girl—walk through the hallway and into the living room. The streetlight shining through the living room windows silhouetted the figure, so I could not be mistaken.

I grabbed my husband's shoulder and shook him. "There's a child in this house!" I whispered.

"There are four children, all asleep," he mumbled.

I quickly told him what I had seen, and he got up. We checked the bedrooms, and our children were asleep.

"Some child must have wandered in here," I said, but I began to shiver.

My husband quickly went through the house and came back shaking his head. "All the doors are securely locked. There is no way a child could come in here. You must have been dreaming."

I knew what I had seen and that it was not a dream, and by this time I had begun to realize it was not a flesh and blood child who had walked through the hallway. I don't frighten easily, yet at that moment I was terrified. We went back to bed, and I insisted we leave the hall light on all night.

I had invited some neighbors to come for coffee the next morning, and over pineapple-ice cream muffins and large cups of coffee I asked some hesitant questions about the house.

Two of the women looked at each other significantly. "The original owners of this house had two daughters," one of them said. "The girls were very happy here. But when they grew into young womanhood, one was killed by her husband; and the other was threatened by her husband. The second daughter left her husband to live at home. One day her father shot the husband as he banged on the door, trying to get in."

"There's been some talk about a ghost," the other neighbor said, "but you don't believe in ghosts, do you?"

That particular child-ghost never returned. So I'm not sure if I believe in her or she was a figment of my imagination.

—Joan Lowery Nixon

Pineapple-Ice Cream Muffins

2 cups vanilla ice cream
1 8¼-ounce can crushed pineapple, drained, juice reserved
2 cups flour
¼ cup sugar

3 teaspoons double-acting baking powder
¼ teaspoon salt
¼ cup salad oil
1 cup topping
1⅔ cups glaze

Preheat oven to 400° F. Soften ice cream slightly and blend with pineapple in an electric mixer. Add flour, sugar, baking powder, salt, and salad oil, and beat until just blended. Line 2 muffin pans with paper baking cups. Fill cups ⅔ full with mixture. Add topping. Bake muffins for 20 to 25 minutes or until golden on top. Remove from pans. Cool on racks and glaze. Yield: 9–12 muffins.

Crumbly Topping:

¼ cup margarine
½ cup flour

¼ cup brown sugar

Mix well until consistency is crumbly.

Glaze:

1½ cups confectioners' sugar

8 teaspoons pineapple juice, reserved from draining

Stir until smooth. Drizzle on tops of cooled muffins.

—Joan Lowery Nixon

Alice's Calorie Deluxe Spoonbread Muffins

1 cup hot water
½ teaspoon salt
1 tablespoon butter
⅔ cup white cornmeal

1 teaspoon sugar
½ cup milk
3 eggs, separated

Preheat oven to 400° F. Combine hot water, salt, and butter. Stir over low heat until butter melts. Stir in cornmeal. Remove from heat and add sugar.

Beat egg whites until stiff. Beat egg yolks. Combine milk and beaten egg yolks. Stir into cornmeal mixture. Gently fold in stiffly beaten egg whites. Pour into small greased iron muffin pans or in muffin pans of other material lined with small paper baking cups. Fill each cup only ½ to ⅔ full. (The muffins should be as small as possible—not more than 2 inches across.) Bake 20 to 30 minutes or until puffed and brown. Yield: 6-12 muffins depending on pan size.

"This was a recipe which was given to me in 'approximates' so to speak, but it worked for me twice and is really delicious."

—Mignon G. Eberhart

Fat Rascals

2 cups flour	⅓ cup currants
Pinch salt	Milk
½ cup butter, very cold	White granulated sugar
1 heaping tablespoon brown sugar	

Preheat oven to 450° F. Sift flour and salt into warm bowl. Cut in butter, add brown sugar and currants. Stir together with enough milk to make a soft dough. With floured hands, put on floured pastry board and roll out ¼-inch thick. With a glass or biscuit cutter, cut into rounds. Dust *heavily* with white sugar. Lay on greased baking sheet and bake 10 to 12 minutes. Yield: approximately 12.

"Fat rascals are only good hot, but they can be made ahead and then reheated. They need neither butter nor honey. On the other hand, they do not spurn either or both."

—Alexandra Roudybush

Dr. Johnson's Scotch Scones

2 cups flour	½ teaspoon salt
4 teaspoons baking powder	4 tablespoons butter, very cold
3 teaspoons sugar, approximately, divided	2 eggs
	⅓ cup cream

Preheat oven to 450° F. Mix flour, baking powder, 2 teaspoons sugar, and salt. Cut in butter. Break eggs into bowl. Reserve approximately 1 tablespoon egg white. Beat remaining eggs with the cream. Add to flour mixture. Mix well. Roll to ¾-inch thickness on floured board. Cut into squares and brush with reserved egg white. Sprinkle with reserved sugar, and place on greased baking sheet. Bake 15 minutes. Yield: 8-10 scones depending on size.

—Lillian de la Torre

Whole Wheat Scones

3⅓ cups whole wheat flour	½ cup raisins
½ teaspoon baking soda	2 eggs
¼ cup butter, very cold	1 cup milk
1½ tablespoons honey	1 tablespoon lemon juice

Preheat oven to 425° F. Combine flour and baking soda. Cut butter into flour mixture. Add honey and raisins. Beat eggs. Add milk and lemon juice. Stir into flour mixture. If dough is too dry for rolling, add more milk. Roll dough about ¾-inch thick. Cut into rounds about 2 inches across, and bake on a lightly greased baking sheet for 20 minutes or until golden. Yield: 25 scones.

—Patrick O'Keeffe

Scones

2 cups flour	2 tablespoons butter, melted
2 teaspoons double-acting baking	2 tablespoons Lyle's Golden Syrup*
powder	3 eggs
1/2 teaspoon salt	1/2 cup sour cream
Grated rind of 1 lemon	2 tablespoons water

Preheat oven to 450° F. Mix dry ingredients and rind. Mix in melted butter and syrup. Beat 2 eggs and add to mixture. Stir in sour cream. Knead lightly for 1 minute. Make 2 balls and roll out on floured surface until 1/4-inch thick. Cut each round into 4 pie-shaped wedges. Beat 1 egg with 2 tablespoons of water . Brush over dough. Bake 15 to 20 minutes or until golden. Yield: 8 scones.

"My first book, *Jump Out,* which was nominated for an Edgar, featured Robert Christopher, a consumer reporter with a weight problem. High on Christopher's list of calorie-laden no-nos is his recipe for scones."

—R. R. Irvine

* Lyle's Golden Syrup is imported from England and is usually available in delicatessens or fancy food stores. However, I'm sure Karo could be substituted.

Devonshire (or Cornish) Splits

1 envelope dry yeast	1/2 cup milk
1 teaspoon sugar	1 teaspoon salt
1 cup lukewarm water	Melted butter
1 1/2 pounds flour, divided	Strawberry jam
1 ounce lard	Cornish or Devonshire cream, optional
1/2 cup butter	

Put the yeast in a bowl with sugar. Add lukewarm water and then a tablespoon of flour. Mix and let this rise in a warm place for about 10 minutes. Put lard, butter, milk, and salt in a saucepan and heat. Put the remaining flour in a mixing bowl, make a well in the middle, and pour in milk mixture and yeast mixture. Mix into a soft dough, cover, and put in warm place to rise for about 1 hour. When risen, knead, roll out, and cut into 2-inch rounds. Place these on a baking sheet and let rise again. Bake in a preheated 350° F. oven about 40 minutes. When cooked, brush lightly with melted butter and place them on a warm blanket, covering lightly with same. (This is to prevent their getting crisp.) To serve, split almost through and serve with strawberry jam. If obtainable, add a thick glob of Cornish or Devonshire cream.

—Alexandra Roudybush

EDITOR'S NOTE: If this blanket business puzzles you, try it. You will become a true believer.

Camembert Bread

4 ounces Camembert cheese
½ cup butter

2 tablespoons dried basil
1 loaf French bread

Preheat oven to 325° F. Put cheese, butter, and basil in a saucepan. Simmer over low heat for 5 minutes. Stir mixture occasionally to blend ingredients. Remove from heat. Cool for 10 minutes, stirring occasionally. Cut into top of loaf, almost slicing it in half vertically. Be careful not to cut loaf all the way through. Stuff cheese mixture into the bread. Drip some of the mixture onto top crust. Wrap bread in foil. Bake in oven for 20 minutes. Open foil to expose top crust and bake for another 10 minutes. Do not allow crust to harden, merely to crisp.

"You need plenty of napkins for Camembert Bread because your fingers get all buttery. Serve hot with drinks, grilled steak or chops. Slice thin (1 inch)."

—Nan and Ivan Lyons

Basic Bread

2 envelopes of dry yeast dissolved in
   3/4 cup of warm (not hot) water,
   with sugar as directed on the
   package
2 cups lukewarm milk
3 tablespoons sugar

1 tablespoon salt
3 tablespoons shortening
8 cups flour, all purpose or bread
   flour
Melted butter

Dissolve yeast. Add milk, sugar, salt, shortening, and half the flour. Mix until smooth. Mix in rest of flour until dough is easy to handle. Knead on floured surface until smooth—10 minutes should do it. Put in greased bowl, cover with dish towel, and let it rise about an hour, until doubled in size. Divide dough in half, shape into loaves, place in greased loaf pans, brush with butter, and let rise another hour. Bake at 425° F. for about 25 to 30 minutes, until brown. To test for doneness, tap to see if they sound hollow. Brush with butter if you like. Yield: 2 loaves.

"Baking bread is one of the ways I relax. I like kneading it, and I love the smell of it, the way it fills the house and makes your mouth water."

—Stephen King

Herb Bread

2 envelopes dry yeast
1/4 cup lukewarm water
1/4 cup plus 1 teaspoon sugar
1 cup milk
2 teaspoons salt
1/4 cup shortening, preferably oil

5 cups sifted flour (approximately)
2 eggs, beaten
1/4 teaspoon dried basil
1/2 teaspoon dried thyme
1/2 teaspoon dried oregano
3/4 teaspoon nutmeg

Soften yeast in water with 1 teaspoon sugar. Scald milk. Put sugar, salt, and shortening into large mixing bowl. Stir in milk, and cool to lukewarm. Add about 2 cups flour to make a thick batter. Add yeast and eggs. Mix well. Crumble basil, thyme, and oregano. Add to batter with nutmeg. Beat well, adding 2½ to 3 cups flour to make a soft dough. Place dough on board and knead until smooth. Place in a greased bowl, cover, and put in a warm place for about 1 hour or until it doubles in size. Punch down and divide into 2 equal parts. Knead the dough again for 2 or 3 minutes, then place in 2 greased pans. Cover. Again, let dough rise until it doubles in size. Do not punch down. Bake until hollow-sounding and brown, about 35 minutes, in a preheated 350° F. oven. Cool and serve. Yield: 2 loaves of bread.

—Dorothy Gilman

Some people are born chefs, others are born writers, and a chosen few are born both. I, however, am not one of the favored; and for those who are merely writers, like myself, I have a recommendation. Marry someone who can help, instruct, and oversee.

There are, however, moments when my wife leaves me to my own flouring in the kitchen, and they can be disastrous.

It happened one lovely summer day. I decided I had attained my maturity as a baker and that I'd reached a point where I could experiment.

Ordinary bread? My familiar and much admired recipe? Sure, but be bold. Add a little something different. Add, say, some soya flour. That will be an advance, even a surprise.

It was.

All proceeded in due course until I kneaded. Try, if you'd like to empathize with me, to knead glue. It sticks to bowl, spoon, hands, forearms and clothes.

I struggled, scraped, pulled, pushed, fought. I ended up in a cast of sticky dough. In desperation I stripped, threw my clothes out of the door and strode forth stark naked, carrying breadboard, bowls, spoons, mixer, flour jars, and whatever else I had touched. I turned the hose on myself and the whole mess.

A few neighbors came to watch the sport. I rejected all their

255

suggestions, stayed with the hose and emerged unscathed, except for my pride. I rescued enough dough to make a small loaf; enough, say, to look like a midget hero sandwich. But the bread was delicious.

My advice: Never bake unless your spouse is within call.

My lesson: Soya flour and all other flours that are low in gluten (rye, cornmeal, buckwheat, etc.) should be added only after the basic dough has been thoroughly beaten.

The following recipe, however, has always received rave reviews.

—Lawrence Treat

Salt-Free Bread

2 envelopes dry yeast
3 cups lukewarm water
1/2 cup plus 1/2 teaspoon dark molasses, divided

1 cup potato water, lukewarm
8 cups white flour, divided
4 cups whole wheat flour
2 tablespoons butter

Dissolve yeast in 1 cup lukewarm water. Add 1/2 teaspoon molasses. Add potato water and remaining water. Mix with 6 cups white flour and 1/2 cup molasses. Beat until smooth, about 150 times. Add butter and rest of flour, and beat until smooth. Knead until dough is rubbery. Place in greased bowl, cover, put in a warm place, and let rise for about 1 1/2 hours, until doubled in bulk. Punch down and put in 4 standard-size greased bread pans and let rise for another hour, until doubled in bulk. Bake 15 minutes in a preheated 450° F. oven. Lower heat to 375° F. and bake for 30 minutes more. Yield: 4 loaves.

—Lawrence Treat

Hobelspänne

3 egg yolks
1 whole egg
2 tablespoons sugar
1 tablespoon sour cream

1 1/4 cups sifted flour
Fat for frying
Sugar and cinnamon

Beat eggs, sugar and sour cream together, add flour gradually and work the dough lightly together. Then roll it out on a floured surface as thin as

256

possible. (It is easiest to do this in small pieces, as the result should be almost transparent.) Cut dough into narrow ribbons, about 1″ × 4″. Fry in deep fat (clarified butter gives the best flavor, but a good vegetable fat will do). Strips will crinkle up, produce bubbles and become very crisp. Lift out with a slotted spoon. Drain and sprinkle immediately with sugar and cinnamon. Delicious hot or cold. Yield: 6-8 servings.

"Hobelspänne means 'wood shavings.' The recipe is an old one, which used to be made by my Bavarian grandmother. I am a mixture of Scottish, Irish, and German, was born in Burma and brought up in England. The cooking in our family, therefore, has always been rather international. I vaguely remember from my childhood that balls made of *Hobelspänne*, wonderfully intricately interwoven (I have no idea how they did it), used to appear in the shops on Shrove Tuesday, and were eaten then as we eat pancakes."

—Elizabeth Ferrars

Tea Brack

8 ounces Sultanas	1 pound self-rising flour
8 ounces currants	4 tablespoons milk
8 ounces soft brown sugar	1 large egg
½ pint cold strong tea	Butter

Soak raisins, currants, and sugar in cold tea overnight. Next day, preheat oven to 375° F. Sift flour into tea mixture. Mix and add milk. Beat well, and then beat in egg. Grease 8-inch cake pan or bread pan and bake in oven for 2 hours or until a toothpick comes out clean. Slice and serve with butter. Yield: 1 loaf.

"You'll find it will slice thinly. But I know people who prefer it sliced thickly and without butter.

"I rather think this title is Irish. The Welsh also make it, and call it *Bara Brith,* which simply means Currant Bread. Don't be deceived, it's more than that."

—Ellis Peters

Welsh Cakes

½ cup butter
4¾ cups self-rising flour
⅓ cup caster sugar
1 tablespoon raisins

1 egg, beaten
Cold water
Flour for dusting

With hands, rub butter into flour. Add sugar and raisins. Add egg. Mix in enough cold water to make a fairly sticky dough, then work it well with heels of hands. Roll out dough, well dusted with flour, to ½-inch thickness. Cut dough into 3-inch rounds. Bake on very lightly greased hot griddle.

"This may be interesting as being peculiar to Wales. I've never seen Welsh cakes outside Wales. These are made on the Welsh farms and keep very well, so there's always something to eat with 'a cup of tea in your hand' for men coming in from hard work. Cakes should be slightly greasy and not need butter."

—Christianna Brand

Crispettes Crippen

1 cup sugar
½ cup butter, softened
1 egg

2 teaspoons cinnamon
2 cups flour
½-1 cup salted almonds, diced

Preheat oven to 275° F. Cream sugar and butter together with an electric mixer, or by hand. Separate egg. Add egg yolk and cinnamon to sugar-butter mixture and beat again. Add flour and mix thoroughly to form a stiff batter. Pat batter into jelly roll pan, approximately 10″ × 18″, smoothing batter into place until it fills pan evenly. With a pastry brush, paint top of dough liberally with slightly beaten egg white. Sprinkle almonds over surface and press lightly into dough. Bake from 60 to 75 minutes, or until top is lightly browned. Do not underbake, as this determines crispness. Cut into squares while still warm. Yield: 5-6 dozen crispettes.

—Elizabeth C. McCoy

Elderberry Blossom Fritters

2 egg yolks	*2 egg whites*
⅔ cup milk	*⅛ teaspoon cream of tartar*
1 tablespoon melted butter	*Elderberry blossoms*
1 cup flour	*Fat for frying*
½ teaspoon salt	

Beat egg yolks well and add milk, butter, flour, and salt. Blend. Beat egg whites and cream of tartar until whites are stiff. Fold into milk mixture. Gather elderberry blossoms with stems about eight-inches long. Wash by dipping into cold water. Dry on paper towels. Using stem as handle, dip blossom in batter and at once plunge into hot fat. Holding stem, flip fritter over when one side is brown. Yield: depends upon number of blossoms used.

"Serve at once with butter and maple syrup, or sprinkle powdered sugar over and eat in your hand. Tiny sausages or crisp bacon may accompany this delicious pioneer dish.

"This early delicacy salutes an ancestress' ingenuity. I like to suppose she had company coming and not much on hand in the way of interesting eatables. Flour and eggs and milk, yes. And for fat, lard left from the winter's hog-slaughter. And there on the edge of the clearing, lifting their lovely heads to the sun, were the elderberry blossoms practically asking to be dipped in batter and then dropped stems up into hot fat to puff up and brown.

"Elderberry Blossom Fritters make a fine excuse for a Sunday brunch. A tray of Bloody Marys and/or Orange Blossoms for the guests to enjoy while dipping Elderberry blossoms in batter and transferring them to the electric frypan. Tiny sausages. A bowl of powdered sugar and maple syrup on the table. Lots of coffee. This is a no-fail party!"

—Amber Dean

English Lemon Curd

½ cup butter
2 cups sugar
Grated rind of 4 lemons

Juice of 4 lemons
6 eggs

Cut butter into small pieces and place with sugar in top of double boiler over boiling water. Add lemon rind and juice. Lightly beat eggs and mix into butter mixture. Stir constantly until consistency of cream—about 20 minutes. Pour into jars and store in refrigerator. Use on toast, between cake layers, or with peanut butter in sandwiches. Yield: 2 cups.

—Patrick O'Keeffe

Norma Gold's Super Eggcream

The eggcreams now being sold in New York City—at what seems like highway-robbery prices to someone who is over twenty-one—may be adequate for visitors from Mongolia. But for a native-born eggcream maven, real eggcreams can only be made in the privacy of one's own occult laboratory.

Start with the syrup. Make your own.

"This recipe is for one 12-ounce glass. Multiply by whatever quantity you want to keep in the back of the refrigerator. One flat teaspoon each of: American cocoa, Dutch cocoa (such as Droste) and Swiss Cocoa (such as Lindt). Add one heaping teaspoon of malted milk powder and two heaping teaspoons of sugar. Mix the dry ingredients thoroughly, then add about a tablespoon of water and an eighth teaspoon of vanilla extract. Mix thoroughly and let stand until

the syrup is smooth and uniform. If necessary, add a bit more water.
Now the technique.

Put the above-noted amount of syrup into a *chilled* 12-ounce glass.
Add 2 ounces of heavy whipping cream (not the ultra-pasteurized
junk). Mix until uniform. Get the *full* syphon (we need maximum
pressure) from the refrigerator and squirt the seltzer *directly* into the
syrup-cream mixture. Rotate the glass to make sure all the syrup is
mixed in (*never* use a spoon, which removes fizz). Fill the glass
three-quarters full. When foam subsides a bit, slowly add enough
seltzer to fill the glass. Now—I didn't want to tell you before, to spare
you the shock, but you have already set up on your lab table a bunch
of opened bottles of your favorite liqueurs: Grand Marnier, Kahlua,
Benedictine, Chartreuse, Creme Yvette (violet), Maraschino, whatever your fancy. Float a drop of two of your choice *on top* of the
eggcream. Quaff the nectar of the gods."

—Herbert Resnicow

Lethal Eggnog

12 egg whites
12 egg yolks
1½ cups sugar, divided
Pinch salt
  1 quart heavy cream, beaten

1 quart milk
1 quart bourbon
1-1½ cups rum
Nutmeg

Beat egg whites until stiff (the whites, not you). Beat in ½ cup sugar and
pinch of salt. Beat egg yolks with remaining cup sugar. Combine and beat.
Beat in cream, then milk. Stir in bourbon, then beat well. Stir in rum.

"This eggnog beats them all. It is even better if you let it "ripen" a week
in your refrigerator. Stir or shake before serving. Garnish with nutmeg. It's for
special occasions, eggnog so rich it's lethal."

—Barbara D'Amato

Pork Liver Cupcakes

(For Felines)

1 pound pork liver	*½ cup wheat germ*
¼ cup salad oil	*Rolled oats*

Open doors and windows. Turn on ventilating fan. Simmer liver in water to cover until tender and repulsively gray. Place in blender with oil, wheat germ and enough rolled oats to make a yukky paste. Freeze individual servings in paper muffin cups. Thaw and remove from paper. Garnish with caviar or whatever. Yield: 12 or more servings (for cats, that is).

"This recipe was developed by the late Antoine Delapierre, chef at the Old Stone Mill in Pickax, for his proposed line of "Fabulous Frozen Foods for Fussy Felines." Readers of *The Cat Who Knew Shakespeare* are aware that the line was never marketed."

—Lilian Jackson Braun

A Message to the Young

It was exactly twenty-nine years ago when, in a frail barque manufactured of happy ignorance and great expectations—or in grandpa's words, spit and coupons—that I set forth on the literary seas, my wife paddling furiously to keep us financially afloat and my wide-eyed young daughter and her pet cat serving as ballast.

That year, 1948, after publication of my maiden mystery, I visited the headquarters of the Mystery Writers of America, signed on as a member, and within a few days attended my first membership meeting. Headquarters, as I recall, was a room somewhere in the middle of the old Gansevoort Meat Market section of Manhattan's West Side, a dingy chamber permeated with an inspiring reek of recently slaughtered carcasses. I also noted at the time that the organization's treasury was kept in a sugar bowl on a shelf in plain view of all; but this, so the then treasurer informed me, represented no risk. Indeed, the only time a thief had been known to invade the premises he had taken no merchandise, but had sympathetically deposited a dollar in the bowl.

The meeting I attended was memorable. Here were not only those awesome camera portraits on book jackets come alive, but made even more awesome by a darkling mood that prevailed. It was the kind of mood that prevails when, far from home, you hear a warning rumble of thunder and suddenly realize you have forgotten your umbrella.

The reasons for it, I gathered that night, were many. The World War II boom in books was over, and the sale of mysteries was below the Plimsoll Line. Television had destroyed the magazine market. Those few intransigents who preferred reading to Uncle Miltie were reading science fiction, not mysteries. Movies were washed up; no more would there be lovely windfalls from them. In brief, as I was informed by a morose and kindly Olympian, this was one hell of a time for anyone to hang up his shingle as a mystery writer.

That was 1948.

Today, three decades later, our headquarters are situated on a treelined street of proper elegance. Our ample funds are stored in a bank. And while the mood at meetings may be volatile, to say the least, it is certainly not darkling. Far from being extinct by now, our organization may mark this as a time when Bullitt and Harper (nee: Archer) affirm on the big screen the vitality of our genre; when the bestseller lists are headed by our people; when the Book of the Month Club has made our anthology one of its selections. It is a time when I could, and did, receive a letter from the director of a University's Center for the Study of Popular Culture which read in part:

We believe that university curricula need to be made, in the tired word, relevant and up-to-date. We think that Popular

Culture—being most of the elements that touch on most of us all the time—should play a more important role in what students study—especially modern mysteries.

Especially modern mysteries. So, all in all, it would seem that this is a fine year for our craft.

—Stanley Ellin
(1978)

Who's Who

JOAN AIKEN, daughter of poet Conrad Aiken, won the 1971 Mystery Writers of America Edgar Award for best juvenile novel for *Nightfall.* Other novels in the same category include *The Spiral Stair, Foul Matter, Mansfield Revisited,* and *Past Eight O'Clock.* (pp. 86, 169)

NORMA AINSWORTH, who died in 1987, was an eminent editor of school-age publications, introducing thousands of young readers to mystery stories. Her own mystery fiction includes *The Ghost at Peaceful End.* (pp. 135–36)

STEVE ALLEN is a well-known television personality and humorist whose books include *Ripoff, Funny People,* and *The Talk Show Murders.* (pp. 223–24)

ISAAC ASIMOV, widely known for his science-fiction novels and stories, has also written much popular mystery fiction including the *Black Widowers* series of short stories. He has written and edited more than 300 fiction and nonfiction books, including *Murder at the A.B.A., Far As Human Eye Could See, The Golden Eye, Azazel,* and the autobiographical *In Joy Still Felt.* (pp. 7–8)

JEAN L. BACKUS often wrote under the name **David Montross,** with *Troika, Traitor's Wife,* and *Fellow Traveller* to her credit. Her short story "The Last Rendezvous" received an Edgar nomination in 1977. She died in 1986. (pp. 139–40)

JOHN BALL won an M.W.A. Edgar Award in 1964 for *In the Heat of the Night,* in which Virgil Tibbs made his first appearance. He is well remembered for his novels *Singapore, Then Came Violence, The Murder Children, Five Pieces of Jade* (an Edgar nominee in 1972), and as editor of *The Mystery Story* and *Cop Cade.* Ball died in 1988. (pp. 110–12)

CATHERINE BARTH was the much-beloved executive secretary of the Mystery Writers of America in the 1950s and 1960s. (pp. 42, 160, 223)

JACQUES BARZUN, outstanding critic and historian, wrote *The Delights of Detection* and (with **W. H. Taylor**) *A Catalogue of Crime,* which received a special M.W.A. award in 1971. (p. 167)

GEORGE BAXT has established a unique reputation for humorous suspense. *A Parade of Cockeyed Creatures* was nominated for an Edgar in 1967. Other novels include *The Tallulah Bankhead Murder, Who's Next?, The Dorothy Parker Murder Case, The Alfred Hitchcock Murder,* and *Strangler's Web.* (p. 97)

JANE BECKMAN is known for her crime short stories, among them, "A Textbook Case" and "Here Comes the Bride." (pp. 25, 53)

D. R. BENSEN has advanced the status of the paperback mystery as both author and editor. He is the author of works such as *Home to the Night, Tempest at Summers End, Nightgleams,*

Tower in the Sea, *Mask of Love* and *Good-Night Irene* as well as numerous shorts in mystery magazines. (pp. 44–45, 165–66)

EVELYN BERCKMAN, concert pianist and composer, wrote *The Crown Estate*, *The Heir of Starvelings*, *The Victorian Album*, *The Nightmare Chase*, *Stalemate*, and *The Evil of Time*, among many other mystery and suspense novels. (p. 139)

GAVIN BLACK, pseudonym for **Oswald Wynd,** born in Tokyo, uses the Orient as background in many of his crime novels, which include *The Golden Cockatrice*, *A Time For Pirates*, *The Bitter Tea*, and *A Big Wind for Summer*. (pp. 148–50)

WILLIAM PETER BLATTY's novel *The Exorcist* made fiction and film script history. Among his other works are *A Shot in the Dark*, *I'll Tell Them I Remember You*, *Twinkle, Twinkle, Killer Kane*, *Legion*, and *The Ninth Configuration*. (p. 87)

ROBERT BLOCH wrote the novel *Psycho*, and many other mystery and suspense novels and stories, radio plays, screenplays, and television plays. You may remember his radio series, *Stay Tuned for Terror*, his stories "Cold Chills" and "Yours Truly, Jack the Ripper," and his novels *Spiderweb* and *American Gothic*. (p. 73)

PAULINE BLOOM, former M.W.A. board member, is a long-established teacher of fiction writing through her Pauline Bloom Workshop for Writers. (pp. 103, 158, 196)

KAGE BOOTON's popular mysteries have included *Quite by Accident*, *Don't Even Whisper*, *Place of Shadows*, *The Toy*, and *Time Running Out*. (p. 190)

CHRISTIANNA BRAND, long one of England's top mystery writers, continues to draw readers after her death in 1988. She earned M.W.A. Edgar nominations for her short stories "Twist for Twist" (1967) and "Poison in the Cup" (1969). Her true crime book *Heaven Knows Who* was nominated in 1960. Her novels include *Death of Jezebel*, *Green for Danger*, and *Death in High Heels*. (pp. 221–22, 258)

LILIAN JACKSON BRAUN has a special affinity for felines. Her mysteries in the "Cat Who. . . ." series have won a devoted following. *The Cat Who Saw Red* was an M.W.A. Edgar nominee in 1986. Others include *The Cat Who Knew Shakespeare*, *The Cat Who Sniffed Glue*, and *The Cat Who Went Underground*. (p. 262)

JON L. BREEN is a mystery critic, novelist, short story writer, and editor. His *Novel Verdicts: A Guide to Courtroom Fiction* (1984) and *What About Murder?* (1981) each won an M.W.A. Edgar. Other works include *Murder California Style*, *Listen for the Click*, and the anthology, *American Murders*. (pp. 49–50)

REX BURNS is a mystery novelist and a professor at the University of Colorado in Denver. He won a first novel M.W.A. Edgar in 1975 for *The Alvarez Journal*. Since then, he has written *Speak for the Dead*, *Strip Search*, and *The Avenging Angel*. (p. 54)

CARLETON CARPENTER, actor and mystery writer, has a number of novels to his credit including *Cat Got Your Tongue?*, *Deadhead*, *Games Murderers Play*, *Only Her Hairdresser Knew . . .* , and *Sleight of Hand*. (p. 247)

PHILIPPA CARR (Victoria Holt, Jean Plaidy, Eleanor Hibbert), has achieved international success under all four names, along with several others. As Philippa Carr, her titles include *The Miracle at St. Bruno's*, *The Lion Triumphant*, and *The Witch from the Sea*. (p. 214)

HERON CARVIC, who died in 1980, wrote the popular Miss Seeton series. Some titles are *Picture Miss Seeton* which was nominated for an M.W.A. Edgar in 1968, *Miss Seeton Draws the Line*, and *Odds on Miss Seeton*. (pp. 40–41)

VERA CASPARY will forever be remembered for *Laura*, a novel, a play, a film, and a haunting melody. Before her death in 1987, Caspary had gone on to write many mystery novels, plays, and screenplays. Her autobiography, *The Secrets of Grown-Ups*, was nominated for an Edgar in 1979.   (pp. 112–14)

THOMAS CHASTAIN has written a series of New York City police procedurals starring Max Kauffman. They include the highly regarded *Nightscape*, and *Pandora's Box, 911, Vital Statistics, High Voltage*, and *The Diamond Exchange*. His *Who Killed the Robins Family?* was a bestseller, and his collaboration with Helen Hayes produced *Where the Truth Lies*. Chastain is the 1989–90 president of The Mystery Writers of America.   (p. 212)

MARY HIGGINS CLARK is a suspense-writing phenomenon. Her first novel, *Where Are the Children?*, was a bestseller, as have been *A Stranger Is Watching, The Cradle Will Fall, A Cry in the Night, Stillwatch, Weep No More, My Lady*, and *While My Pretty One Sleeps*. Clark was 1987–88 president of The Mystery Writers of America, and chairman of the Fourth International Crime Writers Congress.   (p. 43)

MOLLY COCHRAN collaborated with her husband, **Warren Murphy,** in the 1984 M.W.A. Edgar-winning paperback novel, *Grandmaster*, and contributed to the collaborative novel *Caribbean Blues*. Their new novel is entitled *The Temple Dogs*.   (pp. 196–97)

VIRGINIA COFFMAN is highly regarded in the field of romantic suspense with more than eighty novels. Among them are *The Dark Palazzo, The House at Sandalwood, The Stalking Terror*, and *The Ice Forest*.   (p. 19)

STANLEY COHEN's first novel, *Taking Gary Feldman*, won an M.W.A. Edgar nomination in 1970. He followed that achievement with the novels *The Diane Game, 330 Park, Tell Us, Jerry Silver*, and *Angel Face*.   (p. 202)

MAX ALLAN COLLINS was nominated for an M.W.A. Edgar for his critical work *One Lonely Knight: Mickey Spillane's Mike Hammer*. Combining mystery and comic strip, Collins has written *Dick Tracy* since 1977. His many hard-boiled novels include *Primary Target, Bait Money, Fly Paper, Kill Your Darlings, The Silent Scream, Neon Mirage*, and *Shadow of a Tiger*.   (p. 187)

MICHAEL COLLINS (see **DENNIS LYNDS**)

MOLLY COSTAIN, daughter of famed *Saturday Evening Post* editor Tom Costain, is the wife of crime expert **Howard Haycraft.** She has written many historical novels.   (p. 133)

FRANCES CRANE wrote a series of mystery novels involving the husband and wife team Pat and Jean Abbott. All the titles used a "color" identification: *Death-Wish Green, Murder in Bright Red, The Indigo Necklace, Black Cypress*, and so on, for more than twenty titles throughout the 1940s and 1950s.   (p. 189)

JAMES CROSS (see **HUGH JONES PARRY**)

HILDA CUSHING was a short-story writer. "A Flower for Her Grave" and "She Is Not My Mother" have been anthologized. Cushing died in 1987.   (p. 236)

ROALD DAHL is a double M.W.A. Edgar winner for Short Stories for "The Landlady" (1959) and "Someone Like You" (1953). His third Edgar in 1979 was for "Skin," an episode in *Roald Dahl's Tales of the Unexpected* television series. Beyond mystery, his best-known works include *My Uncle Oswald, Switch Bitch, Willie Wonka and the Chocolate Factory* and *James and the Giant Peach*.   (p. 65)

MAUREEN DALY's bestseller *Seventeenth Summer* endeared her to generations of young women. She was married to the late **William P. McGivern,** a noted mystery novelist and past president of M.W.A. Daly now writes short mystery fiction. (p. 52)

BARBARA D'AMATO's novels include *The Hands of Healing Murder*, and *On My Honor*. She also writes musical comedy scripts and lyrics; *RSVP Broadway* ran eight months in Chicago. D'Amato writes a regular column for *Mystery Scene*. (pp. 157, 235, 261)

JEAN DARLING was one of the original "Our Gang" movie kids. After a long acting career, she turned to writing mystery fiction. Many of her stories have appeared in *Ellery Queen's Mystery Magazine*. "The Matchstick Hut" appears in the 1988 M.W.A. anthology, *Distant Danger*. (pp. 190, 197–200)

AVRAM DAVIDSON won a best short-story Edgar for his "Affair of the Lahore Cantonment" and a nomination for "Crazy Old Lady." His "Business Must Be Picking Up" has also attracted praise. (pp. 42, 244–45)

DOROTHY SALISBURY DAVIS is a Grand Master of mystery and a past president of M.W.A. She is equally proficient in the novel and the short-story form. Davis's Edgar nominations include *Where the Dark Streets Go, God Speed the Night, The Pale Betrayer, A Gentleman Called*, "Old Friends," and "The Purple Is Everything." Her Julie Hayes series includes *A Death in the Life, Scarlet Night, Lullaby of Murder*, and *The Habit of Fear*. (pp. 117, 192)

AMBER DEAN has seventeen mystery titles to her credit, among them *Dead Man's Float, Be Home by Eleven, Bullet Proof*, and *Something for the Birds*. Dean died in 1985. (pp. 152–53, 229, 259)

LEN DEIGHTON's crime novels are world famous, and several have been made into films. He has, however, also written cookbooks and dining commentary. His novels include *The Ipcress File, Funeral in Berlin* (a 1965 Edgar nominee), *Billion Dollar Brain, Spy Hook*, and *Mexico Set*. His cookbooks include *Action Cook Book* and *Oú Est Le Garlic; or Len Deighton's French Cook Book*. (pp. 99–100)

LILLIAN de la TORRE, an M.W.A. past president, writes cookbooks (*The 60-Minute Chef*), as well as historic crime novels, stories, and plays. Her full-length fiction includes *Elizabeth Is Missing*, and *The Heir of Douglas;* her true crime book *The Truth About Belle Gunness* earned her an Edgar nomination in 1955. Her several collections of stories about *Dr. Sam: Johnson, Detector* continue in popularity. Among her plays, *Goodbye, Miss Lizzie Borden* chronicles a famous historic murder case. She also writes under the name **Lillian Bueno McCue.** (pp. 27, 31–37, 184, 207, 251)

PETER DICKINSON won M.W.A. Edgar nominations for his novels *The Glass-Sided Ants' Nest* and *The Old English Peep Show*. Among his other mystery novels are *The Lizard in the Cup, Death of a Unicorn, The Poison Oracle*, and *King and Joker*. (pp. 112, 128–29)

DORIS MILES DISNEY wrote forty-seven mysteries in a career that spanned more than thirty years. Her series characters were Jeff DiMarco, David Madden, and Jim O'Neill. Her first book, *A Compound for Death*, appeared in 1943, and her last, *Winifred*, in 1976. In the years between, some of her better-known titles were *The Magic Grandfather, Dark Lady*, and *Do Not Fold, Spindle, or Mutilate*. Disney died in 1976. (pp. 213–14)

HILDEGARDE DOLSON began writing mysteries in 1971 after establishing a reputation as a novelist, juvenile, and nonfiction writer. Her series character, Lucy Ramsdale, was an artist and accomplished cook. Dolson's four mystery titles are *To Spite Her Face* (an Edgar nominee in 1971), *A Dying Fall*, *Please Omit Funeral*, and *Beauty Sleep*, which was published four years before her death in 1981. (p. 77)

DOROTHY DUNNETT's popular "Dolly" series features international portrait painter and spy Johnson Johnson. Some titles in the series are *Dolly and the Bird of Paradise*, *Dolly and the Nanny Bird*, *Dolly and the Starry Bird*. The "Dolly" of all the titles is Johnson's yacht. (pp. 101–02)

MIGNON G. EBERHART, an M.W.A. Grand Master and past president, received a Special Award in 1978 on the fiftieth anniversary of her first crime novel, *The Patient in Room 18*. A recent sampling of her long list of titles includes *Next of Kin*, *Family Affair*, *Casa Madrone*, *The Bayou Road*, and *Nine O'Clock Tide*. Her many short stories have appeared in magazines, collections, and anthologies. (pp. 80–81, 221, 249–50)

R. E. ECKELS is a widely read author of mystery short fiction, one example of which is "Sufficient Unto the Day." (pp. 245–46)

LESLIE EGAN (see **ELIZABETH LININGTON**)

AARON ELKINS is the author of *Fellowship of Fear*, and *The Dark Place* featuring the anthropologist Gideon Oliver. His newest book, *Old Bones*, won a 1988 Edgar for the best novel. *Curses!*, a fourth Gideon Oliver novel, will be published this year. Elkins is an anthropologist and has been a professional boxer. (pp. 68, 234)

STANLEY ELLIN, M.W.A. Grand Master and past president, wrote an unforgettable first story, "The Specialty of the House," which offers a very strange dining experience. He went on to win two Edgars ("The Blessington Method" and "The House Party") and four additional nominations for his stories. He was equally successful with his novels; *The Eighth Circle* won an Edgar in 1958, and *The Valentine Estate* was nominated in 1968. *The Dark Fantastic* (1983) and *Very Old Money* (1984) were his last novels before his death. (pp. 262–64)

JULIE ELLIS wrote many paperback suspense novels before moving on to more serious hardcover fiction. Her popular favorites include *Savage Oaks*, *Eden*, *Rich Is Best*, *The Hampton Heritage*, *The Only Sin*, and *Glorious Morning*. (p. 193)

ELIZABETH FERRARS also writes her mystery thrillers and short stories as **E. X. Ferrars.** With more than fifty novels to her credit, just a few of her titles include *Zero at the Bone*, *The Seven Sleepers*, *The Pretty Pink Shroud*, *Blood Flies Upward*, and *Root of all Evil*. (pp. 256–57)

ROBERT L. FISH, a past president of M.W.A., died in 1981. In recognition of his dedication to helping young writers, M.W.A. and his widow, Mame Fish, present an annual Robert Fish Award to the year's best first mystery short story. Fish received an Edgar in 1962 for his first novel, *The Fugitive*, and another for his short story "Moonlight Gardener," and two additional nominations. Additional titles include *Pursuit*, *The Murder League*, *Always Kill a Stranger*, and *The Hochmann Miniatures*. He also wrote as **Robert L. Pike.** (pp. 21, 24)

JOAN FLEMING, who died in 1980, wrote many psychological crime novels, among them *Midnight Hag*, *Death of a Sardine*, *No Bones About It*, *You Won't Let Me Finish*, *Screams from a Penny Dreadful*, and *Every Inch a Lady*. Her juvenile mysteries include *Dickie Brown and the Zaga Bog*, *Mulberry Hall*, *The Riddle in the River*, and *Button Jugs*. (pp. 226–27) two additional nominations. Additional titles include *Pursuit, The Murder League, Always Kill a Stranger,* and *The Hochmann Miniatures.* He also wrote as **Robert L. Pike.** (pp. 21, 24)

JOAN FLEMING, who died in 1980, wrote many psychological crime novels, among them *Midnight Hag, Death of a Sardine, No Bones About It, You Won't Let Me Finish, Screams from a Penny Dreadful,* and *Every Inch a Lady.* Her juvenile mysteries include *Dickie Brown and the Zaga Bog, Mulberry Hall, The Riddle in the River,* and *Button Jugs.* (pp. 226–27)

LUCILLE FLETCHER won a Special Edgar for her celebrated radio play, *Sorry, Wrong Number.* Other radio plays are *My Client Curley* and *The Hitch-Hiker.* Her crime novels include *Mirror Image, Blindfold, . . . and Presumed Dead, The Strange Blue Yawl, The Girl in Cabin B54,* and *Eighty Dollars to Stamford.* (pp. 74, 77)

STANTON FORBES, who also writes mystery fiction as **Tobias Wells** and **D. E. Forbes,** received an Edgar nomination for her 1963 novel *Grieve for the Past.* As Forbes, she has written, among others, *Terror Touches Me, Bury Me in Gold Lamé, Some Poisoned by Their Wives,* and *If Laurel Shot Hardy, the World Would End.* As Wells, her titles include *Hark, Hark, The Watchdogs Bark, How to Kill a Man, A Creature Was Stirring,* and *The Foo Dog.* (p. 72)

FREDERICK FORSYTH won an Edgar in 1971 with his celebrated thriller *The Day of the Jackal,* and another for his 1982 short story, "There Are No Snakes in Ireland." His "Used in Evidence" was nominated in 1979. Other Forsyth bestsellers have been *The Odessa File, The Dogs of War, The Devil's Alternative, The Fourth Protocol,* and *The Negotiator.* (pp. 142–43)

LUCY FREEMAN, a past president of M.W.A., specializes in psychoanalytic writing. Both her fiction and her nonfiction often deal with the psychology of crime. Some of her titles are *Before I Kill More, Fight Against Fears, The Sorrow and the Fury, Who Is Sylvia?, Too Deep for Tears,* and *What Do Women Want?* She edited the M.W.A. anthology, *Killers of the Mind.* (pp. 69, 101)

MICHAEL GILBERT, an M.W.A. Grand Master, was one of the founders of the British Crime Writers Association. Gilbert has successfully combined his career as a solicitor with his prolific mystery writing. His novel *The Black Seraphim* received an Edgar nomination in 1984. Series characters Inspector Hazelrigg and Patrick Petrella figure in many of his books. Titles include *Smallbone Deceased, The Killing of Katie Steelstock, The Crack in the Cup, The Country-House Burglar,* and *End-Game.* (pp. 66–68, 203)

DOROTHY GILMAN's Mrs. Emily Pollifax has appeared in a number of novels. *The Unexpected Mrs. Pollifax,* was the first of the series, followed by *A Palm for Mrs. Pollifax, Mrs. Pollifax on Safari,* and others. Non-series fiction includes *The Clairvoyant Countess, A Nun in the Closet,* and *The Tightrope Walker.* (pp. 254–55)

JOE GORES, a past president of M.W.A., won Edgars in 1969 for both his first novel, *A Time for Predators,* and his short story "Goodbye, Pops." *No Immunity for Murder,* an episode in the *Kojak* TV series, was awarded an Edgar in 1975. In 1986, his novel *Come Morning* was a nominee. His series novels, *Dead Skip, Final Notice,* and *Gone, No Forwarding,* feature Dan Kearney Associates, a team of auto repossessors. Other crime novels include *Interface* and *Hammett: A Novel.* He has written several screenplays and many short stories. (pp. 122–23)

RON GOULART is prolific in his work as well as his pseudonyms, but much of his mystery

Twice, Hitchhike to Hell, Murder in the Raw, and *One for the Road*. She has also collaborated with **Arthur Moore** under the pseudonyms of **Adam Hamilton** and **Van Saxon**. (pp. 129, 170)

MIRIAM-ANN HAGEN, who died in 1984, was the sister of Grand Master Aaron Marc Stein. She was an accomplished cook as well as a mystery writer. Her Hortense Clinton novels include *Plant Me Now, Dig Me Later*, and *Murder—But Natch*. (pp. 88–89, 180, 227–28)

MILTON HALPERN was for twenty years the Chief Medical Examiner of New York City. He participated in many of the most celebrated criminal cases of the century, and wrote the classic textbook on forensic pathology. His popular book *Autopsy* outlines the work of the Medical Examiners office and some of his famous cases. In 1964, he received a special award from M.W.A. Dr. Halpern died in 1977. (p. 76)

JOSEPH HANSEN occupies a special niche in detective fiction for the strength of his short stories and for his homosexual detective David Branstetter. The Brandstetter series includes *Fadeout, Death Claims, Troublemaker, Skinflick, Gravedigger*, and *Nightwork*. His story "The Anderson Boy" was nominated for an Edgar in 1983. He also writes as **James Colton**. (pp. 132–33)

JOYCE HARRINGTON received an Edgar in 1972 for her first short story, "The Purple Shroud." She has since received three additional short-story nominations for "The Au Pair Girl," "Night Crawlers," and "The Cabin in the Hollow." Her novels are *No One Knows My Name, Family Reunion*, and *Dreemz of the Night*. (pp. 28–29)

HOWARD HAYCRAFT, a past president of M.W.A., received an Edgar in 1947 for Outstanding Mystery Criticism, and in 1974, a Special Edgar for his "distinguished contribution to mystery criticism and scholarship." His *Murder for Pleasure:. The Life and Times of the Detective Story* (1941) was the first book about detective fiction as a literary form to be published in the United States. (p. 133)

PATRICIA HIGHSMITH's first novel, *Strangers on a Train*, was nominated for an Edgar and became a celebrated Hitchcock film. *The Talented Mr. Ripley* also received an Edgar nomination in 1955 and France's *Grand Prix de Littérature Policière*. The Tom Ripley series went on to include *Ripley Underground, Ripley's Game*, and *The Boy Who Followed Ripley*. *The Blunderer* was listed among Julian Symons' *World's 100 Best Mysteries*, and her short story "The Terrapin" was also nominated for an Edgar. (p. 243)

EDWARD D. HOCH, a past president of M.W.A., undoubtedly holds the world's record for short-story writing. The major series characters in his stories are Nick Velvet, Simon Ark, Dr. Sam Hawthorne, Captain Leopold, and Rand of the Department of Concealed Communications. "The Oblong Room," a Leopold story, won an Edgar in 1967, and "The Most Dangerous Man Alive" was nominated in 1980. His novels include *The Shattered Raven, The Transvection Machine, The Fellowship of the Hand*, and *The Frankenstein Factory*. Hoch is the editor of the annual *Year's Best Mystery and Suspense Stories*. (p. 176)

VICTORIA HOLT (see also **PHILIPPA CARR**), the pen name of Eleanor Hibbert, is a worldwide bestseller. Her best-loved titles include *The Bride of Pendorric, The Mistress of Mellyn, The Judas Kiss, The Silk Vendetta, The India Fan, The Demon Lover, The Mask of the Enchantress*, and *Secret for a Nightingale*. (pp. 150–51)

JANE HORNING has compiled *The Mystery Lover's Book of Quotations.*

DOROTHY B. HUGHES, an M.W.A. Grand Master and past president, received an Edgar in 1950 for Outstanding Mystery Criticism. She has been reviewing crime fiction since the 1930's for several newspapers including the *Los Angeles Times* and the *Albuquerque Tribune.* Three of her mystery novels, *The Fallen Sparrow, Ride the Pink Horse,* and *In a Lonely Place,* have been made into major films. Her 1963 novel *The Expendable Man* and her 1978 nonfiction book *Erle Stanley Gardner: The Case of the Real Perry Mason* were both nominated for Edgars. (pp. 55, 164)

MARGARET S. HUNT is a writer of short magazine fiction, and has also written a student guide to anthropology. (p. 132)

R. R. IRVINE has twice been nominated for a paperback Edgar, with *Freeze Frame* and *Jump Cut.* Other novels are *The Face Out Front* and *Horizontal Hold.* (p. 252)

FRED JARVIS (a.k.a. **Fritz Gordon**) is a music critic who writes mystery in a musical vein. His titles include *Murder at the Met, Divas,* and *Tonight They Die to Mendelsohn.* (pp. 75, 156)

VERONICA PARKER JOHNS wrote a number of mystery novels and short stories, including *Murder by the Day, The Singing Widow,* and *Shady Doings.* From 1964 until her death in 1988, she owned and operated Seashells Unlimited, a unique specialty shop where she dealt in and dispensed expert knowledge about seashells from all the world's oceans. (pp. 62–65)

VELDA JOHNSTON'S long list of romantic suspense novels has achieved wide popularity. Just a few of her titles are *Voices in the Night, The Other Karen, The Fateful Summer, The Stone Maiden, A Presence in an Empty Room, The People from the Sea, The Etruscan Smile,* and *A Room With Dark Mirrors.* (p. 138)

JOAN KAHN'S reputation as a mystery editor knows no peer. She has discovered and nurtured many of our foremost mystery writers. She is editor of a number of crime anthologies, including *The Edge of the Chair, Skeleton Keys,* and *Chilling and Killing.* In 1984, she received M.W.A.'s Ellery Queen Award and in 1989 a Special Edgar for her lifetime achievement in the mystery. (pp. 164, 181)

STEPHEN KING has been acknowledged as America's foremost horror writer. Many of his books have been made into popular movies. A list of his titles is a list of bestsellers: *Salem's Lot, The Dead Zone, The Eyes of the Dragon, Firestarter, Carrie, Night Shift, The Shining, Christine, Pet Sematary, Misery, The Dark Tower, The Tommyknockers,* and others. (pp. 254)

TABITHA KING, wife of the horror-suspense author Stephen King, writes herself in somewhat similar vein. Her early novel *Small World* appeared on bestseller lists at the time of its publication. Others are *The Trap* and *Caretakers.* (p. 204)

FLETCHER KNEBEL, whose Washington newspaper column *Potomac Fever* is widely syndicated, wrote (with **Charles Bailey**) the bestseller *Seven Days in May.* His other thrillers include *The Night of Camp David, Trespass, The Zinzin Road,* and *The Bottom Line.* (p. 166)

J. J. LAMB'S series character, Zack Rolfe, has appeared in *The Chinese Straight, Losers Take All,* and *A Nickel Jackpot.* (p. 170)

JANE LANGTON'S New England mysteries feature detective-scholar Homer Kelly. *Emily Dickinson Is Dead* was nominated for an Edgar in 1984. Other titles include *The Transcendental Murder, Dark Nantucket Noon, The Memorial Hall Murder, Murder at the Gardner,* and *Natural*

Enemy. Langton also writes fiction for children; *The Diamond in the Window* was nominated for an Edgar in 1962. (pp. 20–21)

CHARLES LARSON's first novel, *Someone's Death*, was nominated for an Edgar in 1973. It was followed by *Matthew's Hand*, and *Muir's Blood*. (pp. 171–72)

WARNER LAW won an Edgar in 1968 for best short story with "The Man Who Fooled the World." He died in 1979, but his widow, Carol Russell Law, continues writing in the mystery field. (pp. 60, 230–32)

RICHARD LAYMON's novel *The Cellar* appeared in 1980. (pp. 17–18)

ELSIE LEE wrote more than thirty mystery novels in the 1960s and 1970s. She is known, too, for her many books on cooking, including *The Bachelor's Cookbook*, *Easy Gourmet Cooking*, and *Party Cookbook*. Her mysteries include *The Blood Red Oscar*, *The Nabob's Widow*, *Season of Evil*, and *The Wicked Guardian*. (pp. 25, 71–72, 74, 81–82)

GEORGE deLUCENAY LEON is a wine expert and lecturer who writes mystery short stories. His nonfiction book *911* details aspects of police procedure. (p. 206)

CONSTANCE LEONARD's mysteries include *The Other Maritha*, *Steps to Nowhere*, *Hostage in Illyria*, and *Shadows of a Ghost*. She also writes for young readers. (pp. 57–58)

ELMORE LEONARD won an Edgar for *La Brava* in 1983, and was nominated in 1982 for *Split Images* and for *The Switch* in 1978. Other novels include *The Big Bounce*, *The Moonshine War*, *Fifty-Two Pickup*, *Swag*, *Stick*, *Glitz*, and most recently, *Killshot*. He has written screenplays for *The Moonshine War*, *Joe Kidd*, *Mr. Majestyk*, and *Stick*. A few of his westerns are *Valdez Is Coming* and *Gunsights*. (pp. 116–17)

IRA LEVIN's first novel, *A Kiss Before Dying*, won an Edgar in 1953. But it was his second novel, *Rosemary's Baby*, that became a popular sensation and a film classic. It, too, was nominated for an Edgar. Levin's *The Stepford Wives* and *The Boys from Brazil* were also made into movies. A second Edgar was awarded to his play *Deathtrap*; other plays include *No Time for Sergeants*, *Critic's Choice*, and *Drat! The Cat!* (p. 158)

HELEN LILLIE's mystery novels include *Call Down the Sky* and *The Listening Silence*. Born in Scotland in 1915, she writes a regular Washington Letter for the Glasgow *Herald*. (p. 56)

ELIZABETH LININGTON wrote as **Anne Blaisdell, Lesley Egan, Egan O'Neill,** and **Dell Shannon.** Her series characters include the enormously popular Detective Luis Mendoza, Sergeant Ivor Maddox, Jesse Falkenstein, and Vic Varallo. Before her recent death, she had completed more than seventy titles, among them *The Hunters and the Hunted*, and *Little Boy Lost* (both as Lesley Egan), *Murder Most Strange* and *Destiny of Death* as Dell Shannon, and *Skeletons in the Closet* as Elizabeth Linington. Anne Blaisdell's *Nightmare* was nominated for an M.W.A. Edgar in 1961, as were Dell Shannon's *Knave of Hearts* in 1962 and *Case Pending* in 1960. (p. 51)

RICHARD LOCKRIDGE (with his first wife, **Frances Lockridge**) created the Mr. and Mrs. North series, of which there are over twenty-five adventures. The Lockridges's other series novels feature Inspector Heimrich, Nathan Shapiro, and Bernard Simmons. In 1962, Richard and Frances Lockridge were awarded a Special Edgar in honor of their fiftieth novel, *The Ticking Clock*. In 1945, they were nominated for their radio series, *Mr. and Mrs. North*. They were co-presidents of M.W.A. in 1960. Frances Lockridge died in 1963. Lockridge married **Hildegarde Dolson** in 1965. Lockridge died in 1982. (pp. 103–05)

DAVID LOTH, criminology writer, published *Crime in the Suburbs, Chief Justice, Crime Lab,* and *Public Plunder.* He also wrote many fine biographies. (pp. 160–62)

GAVIN LYALL's mysteries appear both in his native England and in the United States. He has twice received the Crime Writers Association Silver Dagger. His titles include *The Most Dangerous Game, Midnight Plus One, Blame the Dead, Judas Country, The Secret Servant,* and *The Conduct of Major Maxim.* (pp. 229–30, 240–42)

DENNIS LYNDS (*a.k.a.* William Arden, Nick Carter, Michael Collins, John Crowe, Carl Dekker, John Douglas, Maxwell Grant, Mark Sadler) writes the Dan Fortune series of novels and stories, and a host of mystery and suspense yarns, including a juvenile series. One of his recent Michael Collins books is *Red Rosa,* and his first novel, *Act of Fear,* won an Edgar in 1967. (pp. 151–52)

DANA LYON wrote a number of mystery novels and short stories. Among her books are *It's My Own Funeral* and *The Frightened Child.* Lyon died in 1982. (pp. 83–84)

NAN and IVAN LYONS together wrote the widely known *Someone Is Killing the Great Chefs of Europe,* followed by *The President Is Coming to Lunch.* (pp. 142, 253)

HELEN McCLOY's first mystery novel, *Dance of Death,* was published in 1938. With it, she established her series character, Dr. Basil Willing, who appeared in most of her novels until the early 1970s, including *Mr. Splitfoot* and *Two-Thirds of a Ghost.* More recent non-series books are *The Smoking Mirror, The Imposter, The Changeling Conspiracy,* and *Minotaur Country.* An early past president of M.W.A., McCloy and her husband, **Brett Halliday,** received an Edgar for outstanding mystery criticism in 1953 and an Edgar nomination in 1951 as editors of *Twenty Great Tales of Murder.* (pp. 131, 215–18)

JAMES McCLURE's South African mysteries, featuring police Lt. Kramer and Sgt. Zondi, have won a devoted following in the United States. His first novel, *The Steam Pig,* won a Gold Dagger from the British Crime Writers Association. It was followed by *The Caterpillar Cop, The Gooseberry Fool, Snake, The Sunday Hangman, The Blood of an Englishman,* and *The Artful Egg.* His non-series novel, *Rogue Eagle,* received a Crime Writers Association Silver Dagger. (pp. 100–01)

ELIZABETH C. McCOY worked with the U.S. missile and space programs, and called herself "a confirmed closet fiction writer." But that was before she was published with such short tales as "Henry's Eighth" and "Heart's Desire." A winner of the Poetry Society of Virginia Award, she has also written television dramas, many of them suspense plays. (p. 258)

THOMAS McDADE received a special Edgar in 1961 for *Annals of Murder,* a collection of true American crimes from Colonial times to 1900. McDade is a lawyer who formerly worked for the FBI. (pp. 24, 208–10)

GREGORY MCDONALD won an Edgar in 1974 for his first novel, *Fletch.* The popular "Fletch" series continued with *Confess, Fletch* (another Edgar winner), and with *Fletch's Fortune, Fletch and the Widow Bradley, Fletch's Moxie, Fletch and the Man Who,* and *Carioca Fletch.* His other mystery novels include the "Flynn" series, and *Who Took Toby Rinaldi.* Mcdonald is a past president of M.W.A. (pp. 41, 43, 44, 45, 54)

JOHN D. MacDONALD wrote mystery fiction for more than thirty-five years. In 1964, he began his acclaimed Travis McGee series with *The Deep Blue Goodbye.* McGee's colorful adventures continued for the next twenty years, with such titles as *The Turquoise Lament, The Dreadful Lemon Sky, The Green Ripper, Free Fall in Crimson,* and *Cinnamon Skin.* He received the M.W.A. Grand Master Award in 1971 and was a past president of the organization. MacDonald died in 1986. (pp. 88, 90–91)

PATRICIA McGERR's series novels and stories featuring Selena Mead, began in 1963 and continued through the early 1980s. She also wrote a number of non-series mystery novels and stories beginning in 1947. A few of her books are *Stranger with My Face, Legacy of Danger, Is There a Traitor in the House?* McGerr died in 1985. (p. 141)

WILLIAM P. McGIVERN was primarily a crime novelist and screenplay writer, although he wrote some short fiction and, with his wife **Maureen Daly,** an account of their travels abroad. His first novel, *But Death Runs Faster,* appeared in 1948; his final two books, *A Matter of Honor* and *War Games,* were published after his death in 1982. In the years between, McGivern wrote *Caprifoil* and *Night of the Juggler* (for both of which he also wrote the screenplay), *Soldiers of '44, Lie Down, I Want to Talk to You, Odds Against Tomorrow, The Big Heat,* and many others. He was a past president of M.W.A. (p. 201)

MILT MACHLIN has written all kinds of fiction and nonfiction. In the mystery field, his three books with **Robin Moore** are *The Family Man, French Connection II,* and *The Set-Up.* (pp. 234–35)

JAMES McKIMMEY has written a number of novels and short fiction since the early 1960s. Some of his titles are *The Man with the Gloved Hand, A Circle in the Water,* and *24 Hours to Kill.* (p. 233)

GARY MADDEROM interrupted a career in publishing to produce such crime novels as *The Four-Chambered Villain* and *The Jewels That Got Away.* (pp. 18, 108–09)

LEO MARGULIES, deftly assisted by his wife **CYLVIA,** was a giant among detective story editors. In pulp fiction's era, he launched many major writers. In 1975, he received a special award as editor of *Mike Shayne's Mystery Magazine.* Margulies died in 1985. (p. 53)

STEPHEN MARLOWE's Chester Drum series includes such titles as *Francesca, Jeopardy Is My Job, Manhunt Is My Mission, Peril Is My Pay,* and many others. Non-series mysteries include *The Valkyrie Encounter, The Cawthorn Journals,* among others. (pp. 126–27, 140)

WHIT MASTERSON is the best-known pseudonym of **Robert Wade,** a prolific author who has been writing novels and short stories since 1946 (with **Bill Miller** until 1961). His more recent titles include *The Slow Gallows, Hunter of the Blood, The Man with Two Clocks, The Undertaker Wind, Why She Cries, I Do Not Know,* and *The Gravy Train.* As **Wade Miller,** the partners were nominated for an Edgar in 1955 for their story "Invitation to an Accident." (p. 89–90)

CLAYTON MATTHEWS (*see also* **Patricia Matthews**) has had a multi-faceted career as actor, carnival barker, animal trainer, and author of paperback mysteries. A few of his titles are *The Negotiator, The Big Score, Nylon Nightmare,* and *The Mendoza File.* (pp. 184–85)

PATRICIA MATTHEWS and her husband, **Clayton Matthews,** have formed the writing team known as **Patricia Matthews.** By herself, she has written a long series of romantic bestsellers. Together, the Matthews have written such recent suspense successes as *The Crystal Window, Horror at Gull House, House of Candles,* and *Mist of Evil.* (p. 211)

MARTIN MEYERS' paperback mysteries in the Patrick Hardy series include *Spy and Die,*

Reunion for Death, Red Is for Murder, Kiss and Kill, and *Hung Up to Die.*   (pp. 129–30, 203)

BARBARA MICHAELS (Elizabeth Peters) is one of today's foremost writers of romantic suspense novels. Under her own name, **Barbara Mertz,** she is a distinguished writer on archaeology. Michaels' books include *Search the Shadows, The Grey Beginning, The Master of Blacktower, Smoke and Mirrors, Shattered Silk, Wings of the Falcon,* and many others.   (p. 178)

PATRICIA MOYES, novelist and short story writer, was once a *Vogue* magazine editor, and worked for eight years for Peter Ustinov Productions, Ltd. Her first novel, *Dead Men Don't Ski,* appeared in 1959 and featured detective team Henry and Emmy Tibbett, as have all her later books. *Many Deadly Returns* was nominated for an Edgar in 1970. Other titles include *A Six-Letter Word for Death, Angel Death, Who Is Simon Warwick?, The Coconut Killings,* and *Season of Snows and Sins.*   (pp. 48–49, 94–95, 211, 212)

WARREN MURPHY (*see also* **COCHRAN**), with wife **Molly Cochran,** won an Edgar in 1984 for *Grandmaster.* Their newest title is *The Temple Dogs.* The following year, Murphy soloed with an Edgar for *Pigs Get Fat.* In 1983, his paperback *Trace* was nominated. Since 1971, Murphy has written the series *Remo Williams, The Destroyer,* mainly with his partner, Richard Sapir. As sole author, Murphy has written *And 47 Miles of Rope, Lucifer's Weekend, Subways Are for Killing,* and many others.

PATRICIA MUSE is the author of *Eight Candles Glowing.*   (p. 26)

JOAN LOWERY NIXON has won three Edgars for her juvenile mysteries—*The Other Side of Dark* (1986), *The Seance* (1980), and *The Kidnapping of Christian Lattimore* (1979). She has also received two nominations for *The Ghosts of Now* (1984), and *The Mysterious Red Tape Gang* (1974). Her latest is *Secret, Silent Screams.* She has generously shared her knowledge of the field in her textbook *Writing Mysteries for Young People.*   (pp. 247–49)

BARBARA NORVILLE is the author of the highly respected text *Writing the Modern Mystery.* Starting her editorial career at the helm of Inner Sanctum Mysteries, she created her own book line, Black Bat Mysteries. Edgar-winning authors who have worked with her include Robert L. Fish, Ed McBain, Gregory Mcdonald, Emma Lathen, and Dorothy Uhnak. Over 150 successful mystery writers made their first sales under her guidance.   (p. 202)

SHANNON O'CORK, wife of novelist **Hillary Waugh,** specializes in the adventures of T. T. Baldwin, a female sports photographer. Her titles include *End of the Line, Sports Freak, Hell Bent for Heaven.*   (p. 70)

LENORE GLEN OFFORD for many years wrote the mystery book column for the *San Francisco Chronicle.* Her own mysteries, which appeared from 1938 through 1961, include *Murder on Russian Hill, Clues to Burn, Skeleton Key, The Glass Mask, The Smiling Tiger, Walking Shadow, . . . My True Love Lies,* and *The Girl in the Belfry,* which was nominated for an Edgar in 1955. She received a Special Edgar in 1951 for outstanding mystery criticism.   (p. 179)

PATRICK O'KEEFFE was the author of many short magazine stories, a majority of them with the salty sea background from his years as a wireless operator on various ships.   (pp. 251, 260)

EDITH PARGETER as **Ellis Peters** won an Edgar in 1962 for her novel *Death and the Joyful Woman,* the first of the Felse family series. After a number of Felse novels, Peters began the Brother Cadfael series, which includes *The Pilgrim of Hate, Dead Man's Ransom, The Devil's*

Novice, The Sanctuary Sparrow, and many others. As **Edith Pargeter,** she has written *This Rough Magic, A Bloody Field by Shrewsbury, The Hounds of Sunset, A Means of Grace*, and much more. (pp. 159, 183, 238, 257)

PERCY SPURLARK PARKER has written *Good Girls Don't Get Murdered*, and many short stories. He is a regular contributor to *Alfred Hitchcock's Mystery Magazine.* (pp. 120, 185)

HUGH JONES PARRY, better known to readers as **James Cross,** is a novelist as well as a prolific short story writer. His 1957 novel, *Root of Evil*, was an M.W.A. Edgar Nominee. His other novels include *To Hell for Half-a-Crown, The Grave of Heroes*, and *The Dark Road*. His wife, **Betty Parry,** has also contributed to this book. (pp. 115, 119–20, 144–46)

HUGH PENTECOST (Judson Philips) has on his long list of mysteries *Nightmare Time, Murder Out of Wedlock, Random Killer, The Copycat Killers, Backlash, Remember To Kill Me, The Price of Silence*, and many others. (pp. 11–12)

OTTO PENZLER, along with Chris Steinbrunner, Marvin Lachman, and Charles Shibuk, produced the Edgar-winning *Encyclopedia of Mystery and Detection* in 1976. Penzler is best known in mystery circles as the owner of The Mysterious Bookshop and as publisher, through The Mysterious Press, of many of our top mystery authors. He also publishes *The Armchair Detective.* (pp. 20, 105–06)

GERALD PETIEVICH's crime novels owe their hard honesty to his earlier career as a U.S. Treasury Agent. His titles include *Money Men, One-Shot Deal, To Die in Beverly Hills, To Live and Die in L.A., The Quality of the Informant*, and *Shakedown.* (pp. 114–15)

ELIZABETH PETERS (*see also* **BARBARA MICHAELS**). Peters's detective/ suspense novels are divided into three separate series: Vicky Bliss, Amelia Peabody Emerson, and Jacqueline Kirby. Bliss novels include *Silhouette in Scarlet, Street of the Five Moons*, and *Borrower of the Night*. Emerson appears in *The Curse of the Pharaohs* and *Crocodile on the Sandbank*. Kirby books include *The Murders of Richard III* and *The Seventh Sinner*. Just a few of Peters's non-series novels are *The Copenhagen Connection, Summer of the Dragon*, and *The Jackal's Head.* (p. 128)

ELLIS PETERS (*see* **EDITH PARGETER**)

ROBERT L. PIKE (*see* **ROBERT L. FISH**)

CHARLES M. PLOTZ, a physician, has collaborated on mysteries with **Lawrence Treat.** (p. 157)

RONA RANDALL is widely popular in England and the United States for her colorful romantic suspense novels. Just a few of her many titles are *The Mating Dance, Curtain Call, The Potter's Niece, Broken Tapestry, Dragonmede, The Eagle at the Gate, The Drayton Legacy*, and *The Watchman's Stone.* (p. 204)

ALICE SCANLON REACH is a short story writer and the widow of the mystery writer **James Reach.** (p. 178)

HERBERT RESNICOW's first novel, *The Gold Solution*, was nominated for an Edgar in 1983. Since then, Resnicow has written *The Seventh Crossword, The Dead Room, The Gold Gamble, The World Cup Murder* (with Pelé, the international soccer star), *Murder at the Superbowl* (with Fran Tarkenton) and more. (pp. 260–61)

PRISCILLA RIDGWAY is Executive Secretary of M.W.A. Her invaluable services to the organization include much helpful work on this volume. (pp. 121–22)

PETER RILEY has written *The Love-Strife Machine* and *Strange Family*, among others. (p. 205)

WILLIAM RIVERA's paperback mystery *Panic Walks Alone* was published in 1976. (pp. 86–87, 232)

KELLEY ROOS is the joint pseudonym of **Audrey Roos** (née Kelley) and **William Roos.** Audrey Roos died in 1982. Their series characters, Jeff and Haila Troy, appeared in many of their novels. Non-series books include *Murder on Martha's Vineyard, What Did Hattie See?, Necessary Evil,* and *Requiem for a Blonde.* They received an Edgar in 1960 for their television play *The Case of the Burning Court.* (pp. 218–19)

DAN ROSS, under his own name, has written several mystery novels that include *Murder at City Hall, The Mystery of Fury Castle,* and *Out of the Night.* As **Marilyn Ross,** he has written novelizations of the "Dark Shadows" television series, and a long list of suspense novels including *Delta Flame* and *This Frightened Lady.* (p. 82)

ALEXANDRA ROUDYBUSH, a gourmet cook and mystery writer, lives in France, where she writes American mysteries, many of them with culinary plot devices. A few of her books are *A Sybaritic Death, Suddenly in Paris,* and *A Gastronomic Murder.* Her first mystery novel, *Before the Ball Was Over,* was nominated for an Edgar in 1965. (pp. 158–59, 182, 188, 246, 250, 252–53)

NORMA SCHIER is a psychologist who has made a dual career of constructing crossword puzzles and writing mysteries. Her books include *The Anagram Detectives, Death Goes Skiing, Death on the Slopes, Demon of the Opera,* and *Murder by the Book.* (p. 195)

DELL SHANNON (*see* **ELIZABETH LININGTON**)

MICHELE SLUNG edited M.W.A.'s anthology *Crime on Her Mind.* She has worked with writers and books since starting out in book stores in Philadelphia. She was on staff at *Ms.* magazine, and has written her own free-lance column, "Mystery Tour." Recently, she stepped away from mystery to write her own comic bestseller, *Momilies.* (p. 191)

JULIE SMITH's San Francisco detective, Rebecca Schwartz, has starred in a number of her novels, which include *Huckleberry Fiend, Tourist Trap, The Sourdough Wars,* and *Death Turns a Trick.* (pp. 186–87)

KAY NOLTE SMITH's first mystery novel, *The Watcher,* received an Edgar in 1980. Subsequent titles include *Catching Fire* and *Mindspell.* (p. 189)

AARON MARC STEIN, an M.W.A. Grand Master and past president, had written more than one hundred mystery novels before his death in 1985. His best-known pseudonyms were **Hampton Stone** and **George Bagby.** As Stein, he wrote the Matt Erridge series and his non-series books; as Stone, his series character was Jeremiah X. Gibson; and as Bagby, he wrote about Inspector Schmidt. His titles include *Body Search, Pistols for Two, The Second Burial, Mugger's Day, The Cheating Butcher, The Kid Was Last Seen Hanging Ten, Chill Factor,* and *Better Dead.* (pp. 136–37, 179–180, 181–82, 207–08)

RICHARD MARTIN STERN won an Edgar in 1958 for his first mystery novel, *The Bright Road to Fear.* Some of his later titles are *Cry Havoc, High Hazard, Merry Go Round, Manuscript for Murder, You Don't Need an Enemy,* and *Death in the Snow.* Stern began writing general fiction in the 1970s. His 1973 novel *The Tower* was the basis for the film *The Towering Inferno. Tsunami!* is his latest. He is a past president of M.W.A. (pp. 16–17, 109, 173)

278

HAMPTON STONE (*see* **AARON MARC STEIN**)

ELEANOR SULLIVAN is the editor of *Ellery Queen's Mystery Magazine*, and has discovered many of the new and more widely known writers of short mystery fiction. In 1986, she received M.W.A.'s Ellery Queen Award. (p. 160)

FRED S. TOBEY became popular for his short crime puzzles. (p. 71)

LAWRENCE and ROSE TREAT, working together, frequently perform home cooking miracles. A founding member and past president of M.W.A., Larry Treat's first mystery novel *Run Far, Run Fast*, was published in 1937, and he hasn't stopped turning out books and stories since. In 1964, his short story "H as in Homicide" won an Edgar, and in 1977, Treat received a Special Edgar for his work as editor of *The Mystery Writer's Handbook*. Just a few of his many titles are *Venus Unarmed, Weep for a Wanton, Trial and Terror, V as in Victim*, and *Q as in Quicksand*. (pp. 9, 19, 255–56)

CALVIN TRILLIN has written the novel *Runestruck*, as well as several books of humor. He is a frequent contributor to *The New Yorker* magazine and *The Nation*. (pp. 50–51)

THOMAS TRYON, actor and writer, is a star in both fields. His hit novels have included *Harvest Home, The Other, Lady*, and *Crowned Heads*. (p. 110)

DOROTHY UHNAK was once a member of New York City's police force. Her crime novels have all borne the stamp of her experiences. They include the 1968 Edgar winner *The Bait*, as well as *The Witness, The Ledger, Law and Order, The Investigation*, and *False Witness*. Before turning to fiction, Uhnak wrote *Policewoman: A Young Woman's Initiation into the Realities of Justice*, a nonfiction account of her early years on the force. (pp. 219–20, 243–44)

GEORGE WARREN has published more than thirty books. As coeditor of *Bookwest*, he reviews mystery fiction in its pages. Two of his novels are *Last Stage to Benbow* and *Big Rig Blues*. (pp. 91–93)

HILLARY WAUGH, a past president of M.W.A., has been writing mystery fiction since his first novel, *Madam Will Not Dine Tonight*, was published in 1947. While most of his work appears under his own name, he also writes as **H. Baldwin Taylor** and **Elissa Grandower**. Some of his titles are *Madman at My Door, Parrish for the Defense, Last Seen Wearing, Finish Me Off, A Rag and a Bone*, and *The Odds Run Out*. (pp. 134–35)

JEAN FRANCIS WEBB has written such mysteries as *No Match for Murder, Is This Coffin Taken?, Tree of Evil* (as **Roberta Morrison**), *Somewhere Within This House, The Craigshaw Curse, Caveron's Castle, Roses from a Haunted Garden*, and *The Empty Attic*. With Nancy Webb, he coedited *Plots and Pans*, and other nonfiction. (pp. 13, 29–30, 121, 237)

NANCY WEBB worked with her husband **Jean Francis Webb** on *Plots and Pans*, as well as on *Kaiulani, Will Shakespeare and His America*, and *The Hawaiian Islands from Monarchy to Democracy*. She has written one novel alone (*Marcia Blake*), two other cookbooks, *Blackstone, The Magic Detective*, a radio crime series, and *Chick Carter, Boy Detective*, also on radio. As a public relations counsel, she specialized in prominent food accounts. (pp. 69, 107, 118, 152)

HELEN WELLS was known widely for her short mystery fiction, but more so for her Cherry Ames and Viki Barr series of juvenile mysteries. Two among many of these adventures were *Escape by Night* and *The Girl in the White Coat*. She also wrote many biographies of outstanding Americans for juvenile readers. Wells died in 1986. (pp. 26, 60, 168, 183, 228)

279

TOBIAS WELLS (*see* **STANTON FORBES**)

LIONEL WHITE began writing mystery fiction in the 1950s, having edited *American Detective* magazine, *World Detective*, and *Homicide Detective*. His many novels include *The House Next Door*, *Rafferty*, *Hijack*, and *The Money Trap*. (pp. 58–59)

TED WILLIS (Lord Willis of Chiselhurst) is a stage, movie, and television script writer as well as a mystery novelist. His novels include *The Most Beautiful Girl in the World*, *Death May Surprise Us*, *The Left-Handed Sleeper*, *Man-Eater* and *Backlash*. His motion pictures include: *The Blue Lamp*, *Woman in a Dressing Gown*, and *Hot Summer Night*. (pp. 106–07)

GAHAN WILSON is both an artist and an illustrator. His work has appeared in magazines ranging from *Playboy* and *The New Yorker* to *Punch* and *Paris Match*. He is the author of *Everybody's Favorite Dog*, *Eddy Deco's Last Caper*, *Gahan Wilson's America* and *The Man In the Cannibal Pot*.

PHILIP WITTENBERG, who died in 1987, received an M.W.A. Raven in 1960 for his long and dedicated service as the organization's legal counsel. He was the author of *The Protection of Literary Property*, the "bible" on literary law. (pp. 99, 116)

OSWALD WYND (*see* **GAVIN BLACK**)

STEPHEN WRIGHT has edited the specialized anthology *Different*. (pp. 27–28)

NANCY WYNNE has published *An Agatha Christie Chronology*. (p. 165)

MARGARET TAYLOR YATES, who died in 1952, wrote a number of mystery novels in the 1930s and 1940s, featuring series character Anne Davenport McLean. These include *Death Sends a Cable*, *The Hush-Hush Murders*, and *Midway to Murder*. (p. 31)

Index

Index

Index

Index